706.

CARL BARKS AND THE DISNEY COMIC BOOK

UNIVERSITY PRESS OF MISSISSIPPI / JACKSON

CARL BARKS
AND THE DISNEY COMIC BOOK
UNMASKING THE MYTH OF MODERNITY

THOMAS ANDRAE

www.upress.state.ms.us

The University Press of Mississippi is a member of the
Association of American University Presses.

Illustrations courtesy of the collection of
Thomas Andrae unless otherwise noted

Information on Carl Barks's animation work appearing in "The
Duck Man" was previously published in *Animation Journal*
(Spring 1997).

First Edition 2006
∞
Library of Congress Cataloging-in-Publication Data

Andrae, Thomas.
  Carl Barks and the Disney comic book : unmasking the myth
of modernity / Thomas Andrae.— 1st ed.
     p. cm.
  Includes bibliographical references and index.
   ISBN 1-57806-857-6 (cloth : alk. paper) —
ISBN 1-57806-858-4 (pbk. : alk. paper) 1. Barks, Carl, 1901– —
Criticism and interpretation. I. Title.
   PN6727.B35Z53 2006
   741.5092—dc22   2006001963

    British Library Cataloging-in-Publication Data available

CONTENTS

ACKNOWLEDGMENTS

Writing a book involves the aid of many people, and this volume is no exception. First, I would like to express my gratitude to the late Carl Barks for his great patience and generosity in answering a plethora of questions over many years and for creating the stories that have meant so much to me and millions of others. I also owe a debt of gratitude to David Smith and the Walt Disney Archives for invaluable assistance in hunting down rare Barks art and to the late Bruce Hamilton, my former publisher at Another Rainbow, for giving me the chance to write about and research Barks's work.

Thanks also to my editor at the University Press of Mississippi, Seetha Srinivasan, for having confidence in this project through its many years of gestation; to David Kunzle, for his invaluable feedback and cogent editing suggestions as reader of my manuscript; to Geoffrey Blum, who cowrote with me some of the material on which this book is based; to Donald Ault, for interview material; to Mark Evanier, for important information about Chase Craig and Western Publishing; to Mary E. Whitney and Dr. Peter Demyan, for information about William F. Whittier and the towns of Hemet and San Jacinto; to Robert Norman and Andrew Hastings, for their wonderful photographs; to Rory Root and Comic Relief in Berkeley;

to Dana Gabbard; to David Gerstein; to Peter Kylling; to All Star Auctions; to Ellen D. Goldlust-Gingrich; and last but not least to my wife, Robin, for putting up with an author who was as obsessive in his scholarship as Uncle Scrooge in hoarding wealth.

ABBREVIATIONS

DD	*Donald Duck*
FC	Four Color
GG	*Gyro Gearloose*
JW	*Huey, Dewey, and Louie Junior Woodchucks*
MOC	*Boys' and Girls' March of Comics*
US	*Uncle Scrooge*
WDC&S	*Walt Disney's Comics and Stories*

CARL BARKS AND THE DISNEY COMIC BOOK

REREADING
DONALD DUCK

efore television, rock music, and video games, comic books were the mainstay of children's entertainment in America. Their ten-cent price and massive print runs made them a near universal experience of children who grew up from the Great Depression through the baby boom years. Printed on pulp stock sandwiched between slick paper covers, comics epitomized the junk aesthetic of mass-produced culture and were never intended to survive more than several readings. To think of them as worthy of being saved, let alone collected for their artistry and monetary value, would have seemed ridiculous to adults who threw them away by the thousands during paper drives and fits of house cleaning. Yet the children who read them saved and collected them, treating them as rare treasures that gave voice to their experiences and longings like nothing else in the culture.

Since the 1960s, a revolution in taste has occurred. Comic books, like other pop cultural ephemera, have become highly priced collector's items in a booming nostalgia market. However, comics are valued for more than sentimental reasons or monetary value. They are now celebrated as works of art, and an audience of aficionados has enshrined a pantheon of artists as the medium's greatest auteurs. Chief among these is Carl Barks, an ex-Disney storyman who has been hailed as the foremost cartoonist and storyteller of his era.

At the time, few readers would have understood the significance of "Barks' Jiffy Chicken Dinner" written on the side of a box on the cover of the March 1947 issue of *Walt Disney's Comics and Stories*. Nor would they have known that a can in Donald's cupboard labeled "Barks' Dog Food" in a 1946 Donald Duck story named its author. The policy of both the Disney Studio and its comic book licensee, Western Publishing, was to keep artists' identities secret. This maintained the illusion that Walt Disney was responsible not only for the animated cartoons that bore his name but also for the myriad of children's books and comics that carried the Disney logo. Barks's name never appeared on his stories during the period from 1942 to 1966 that he drew the Disney ducks. But children knew the distinctive style of the person they called the "good artist" and were quick to complain when he was replaced by lesser talents.

Unfortunately, Barks never saw anyone buy one of his comics: "I used to go to the drugstore or wherever there was a newsstand, and if I happened to have a little time on my hands, I would stand around . . . pretending I was looking at *Popular Mechanics* or something, and watch the kids who would come in. . . . And I always hoped that I would see some kid buy a *Walt Disney's Comics* or an *Uncle Scrooge*. I never did. They always picked up *Superman* or a Harvey comic or an *Oswald Rabbit*, but never did one of them even look at an *Uncle Scrooge* or a *Donald Duck*. . . . I guess that would have been the greatest thrill of my life, to see some kid pay ten cents for an *Uncle Scrooge*."[1]

Barks invented a whole family of relatives for Donald, including his cousin, Gladstone Gander, a wavy-haired dandy who lived without working due to his incredible luck; the daffy inventor, Gyro Gearloose; the zillionaire skinflint, Uncle Scrooge, and his archnemeses, the inept gang of burglars, the Beagle Boys; and the Italian sorceress, Magica de Spell. Donald's nephews and his girlfriend, Daisy Duck, holdovers from animation, rounded out the cast. In general, there were two types of Barks stories. One was a series of ten-page Donald Duck tales that ran monthly in *Walt Disney's Comics and Stories*. These usually were situated in the fictional city of Duckburg that Barks had created for his feathered clan and primarily concerned Donald's everyday life. The other type of Barks tale was the longer Donald Duck Four Color Series and Uncle Scrooge adventures, which took the ducks to foreign locales in search of hidden treasure and lost civilizations. Barks wrote and drew more than five hundred stories at a rate of one story every two weeks, an incredibly prolific record for any author or artist.

Barks's imaginative storytelling made fans eager to learn more about the mysterious chronicler of the ducks' lives. In 1960 a fan named John Spicer used a ruse to pierce the veil of silence, and Western Publishing revealed Barks's name to a reader for the first time. When Barks received his first fan letter, he was so unused to recognition that he thought that it was a prank concocted by his friend, Bob Harmon, a gag writer for *Dennis the Menace* known for practical jokes. Only after Harmon repeatedly denied writing the letter and after "eyeing it with dark suspicion for several weeks" did Barks decide to answer it on the chance that it might be genuine. He later commented, "The front office tells me they get many letters, but over the past 17 years I can only recall three . . . two of which were pan letters that left my head shrunk for weeks."[2] Critics have speculated that Western kept Barks in the dark about his fan mail to keep his head from swelling and to keep him from demanding more recognition and a higher salary. But most of Western's writers and artists worked anonymously on the various franchised characters that were the publishing company's stock-in-trade.

Since his identity was uncovered, Barks's fame has mushroomed. His work has been the subject of museum shows, and *Time*, *Newsweek*, and the *New York Review of Books* have lauded him as a major American humorist. Barks has also had an important impact on American popular culture. The doyens of the fantasy film, George Lucas and Steven Spielberg, have acknowledged his adventure stories as the inspiration for their Indiana Jones films. Beginning in the 1980s, a syndicated television series, *Duck Tales*, featured Barks's creation, Uncle Scrooge, and adaptations of some of his most famous stories. Barks's work has been in publication through reprints in the United States for a number of years, adding to his recognition. However, he has achieved his greatest popularity in Europe, where his stories are reprinted in weekly editions of Donald Duck comics and Barks's name is a household word.

Disney comics were originally published in the *Mickey Mouse Magazine*, which originated in 1935. This was an oversized tabloid that contained games, jokes, and reprints of the Mickey Mouse and Donald Duck newspaper strips. The enormous success of Superman in the late 1930s transformed comic books from a cottage industry into a thriving mass medium. K. K. Publications, which printed the magazine, sought to capitalize on the booming comic book market and began changing its size and content. By its last issue in 1940, the *Mickey Mouse Magazine* consisted almost entirely of comic strip reprints and had become identical in size to a comic book. *Walt Disney's Comics and Stories* took over the format when it debuted in October 1940. Before Barks came on the scene, Donald Duck's appearances in comics were confined to the gag-a-day newspaper strips drawn by Al Taliaferro. Barks drew the first original Donald Duck comic book story ("Donald Duck Sails for Pirate Gold," FC #9) in 1942, when he was still employed by the Disney Studio. He was subsequently asked to draw the first original Donald Duck story in *Walt Disney's Comics and Stories* #31 (April 1943). He continued writing and drawing Disney comics for the next twenty-three years.

During their heyday in the 1940s and 1950s, Disney comics were highly popular. *Walt Disney's Comics and Stories* had grown from a circulation of 252,000 for its first issue to more than a million in 1942.[3] By 1947, after Barks had been doing stories for several years, the publication's circulation had risen to 2 million. The peak came in 1953, when the title sold more than 3 million copies a month, making it the most popular comic book ever published. More than one in five Americans read Barks's stories, and Disney comics ranked second in popularity only to *Time* and the *Saturday Evening Post*. Such influence led film critic Leonard Maltin to claim in 1983 that Barks was "the most popular writer-artist in the world."[4]

Part of the success of Barks's comics resulted from the fact that he never talked down to his young readers. Indeed, his stories could be read on multiple levels, appealing to both children and adults. "Kids are not empty-headed dolls, and they weren't thirty years ago," Barks remarked. "I can't recall a time when I was young enough to be ignorant of most worldly things. Nor did I ever know a kid who didn't know quite a lot about mechanics, geography, animals, values, morals, responsibility, etc. The vapid little Bobbies and Billies and Janies of the standard children's books are figments of the imaginations of old-maidish editors who long ago forgot what filled their minds when they were children."[5] As James Freeman points out, Barks's stories deal almost exclusively with adult desires and concerns: "Donald is swindled in real estate; Donald loses job after job; Donald only wants a pedigreed dog; . . . Donald is pestered on his vacation by salesmen; Donald tries to impress Duckburg society by giving a lunch jungle party; and so on."[6] But these concerns resonated with children desiring to become adults and living in a world dominated by them. This elision between adult and child would become a central feature of Barks's work.

The comic book market typically has been segregated by age and gender. Young children gravitate to funny-animal comics, girls prefer teen and romance comics, and more boys than girls read superhero and science fiction comics. Barks's comics were unique in transcending these divisions. A 1950 study of the reading habits of children and adolescents, for example, found that Donald Duck was mentioned most often as read by all age groups and both genders.[7] These facts testify to the universal appeal of Barks's stories and to their ability to transcend barriers of age, gender, and nationality.

Since Superman became a popular icon in the late 1930s, the superhero genre has dominated the comic book industry. These comics dish out adolescent fantasies of crime fighters with flamboyant costumes and magical powers, offering readers an escape from the restrictions and banality of their everyday lives. Barks's work instead was more realistic and down-to-earth. His short stories offered a portrait of ordinary mortals trying to cope with the travails of quotidian life. And while his longer epics contained enough high-spirited adventure for children, these stories really addressed adult longings and anxieties. Barks's work required a more complex moral and social vision than that of superhero comics, and he eschewed good guy/bad guy conflicts, making the ducks morally ambiguous characters with human failings and illusions. Commented Barks, "The thing that is most important about my comics is this: I told it like it is. I told the kids that the bad guys had a little bit of good in them, and the good guys have a lot of bad in them, and that you couldn't depend on anything much, that nothing was going to always turn out roses."[8]

Barks's stories deconstruct a myth long held by the general public and comic book censors: that comic books are read almost exclusively by children. However, studies of reading habits reveal that although comic books were primarily a children's medium, they also had a large adult audience. Although about 90 percent of children were regular readers of comic books, an astonishing 41 percent of men and 28 percent of women were also regular comic book consumers in the 1940s.[9] Comic books, in fact, had been the most popular reading material among the armed forces during World War II.[10] The postwar era saw an increasing use of sophisticated material in comics and an explicit appeal to adult audiences, and Barks's stories helped spearhead the medium's growing sophistication and complexity, making him one of the most innovative graphic artists of his time.

This book covers the major phases of Barks's career as a Disney artist, from his work on the Donald Duck animated cartoons to his work on Disney comics. Such a book is an innovation in popular culture studies. While film, jazz, and video have been elevated to the level of art, comics have traditionally been considered subliterature. As a result, few studies exist of individual comic book artists. Moreover, scholarship on comic books has been dominated by studies of superheroes and their creators. The funny-animal genre within which Barks operated has been neglected because of the misperception that because such magazines were targeted at younger readers, their content is less sophisticated than that of other genres. This assumption governs Bradford Wright's *Comic Book Nation*, a major cultural history of comic books. According to Wright,

> I chose not to include the many funny animal, cartoon, and teen-humor series in this study. While titles like *Donald Duck*, *Richie Rich*, and *Archie* have enjoyed very large preteen audiences, they all possess a certain timeless and unchanging appeal for young children that makes them relatively unhelpful for

the purposes of a cultural history. . . . [T]here is more fertile ground in exploring those comic books aimed at a slightly older audience—readers who, in
other words, have reached a developmental stage at which they are capable of
perceiving texts within a broader social and political context.[11]

In other words, funny-animal comics are for kids, while superheroes appeal
to adults. However, Barks's stories break down this adult/child dichotomy
and are universal in their appeal, offering profound insights into American
culture and society.

Part of the problem is the lack of scholarly work done on Barks's
work. Ariel Dorfman and Armand Mattelart's *How to Read Donald Duck:
Imperialist Ideology in the Disney Comic* is the only critical examination
of Disney comics in English. Written at the height of Chile's attempt to
free itself from U.S. domination, Dorfman and Mattelart's book has been
called the "classic work on cultural imperialism and children's literature"
and "of all analyses of comics perhaps the most important."[12] However,
the book has serious flaws, and critiquing it enables us not only to correct misjudgments about Barks's work but also to gain insights into more
appropriate methods of studying comics.

How to Read Donald Duck was published in Chile in 1971, one year
after the ascension to power of Salvador Allende's socialist government.
Both Dorfman and Mattelart were advisers to the Chilean state publish-
ing house, Quimantú (literally "Sunshine of Knowledge"), and saw their
work as an important part of the process of bringing socialism to Chile.
The government was overthrown by a 1973 military coup abetted by the
United States, and a junta led by the brutal dictator General Augusto
Pinochet came to power, forcing Dorfman and Mattelart into exile.
The book was translated into English and initially banned in the United
States because Disney corporation lawyers alleged copyright violations.
Subsequently released in America and throughout the world, by the time
of its second edition in 1984 it had been translated into fifteen languages
and had sold more than half a million copies.

As the title suggests, Dorfman and Mattelart attempt to reveal the
imperialist worldview contained behind the seemingly innocent, wholesome facade of Disney comics. The authors claim that Disney comics are

a powerful tool of American imperialism precisely because they pretend to be harmless entertainment produced for children. Dorfman and Mattelart argue that Disney comics are forms of capitalist propaganda and merchandising tools of the global Disney empire.

The authors note the curious absence of fathers and mothers in Disney comics. Numerous uncles, nephews, and cousins populate the comics, but they efface all references to biological paternity or motherhood. Dorfman and Mattelart take this not only as an example of Disney's prudery but also as a means of ensnaring children within the webs of patriarchal power. They note that the irresponsible, incompetent Donald takes the role of the child-adult in the stories, while the nephews are cast as the true adults, more mature, moral, and capable than their uncle. Consequently, when the nephews rebel against Donald's misdeeds, they do so in the name of adult values. By identifying with the nephews, child readers come to adopt these values while abandoning their natural proclivity for spontaneity, imagination, and subversion of adult authority. "Since the child identifies with his counterpart in the magazine," the authors argue, "he contributes to his own colonization. The rebellion of the little folk in the comics is sensed as a model for the child's own real rebellion against injustice; but by rebelling in the name of adult values, the readers are in fact internalizing them."[13] Thus, Disney comics' "inversion" of child and adult entraps children within a circular inflexible system of rule from which they cannot escape.

Dorfman and Mattelart argue that imperialist ideology in Disney comics draws a homology between children and citizens of the Third World that infantilizes them and keeps them "underdeveloped." Third Worldlings are childlike "noble savages," friendly, carefree, naive, trustful, and happy. Unlike the urban child-adults of Duckburg, who are forever correcting their adult kin, those in the Third World lack "intelligence, cunning, discipline, encyclopedic knowledge and technical skills."[14] Unaware of the market value of their country's wealth, they gladly allow the ducks to dispossess them of their riches in return for trinkets. By leading Third World readers to internalize images of themselves as gullible primitives, argue Dorfman and Mattelart, Disney comics reinforce a relationship of dependency between America and the underdeveloped world that legitimates western "imperialist plunder and colonial subjection."[15]

Just as Disney comics repress sexuality and biological reproduction, they also elide images of industrial workers and the production of wealth and substitute a world of consumers and consumption, claim the Chileans: "In the world of Disney no one has to work in order to produce. There is a constant round of buying, selling and consuming, but to all appearances, none of the products involved has required any effort to make."[16] This occlusion of industrial labor draws on Marx's notion of the fetishism of commodities according to which the value of products is displaced from the labor that produces them and is thought to emanate from the product itself. The authors argue that Disney comics depict work primarily in the service sector: the citizens of Duckburg are hairdressers, salespeople, night watchmen, delivery boys, and the like but never blue-collar laborers. Consequently, Dorfman and Mattelart argue, the stories efface the realm of industrial production and the working class, which is the real generator of wealth in capitalist society.

Doesn't Donald suffer from being an underpaid, alienated worker, we might ask. But Dorfman and Mattelart argue that he never works for need—to pay the rent or the phone bill. Rather, he works only to consume—to buy a television set or a present for someone. In Disney's world, all speech is an advertisement, and the characters are engaged in an intense compulsion to consume. Consumption thus replaces production as the focus of interest, claim the authors. "This is the world the bourgeoisie always dreamed of, one in which a man can amass great wealth without facing producer and product: the worker."[17]

Poverty and unemployment are abolished in the Disney utopia, claim Dorfman and Mattelart. Although Donald continually loses jobs because of his incompetence, he is always able to find work and never suffers the fate of being unemployed. Disney comics thus reinforce the mythology of labor and hide the employee's exploitation in producing surplus value for his employer. Donald is "sensed as the true representative of the contemporary worker," the Chileans argue, but in fact "he is the bastard representative of all workers."[18]

How to Read Donald Duck is densely argued and cannot be fully explicated here. But this summary offers a basis from which to launch a number of criticisms. In assuming the validity of the Chileans' arguments, critics have failed to understand the major differences between comics produced for a Latin American audience and those intended for North American readers. In fact, Latin American publishers rewrote the original versions of these comics and sometimes added conservative slants absent from those published in the United States. In Barks's story, "Lost in the Andes," for example, the blockheaded natives of an imaginary, antebellum square-worshipping society ask Donald and the nephews to teach them "somethin' to improve theath good spirits!" In Barks's story, the nephews reply, "We'll teach 'em *square* dancing!" In the Chilean comic, the nephews say, in Spanish, "We will teach them to stand to attention before their superiors!"

Dorfman and Mattelart were writing from and for the perspective of the Third World and lacked access to U.S. libraries and literature. Consequently, they did not know about the existence of Barks as an individual author, and their book does not distinguish Barks's work from that of other Disney artists. Although the translator, art historian David Kunzle, briefly mentions Barks in the introduction, Dorfman and Mattelart never refer to Barks in their analysis. In addition, their sample was confined primarily to comics from the 1960s, thereby skewing their interpretations: during the mid-1950s, Barks was hemmed in by what Barks biographer Mike Barrier calls a "growing thicket of taboos."[19] Dorfman and Mattelart's critique was based on these tamer stories.

Dorfman and Mattelart also failed to distinguish the worldview in Disney animation from that in Disney comics, erroneously assuming that the studio controlled the production of both media. In fact, Barks's status at Western was unique. After initially establishing his ability as a storyteller, he, unlike other writers, did not have to submit scripts for approval to his editors: as Barks remarked, "I started drawing with no-one's okay but my own (what a change from my years in the Disney story Department!)."[20] Barks received a degree of autonomy unique in the Disney empire. He was one of the few comic book producers to both write and draw his stories and had little editorial supervision during much of his career. Convinced that comic books could rise to the status of great literature, Barks valued his autonomy so much that he was willing to accept less money than some other Western Publishing artists to retain his artistic freedom: "I know there were a number of guys getting higher rates than I was. But they were more under the thumb of the editors. They had to make more corrections, and the work they were doing was not so interesting as what I had. I had that freedom. It was worth $10 a page to me to have the freedom to write whatever I wanted to write."[21]

Bark's integrity showed. In his introduction to *How to Read Donald Duck*, David Kunzle acknowledges that the author was an exception to the sugarcoated innocence of most Disney products: "There are elements of satire in Barks's work which one seeks in vain in any other corner of the world of Disney," claims Kunzle, "just as Barks has elements of social realism which one seeks in vain in any other corner of the world of comics."[22] In an account of his work on Dorfman and Mattelart's volume, "The Parts That Got Left Out of the Donald Duck Book," Kunzle notes that he was forced to qualify his praise of Barks's stories as an exception to a uniform Disney imperialist ideology.[23] Unfamiliar with Barks's work and wishing to maintain political orthodoxy, the publisher and both authors asked Kunzle to rewrite and cut back his praise of Barks in the introduction to one paragraph. Karl Marx thus supplanted Carl Barks.

There are also a number of problems with Dorfman and Mattelart's textual analyses. *How to Read Donald Duck* is premised on a reductionistic Marxist model of culture in which the cultural superstructure is merely a reflex of the economic base. This paradigm allows no contradictions or oppositional discourses in popular culture, subsuming it under a single, monolithic imperialist ideology. This concept of imperialism is ahistorical and admits no change over time. As Raymond Williams notes, the economic base contains multiple contradictions and the Marxist method is inherently historical, so even their use of this model contravenes a truly Marxist approach.[24]

Economistic Marxism installs a "hierarchy of oppression" in which the working class is viewed as the most oppressed sector of society whose emancipation would constitute the liberation of all social groups. "The element which truly challenges the legitimacy and necessity of the monopoly of wealth, and is capable of destroying it," write Dorfman and Mattelart, "is the working class, whose only means of liberation is to liquidate the economic base of the bourgeoisie and abolish private property."[25] This essentialist model reduces gender, racial, and other forms of domination to those of class.

Dorfman and Mattelart's concept of class is directed at readers in the Third World. However, interpreting Barks's tales requires taking into account the social context of the American audience for which he was writing. While industrial workers predominate in the underdeveloped counties, four-fifths of U.S. employees were service workers during the 1950s.[26] Thus, Barks's representation of labor in Duckburg was accurate rather than an ideological mystification of class realities. Moreover, it is arrogant to argue that just because providing services is not industrial labor, that it is not really work. Donald's alienation, oppression, and lack of control of his labor are key elements of his persona in Barks's universe.

Dorfman and Mattelart's model of cultural imperialism implies that Disney comics indoctrinate Third World readers into an imperialist ideology and that a distinct media effect has taken place. However, their argument for this effect is vague and is grounded in the wider context of Third World dependency on western imports. "Our countries are exporters of raw materials and importers of superstructural goods. . . . [W]e send copper, and they send the machines to extract copper, and of course, Coca Cola. Behind the Coca Cola stands a whole superstructure of expectations and models of behavior, and with it, a particular kind of present and future society and an interpretation of the past."[27] Thus, imported goods from the West indoctrinate native consumers into the values and inferior subject positions given to them by the West by instructing them "in the way they are supposed to live and relate to the foreign power center."[28] However, Dorfman and Mattelart simply assume that these values are transmitted and nowhere provide evidence about an audience's actual responses.

This dependency model of cultural imperialism has been criticized for its mediacentric perspective and unilateral view of media effects, which assumes that audiences are merely passive recipients of media content and do not alter or resist its messages. Recent evidence points to the importance of the audience as an active agent in the consumption process, with the power to interpret and adapt cultural meanings to their situations.[29] Dorfman and Mattelart's model is elitist, characterizing the readers whose liberation they champion as passive dupes to whom intellectuals like the authors must show the truth. In a brutally frank memoir, Dorfman has acknowledged the error of this position:

> In my pursuit of purity and national autonomy, in my desire for a rebellious Chile that would totally expel the American part of me . . . I have exaggerated the villainy of the U.S. and the nobleness of Chile. I have not been true to the complexity of cultural interchange, the fact that not all mass-media products absorbed from abroad are negative and not everything we produce at home is inspiring. And I have projected my own childhood experience with America onto Chile and the Third World, assuming that because I have been so easily seduced, so willingly ravished and impregnated, millions of people in far-away lands are empty, innocent, vessels into which the empire passively pours its song, instead of tangled, hybrid, wily creatures ready to appropriate and despoil the messages that come their way, relocate their meaning, reclaim them as their own by changing their significance.[30]

Ironically, his attack on Disney turned Dorfman into "an object of hatred" for thousands of indignant Chilean fans. Portly grandmothers tried to run him over with their cars, and one night his bungalow in Santiago was stoned by irate mobs of children and parents holding up placards and shouting, "Viva el Pato Donald!"

One of Dorfman and Mattelart's biggest mistakes is their failure to examine the reasons for Disney comics' great popularity. British cultural studies offers an alternative approach to the study of ideology in comics. In place of the concept of a dominant ideology, with its implication of economic manipulation or unconscious interpellation, cultural studies suggests that we turn to the model of ideological hegemony proposed by Italian political theorist Antonio Gramsci. Hegemony is the ongoing process by which a particular historical bloc maintains or comes to power by mobilizing broad public support for its projects. A hegemonic elite leads rather than dominates, its power resting on its ability to persuade disparate groups to accept its rule and definitions of reality. Hegemony refers to a process, not a fixed condition, and is based on a dynamic analysis of how relations of dominance and subordination change over time rather than a static, synchronic account of power relations at any single point. According to this logic, hegemony can never be complete but must be continually renegotiated through an ongoing process of attaining consensus among contending coalitions and groups. This historicization of media representations allows for the recognition of difference, antagonism, and change where manipulation theory does not.

The notion of hegemony rejects the premises of manipulation theory that audiences are cultural "dopes" on which is imposed a dominant ideology. Media texts must appeal to the desires, tensions, and anxieties of the populace to secure consent to its definitions of reality. Cultural studies theorists argue that media culture has polysemic texts whose multiple meanings and conflicting discourses allow for different readings according to an individual's race, class, gender, and nationality. Gramsci constructs a dialectical model in which popular culture is neither produced by the people nor a dominant ideology imposed on unwitting audiences. Rather, it is a site "in which dominant, subordinate and oppositional values and ideologies meet and inter-mingle, in differing mixes and permutations, vying with one another in their attempts to secure spaces within which they can become influential in framing and organizing popular experience and consciousness."[31] Media culture is not simply a reflection of popular needs or an imposition on a passive public but a contested terrain, a site of struggle that can only be understood within a sociohistoric context.

Cultural studies foregrounds the intersection of multiple axes of oppression within patriarchal capitalism, charting the way class, race, gender, sexuality, and other social categories intersect to produce social domination. Such analyses avoid reductionism by attempting to synthesize multiple approaches to texts rather than single critical theories. Marxism is good for examining class relations, feminism for thematizing gender, and deconstruction for the play of significations within a text. But each critical method has its strengths and limitations, privileging one aspect of culture or social life while marginalizing or excluding others.

As Douglas Kellner notes, a multiperspectival approach to media culture elucidates a fuller range of textual meanings and ideological discourses than single theories alone and allows us to view texts from the multicultural perspectives of race, class, and gender.[32]

Dorfman and Mattelart also fail to deal with the ways in which changes in capitalism undermined patriarchal power and, along with the rise of permissive child rearing, helped pave the way for the heroization of the child-adult in comics. In these terms, the inversion of adult and child perceived by Dorfman and Mattelart represents not merely a ruse to subordinate children and adult readers but an important diminution of the power of patriarchy that allowed children (albeit imperfectly) a space of rebellion and empowerment within a culture ruled by adults. As Stephen Kline points out, whereas books for children were often chosen, paid for, and read to them by adults, comic books were the first cultural products for children that were priced cheaply enough to be bought by them. Thus, they offer an important perspective on children's culture.[33]

The basic premise of this book is that although continuities of plot and characterization exist, the Barksian corpus has a depth and complexity found nowhere else in Disney's output. Indeed, Barks's work has elements of irony, satire, and cynicism that run counter to the saccharine Disney ethos. Barks's stories subvert social hierarchies, contesting the power of parents over children, males over females, the rich over the majority, the West over natives, and the technological domination of nature. Barks closely hewed to political realities of the most topical kind and ingeniously inserted them into comics largely forbidden to tackle such realities. Rather than being an apologia for capitalism, Barks's tales offer one of the most critical views of urban industrial civilization in popular culture. "I think the conquest of the West was a disgusting shame," Barks remarked. "The senseless fecundity of white immigrants to the New World is the calamity of the ages."[34] Barks's stories consistently satirize the homogenization and deracination of traditional societies by American consumer culture and profiteering.

Cultural imperialism raises deeper questions about the nature of cultural identity and thus cannot be fully understood within the terms of "media imperialism."[35] Cultural identity cannot be understood in terms of national domination but requires attention to historical processes of cultural change—in particular, to processes of modernity. Capitalism is only one aspect of the types of changes undergone by traditional societies in the transition to modernity. These processes also include industrialism, urbanism, a system of nation-states, mass communication, a technical-scientific-rationalist ideology, and the dominance of the nuclear family.[36]

Such nineteenth-century European social theorists as Marx, Weber, Durkheim, and Tönnies constructed their theories around the idea of a set of dramatic changes in European societies that resulted in the creation of a "modern" world. Crucial differences existed in the way in which these theorists understood this transition—"tradition" versus "modernity," "mechanical" versus "organic solidarity," "precapitalist" versus "capitalist," "*Gemeinschaft*" versus "*Gesellschaft*"—but all agreed that societies were becoming "modern" in a sense not merely in terms of chronological succession but also in terms of a social order entirely different from anything that had preceded it.

These theorists were also quite skeptical about the modern world's capacity to fulfill its promises to bring humanity autonomy and happiness. Modernity had spelled the end of feudal hierarchy, the decline of dogmatic religious superstitions, the assertion of political rights, and a greater degree of material abundance. But it had failed to deliver emancipation from many forms of domination. These authors wrote plaintively about the high costs of modernity, describing its new configurations in terms of social pathology: "alienation" "anomie," and the "iron cage" of instrumental rationalization. All agreed that modernity resulted in a fragmentation of community and the loss of tradition. Thus, the cultural impact of capitalist modernity can be seen in terms of loss rather than just imposition. From this perspective, "the process of the spread of capitalist modernity involves not an invasion of 'weak' cultures by a 'stronger' one [as in the cultural imperialism hypothesis], but almost the opposite—the spread of cultural decay from the West to the rest of the world."[37]

Barks's work operates within the funny-animal genre that derives from the beast fable, a type of didactic tale going back to Aesop (and earlier) that parodies human folly by representing types of people as animals.[38] Barks's treatment of the ducks was ambivalent. On the one hand, he thought of them as people: "I never thought of them as ducks. I always thought of them as people. Like when I named Uncle Scrooge 'Only a Poor Old Man'—the title of a story—I never thought of 'Only a Poor Old Duck.'"[39] On the other hand, the characters in his stories continually refer to themselves as ducks, mentioning their feathers, tails, and webbed feet. This slippage functions as a running gag in the comics, parodying human foibles by mocking the hubris and absurdity of ducks trying to talk, think, and act like humans.

Barks's stories also concern an examination of the structure of desire that forms the social imaginary of modern times. Barks's view of human nature was pessimistic, and his stories reveal the way in which we are governed by illusions that enthrall and deceive us. A recurring theme is the way in which characters' desires become obsessive and spiral out of control, culminating in nightmarish outcomes that mock their authors' original intentions. Barks's work offers a sustained interrogation of the assumptions and conflicts within capitalist modernity. His stories examine the American dream and our preoccupation with wealth, power, and technological control. They reveal the ironies and contradictions of the myth of the self-made man and question the fetishism of money and success on which this myth was based. Through satire and parody, Barks's stories also deconstruct media images of heroism and glamour, self-reflexively examining the grounds of comics books' popularity and appeal.

However, Barks's work has a broader perspective. He was a self-described conservative and traditionalist, and those sensibilities inform his work in both animation and comics. Speaking about his comic book tales, he observed, "I think a lot of the philosophy in my stories is conservative—conservative in the sense that I feel that our civilization reached a peak around 1910. Since then we've been going downhill. Much of the older culture had basic qualities that the new type of stuff we keep hatching up can never match."[40] Barks's conservatism is manifested in a fondness for the "long ago and far away." Many of his stories are set in the past, when individuals were less confined by the restrictions of civilization. Calling attention to the untoward consequences of the Enlightenment myth of progress, his stories question our faith in western civilization's project of dominating nature, undermining our complacent faith in science and technological progress. Indeed, Barks is one of the few comic book artists to invoke an ecological critique of modernity. Even before an ecological consciousness emerged in the 1960s, Barks had written stories about the effects of industrial civilization on nature, the modern psyche, and traditional societies.

These themes also include an exploration of the contradictions within patriarchy. Many of Barks's stories deal with the deauthorization of the male in contemporary times and the fears of loss of control, emasculation, and failure that are regarded as inimical to the achievement of traditional masculinity. His works reveal a crisis in male identity, presenting compulsory masculinity as a nightmare of anxiety, humiliation, and abuse. By dwelling on the fractured male subject, Barks reveals the inadequacy of achieving a coherent and satisfying male identity within the terms of patriarchal definitions of masculinity.

To examine the evolution of Barks's humor, we shall analyze the formulas of parent-child conflicts that dominate the duck shorts and Barks's application of them in his first comic book stories. Subsequent chapters will describe the way Barks's tales began to break from these formulas during the postwar era to invoke a darker portrait of America during the years when the contours of the American empire were definitively established. At this time, the nation reached a zenith of power, affluence, and self-confidence, yet it was also a time of psychological dislocation, anxiety, and alienation, marked by the beginnings of the Cold War, the creation of the Bomb, unsettling changes in gender roles and race relations, and widespread concern regarding the undermining of individual autonomy and male authority by the rise of corporate conformity, consumerism, and mass culture.

The wartime and postwar crisis served as a catalyst for a new venue for Barks's antimodernist sentiments. At the same time that America was consolidating its empire, Barks's stories began investigating the roots of this empire and its unseemly history of conquest. Long before settlement of the New World, tales of exploration and colonization described America as an earthly paradise. This image continued in notions of American exceptionalism that conceived of the nation as a virgin land whose abundance of free territory seemed to guarantee the equality that did not exist in a hierarchically ordered Europe. The image surfaced again in myths of America as an agrarian garden populated by virtuous yeomen or a frontier free of civilized restrictions in the process of being tamed by pioneers, Indian fighters, and cowboys.

Barks's stories invoke this pastoral ideal. His tales of elfin little people and utopian villages cut off from civilization contrast the generosity, tranquillity, and fraternity of the close-knit communities of the past with the acquisitiveness, stress, and alienation of urban America. However, rather than evoking a simplistic nostalgia for the past or merging with an apotheosized nature, Barks's antimodernism is complex and ambivalent, revealing both the worth and limits of our Arcadias. Rejecting simplistic notions of linear progress, Barks reveals the way in which Eden both prefigures and constitutes an alternative to modernity.

In the late 1950s and 1960s, Barks's stories anticipate the arrival of a postmodern culture that signals a transformation in the modern paradigm. This period ushers in the increased penetration of capital into both American and Third World cultures and the growth of a global media-based consumer culture. The era saw social and cultural fragmentation embodied in a decline in the credibility of the adventure mythos and an atrophy in the pastoral ideal in his little people tales. With the coming of the tumultuous political upheavals of the 1960s, Barks's stories grew increasingly topical, no longer able to maintain the veneer of their former innocence and sense of coherence.

Understanding the origins of Barks's stories requires looking at the details of his life. He was born on March 27, 1901, on a small grain ranch near Merrill, Oregon. His ancestors were Scotch and Dutch of the hardworking, thrifty sort of whom Uncle Scrooge would have approved. The Barkses had originally settled in the mountains of North Carolina, where they were said to have been moonshiners during the Revolutionary War.

Carl's father was a homesteader from Missouri who came to California in the 1880s, settling briefly in the San Joaquin Valley, where he worked as a blacksmith. When the government offered parcels of land to settlers across the Oregon border, he moved to Merrill and started a wheat ranch. Carl and his brother, Clyde, grew up on that windy, arid land and led an isolated life with little access to movies, books, and art. "We had to work all the time," Barks recalled, "so we had very little time to play. We went to school in a little one-room schoolhouse, and there were very few kids to play with. The school was several miles away from a town of any kind— just a little old schoolhouse sitting out there in the sagebrush." [41]

Art supplies were scarce, so young Carl drew on anything he could find. He drew cartoons on scraps of paper, the margins of newspapers, and in the dust of horse's harnesses when he plowed the fields. "Pencils and paper were quite rare," Barks explained, "so very little of my stuff was ever permanently done. I'd pick up a piece of charcoal out of the stove and draw on the walls of the house—get my butt spanked." [42] Barks never had any formal art training but followed the Sunday comics. From the beginning, he was interested only in cartoon art and would practice by creating daily strips featuring his own characters. He read the Sunday funnies, following the antics of Happy Hooligan, Old Dock Yak, and his favorite, Windsor McCay's Little Nemo. "That's how I originally started to draw," he explained. "I tried to copy figures like Happy Hooligan and various other characters." [43] Barks was a natural satirist, a skill manifested in his drawings in his grade-school reader. Next to the word *butcher*, he drew a doctor's shingle; the word *ivory* inspired a man with a gleaming bald pate; and *icicle* brought to his mind an old hag with a long nose and hooked chin. The entries for *honey*, *chicken*, *peaches*, and even *usher* provoked drawings of pretty women, prefiguring his later penchant for drawing sexy females.

Barks's parents, William and Arminta, married late in life and were past forty when Carl was born. They had known each other in childhood and carried on a relationship by mail for more than twenty years before marrying. In 1908, William moved to Midland, where a town had grown up around the new railroad line. He built holding pens and feedlots for the cattle that began streaming in from the ranches to the east. Carl and his brother were responsible for feeding the animals and bedding down the train cars with straw. When the boys had a few minutes to spare from their chores, they liked to hang around the cowboys who herded the cattle and were fascinated by their colorful names and vulgar vocabularies. "My brother and I just idolized those fellows. . . . One was called Windneck Mitchell," Barks recalled. "He had a sort of goiter on the side of his neck, and it seemed as if there was an extension of his vocal chords, or his voice box, that went out into that, so any time he talked he had a reverberation. He could speak profanity with the loudest basso you ever heard."[44] Barks's fascination with lost civilizations and frontier life grew out of these experiences growing up in rural Oregon: "I have a love of the Old West, the wide-open spaces. . . . I can remember when I myself was a young kid with plenty of room to roam around in, a gun to shoot, horses to ride. All those things were part of the formation of my character, I guess."[45]

Barks received little appreciation for his budding artistic skills: "My parents had little patience with the yearnings of a small boy, both being old enough to be my grandparents, and my slightly older brother had little patience with my 'sissy' fascination with drawing and reading so, other than the farm animals, I had little companionship."[46] The notion that literature and cartoon art were unmanly interests undoubtedly made the young Carl retreat inward into the world of his imagination through which he might temporarily transcend the harshness and emotional barrenness of his life. "My dad was never much of a fellow to talk," Barks remembered. "He would read his Bible—that was about the extent of his life."[47] One can imagine the young Barks speaking to the farm animals as if they were human beings, anticipating his future creation of a universe of humanized duck characters.

The sagebrush out on the prairie, the blazing sunsets, and the desolated badlands in Barks's comics were not portraits that Barks gleaned from reading Western pulp magazines but aspects of daily life in the frontier environment in which he grew up. His was not a nostalgic vision of the Old West but a realistic picture of loneliness and a harsh struggle to survive: "I guess I found it natural to satirize the yearnings and pomposities and frustration of the ducks because of my early contacts with people in the rougher walks of life. The cowboys, ranchers, loggers, and steel workers with whom I worked before I broke into the 'soft' field of cartooning were all satirists. They had the ability to laugh at the most awesome miseries. If they hadn't seen humor in their hard-bitten lives, they'd have gone crazy." [48]

In a few years, William had expanded his homestead to a square mile of property with a farmhouse, a blacksmith shop, and a crew of hired hands. In 1911 he rented out the wheat ranch at Merrill and the feedlot at Midland. Hoping to capitalize on his fortune, he moved the family again, investing eight thousand dollars in a four-acre prune orchard in Santa Rosa. At this time, Carl decided to become a cartoonist. He was enthralled by the artistry of the schoolmate who sat next to him and recalled watching in amazement as the boy drew caricatures of Woodrow Wilson and Teddy Roosevelt: "I thought that was the most wonderful thing in the world, to draw like that kid could draw. I think I hadn't quite turned sixteen yet when I talked my dad into letting me subscribe to that Landon School of Cartooning." [49] But the nearest post office was five miles away, and a mail-order course proved impractical. However, Barks insisted that "the thorough basics outlined in those few Landon lessons have been the foundation beneath my whole concept of dramatic and humorous presentation." [50]

The Barks family followed a pattern of attempted expansion and retrenchment similar to those of other hardscrabble entrepreneurs. William's fortunes changed dramatically when the price of prunes dropped suddenly one year and the rains dried up in Oregon. These financial setbacks and Arminta's health problems—she was diagnosed with cancer and had to have an operation—caused William to have a nervous breakdown. "We ran into pretty hard times," Barks allowed. [51] After William recovered, the family moved back to Midland to run the feedlot, their only source of income. When its lease expired, they returned to the family ranch, where Barks's mother died. Years later, Carl would write stories about Scrooge's mental anguish at the thought of ending up a "poor old man." For his entire career as a Disney artist, Barks would live with the specter of poverty and lack of recognition, never able to make enough to get ahead or to sign his name to his work.

Carl completed the eighth grade in 1916, when he was fifteen: he had lost two years because the family moved around so often. Barks "would have loved to go on to high school," but it was five miles away. Also, a childhood bout with measles had caused a deterioration in his hearing, making it "difficult . . . to pick up things in class."[52] Moreover, World War I meant that there was money to be made: he was earning an adult's pay of five dollars a day doing farm work for his neighbors and had to put his career as an artist on hold.

But Barks never forgot his desire to become a cartoonist. In December 1918, he left home and went to San Francisco to try to break into the cartooning profession. He worked for a year and a half as an errand boy in a print shop, earning $12.50 per week, while trying to interest editors in his samples. Barks took his work, including his first major comic strip character, Burlock Bungle, a parody of a bungling detective, to various San Francisco newspapers but failed to find a job as an artist: "They had good cartoonists working for them in those days; they didn't have to take on some kid who didn't have any training."[53]

During his sojourn in San Francisco, Barks sold his first art: "It was a drawing of the sleeve of a soldier's coat that I did as a poster," he recalled. "This was right after World War I had ended, and all the soldiers and sailors were being discharged. And there was a particular chevron that was given to them when they had been discharged that they could put on their sleeve [so] that they could still wear that uniform . . . and would no longer have to salute the officers when they met them. . . . They were going to put the poster in all the streetcars, and so on, and asked me to do it."[54] San Francisco also gave Barks his first taste of big-city life: "The first bare-legged chorus girl I ever saw was in the 1920s, in a musical revue," he recalled.[55] Barks's father subsequently became ill, and Carl returned to Oregon to help with work on the ranch, all the while continuing to hope for a career as a cartoonist.

In 1921, he "foolishly got married."[56] Barks was only twenty, while his new wife, Pearl Turner, the daughter of a Merrill logger, was sixteen. Barks went to work in his father-in-law's logging camp as a swamper, trimming branches off the felled trees. Within a year, Carl had a new daughter,

Peggy. But the logging season ended and Carl was out of work again. The young couple drove to Coalinga, California, in his rattletrap Ford, looking for work. A friend got Carl a job at in the railroad shops at Pacific Fruit Express, first swinging a sledgehammer, then heating rivets. "I was there for about six and a half years, working on that lousy riveting gang," Barks recalled.[57] During this time, Dorothy, another daughter, was born, and Barks found himself with a family to support but little money to do it.

In 1928 he sold his first cartoon to a mildly risqué men's humor magazine, the *Calgary Eye-Opener*. Encouraged by his success, he sent more and more cartoons to publishers, writing gags to go along with his art. By the late 1920s, his marriage had gone sour. "I was always trying to figure out a comic strip or something I could do," Barks explained. "That's what used to irritate my wife at that time. She was satisfied just being the wife of a laborer on the railroad; that's all she wanted out of life. I was using our evenings and all of our spare time working at this darned stuff, and she would rather have been socializing, and so we got to fighting all the time."[58] In early 1930, Carl and Pearl separated, and he returned to Oregon while she and the children remained in California. To make ends meet, Barks boarded with his in-laws and found a job working with his father-in-law at a box factory. Because of the Depression, Barks was soon laid off and took the gamble of going into cartooning full-time.

For the next year, Barks supported himself by freelancing cartoons. But he began to feel that he was imposing on his in-laws, and he took his children and moved to Medford. He decided that his daughters would be better off with him since "my wife had just sort of become the town tramp."[59] One evening, the girls failed to return home from school. A neighbor reported seeing a car drive up and a man and a woman take the girls away: Barks did not know it at the time, but Pearl and her boyfriend had taken the girls to her parents. "I found out afterwards," Barks recalled, "but I spent some pretty hard days there. I had no money, I didn't even have fifty cents to send them a telegram or anything. I was so sure that was what happened, so I just let it blow over, and after two or three weeks, one of my brother-in-laws wrote and told me that they were safe and sound. . . . After that, I didn't feel I owed anybody a hell of a lot, because they let me be hurt like I was hurt in those weeks of uncertainty." [60] This was the only time that Carl ever used the word *hurt* in any interview. His early hearing loss and the loneliness of the ranch gave him a lifelong habit of holding in the pain and withdrawing into himself and the fantasy world of his work.

Barks spent the summer in Midland, freelancing for the *Eye-Opener*. He was unaware that the magazine was in for a shakeup. The *Eye-Opener* had been the creation of Robert Edwards, a Canadian M.P. When "Old Bob," as he was known, died in 1922, Harry Fawcett of the Fawcett publishing empire bought the publication and moved it to Minneapolis. Fawcett turned it into a men's humor magazine modeled after *Captain Billy's Whiz Bang*, which was published by his brother and whose popularity had ushered in a boom in men's joke books. In 1931, Fawcett sold the magazine to Henry Myer, who decided to bring in a new staff. According to Barks,

> Meyer was enough of a businessman to see things weren't being run right around there, so he decided to clean house. There was too much drinking and playing around and not enough production, so he looked over the list of gag men and decided that hell, I was a hardworking son-of-a-gun. So he sent a letter to me, asking if I would come back there. I had enough money to send a telegram saying I didn't have enough money to get back there. He sent me the money, and I closed my affairs very rapidly and gave away the big stack of joke magazines I had. What I could carry in a valise, I carried with me. I got into Minneapolis in November of 1931. [61]

When he arrived, Barks found that the "entire staff consisted of a bookkeeper, a stenographer, an errand boy, the editor, and me. My responsibility was to draw as many drawings as I could to help make the book cheaper to publish, and to write as many gags as I could." [62] In time, Barks was practically writing and drawing most of it. To make it seem like the magazine was not a one-man operation, he would sign various pseudonyms to his art. Barks enjoyed working indoors, heated by the fire of a wood-burning stove, instead of working outdoors and braving the elements. He was making the sizable salary of $110 a week at a time when he could look down from his office window and see unemployed workers rioting on the steps of city hall amid clouds of streaming tear gas.

During the 1920s, humor magazines flourished in the United States. "[M]agazine humor ranged from ingenious slapstick to juvenile 'rah rah' and impassioned social protest, utilizing both crude and amateur efforts and slick professionals."[63] All humor magazines were topical and sought to keep in close proximity to recent events, fads, and fashions. Next to jokes about liquor and crime, the topic that attracted the most attention was gags about women and sexuality. Women had previously been less prominent in cartoons because they were less evident in the social life of the times. The 1920s changed all that. This period saw the collapse of the Victorian morality that had enforced Puritan ideas about femininity and sexuality and witnessed the flowering of a consumer culture based on celebrity, conspicuous consumption, and erotic spectacle. The collapse of Puritan ideals opened up a secret world of masculine daydreams and forbidden desires. Humor magazines responded with a flood of sexual fantasy: voyeuristic plumbers surprising ladies in bathtubs, exhibition-istic maidens struggling to keep their clothes on, and college girls tanta-lizing their beaux with brief costumes and candid speech. Their humor thus contained female sexual freedom within the male gaze, transforming women into sexual objects of male pleasure.

With her rouged cheeks, bobbed hair, and rolled stockings, the central incarnation of the new sexuality was the flapper. She embod-ied a more active and open form of sexuality, epitomizing the "flaming youth" of the 1920s. While magazines such as *Judge* and *Life* portrayed a somewhat decorous version of the new explicitness, men's humor magazines expressed cruder versions of the changes in fashions and morals.

The New Woman was not only sexually freer than her predecessors but also more independent. The 1910s and 1920s saw a dramatic increase in women's entry into a previously male-dominated public sphere with the coming of women's suffrage, increased employment of women in the workforce, and the ability for women to go out unchaperoned in public. While the new sexual frankness promised more sexual pleasures for men, it also aroused anxieties about a loss of male authority, autonomy, and power that female independence portended. Magazine humor thrived on images that subordinated and ridiculed women yet also pandered to their increased eroticization.

Barks's cartoons in the *Eye-Opener* expressed this ambivalence, depicting multifarious images of seductive young women in various stages of undress who functioned as objects of voyeuristic pleasure for the magazine's male readers. These images operated with a different set of conventions for domestic relations, oscillating between what Barks called "fat bags" and "old hags." [64] Wives were huge, obese harridans who tyrannized their diminutive husbands. Once a man married, so the stereotype went, women ceased to be sexually alluring and immediately constituted a threat to his autonomy, becoming the proverbial ball and chain. Conversely, Barks drew older, unmarried women as withered old spinsters who pined for young, virile males.

Barks also indulged in the invidious ethnic stereotypes prevalent in the joke magazines of the era. He drew black males as minstrelsy coons too lazy to get out of bed or get a job, sexually jaded or grossly fat black women, and hook-nosed Jews. These cartoons propped up the self-identities of white males threatened by anxieties about women's dominance or the inability to be good providers during the Depression. Fear of emasculation provoked by this crisis in masculinity also inspired drawings of wispy, effeminate males. However, Barks was too creative an artist to merely replicate gender clichés in his mature work. Although he would continue to utilize such stereotypes in his comics, he would problematize them by satirizing and subverting them.

Barks and the *Eye-Opener*'s editor, Ed Sumner, got along well and in 1932 tried to launch a more respectable humor magazine, *Coo-Coo*, which folded after only one issue. A year earlier, Barks had met Clara Balken, a telephone operator in the hotel where he lived, and they began to date. He was immediately taken by her charms: "She was a very beautiful woman, who in Hollywood circles could have been a stand-in for Marlene Dietrich," he recalled. [65]

In 1932, Annette Fawcett, William Fawcett's ex-wife, bought the *Eye-Opener* with her recently received alimony. She fired Sumner, bringing in a new staff. Annette's byline was the "Henna-Haired Hurricane of Joy and

Laughter," and it fit. "She wanted to put in her own type of heavy drinkers," Barks recalled. "Quite a lot of the time, there wasn't enough left after Annette got her fingers into the incoming checks. . . . She lived in the Radisson Hotel in a very expensive suite, and she entertained very lavishly whenever there were any visiting celebrities from Hollywood in town. She would just take everything that came in and spend it. . . . Some of us poor devils— there was myself, and there were three girls in the office—would get half of our checks, maybe."[66] The magazine finally became so much in arrears that the printers forced Annette Fawcett to let them run the business.

Fearing that the *Eye-Opener* would never become solvent, Barks cast around for other jobs as a cartoonist. Disney animation played a key role in his life, convincing him to become a funny-animal cartoonist. "I had become very interested in funny animals in watching the Disney shorts at the movies. I just split my sides for weeks laughing at the Big Bad Wolf. I really wanted to do that stuff."[67] In November 1935, he read in a newspaper advertisement that the Disney Studio was looking for artists and immediately applied. "I didn't have any particular style," he admitted. "You see, I'd been drawing all kinds of different people's styles when learning to draw, and nothing ever came of it that was individual, except something that looked a little like Disney's style. That's what started me on trying out for them. I would look at those Mickey Mouse newspaper strips and think, 'Hell, I'm drawing things like that. . . . I'll try out and send them cartoons and see what they think of them.'"[68] After seeing his samples, Disney quickly replied with a job offer. "When George Drake hired me, I hadn't even quit my job at the *Eye-Opener*," Barks recalled. "I had to write [to the editor] and tell him I had to get a replacement for myself, and instantly they offered me a raise if I'd stay on back at the *Eye-Opener*." Thinking that they were going to lose their star cartoonist, the *Eye-Opener* upped Barks's salary to $160, double the wage he would get as a starting artist for Disney. But the magazine had no guarantee of solvency. "I had a little trepidation about taking that offer and going to work for Disney for $20 a week, but I did it," Barks admitted.[69] Throughout his life, Barks would demonstrate the ability to take decisive action and engage in "reckless daring" to uproot himself and gamble on starting life anew.

THE DUCK MAN

In contrast to his comic book career, Barks's work in animation has received little attention. The most comprehensive account of his career as a Disney storyman appeared in Michael Barrier's *Carl Barks and the Art of the Comic Book*. But this is primarily a bibliography of his comic book stories, with only passing references to animation. To complicate matters, Disney cartoons have always been team efforts, making it difficult to single out the contribution of any individual. Since Barks's stature as a comic book artist has overshadowed his other work, artists such as Jack Hannah, who labored primarily in animation, are considered the auteurs of the Duck shorts. Nevertheless, Barks, along with Hannah and Harry Reeves, his partners in the Disney Studio's Duck unit, wrote many of the classic Donald cartoons of the 1930s and 1940s and created the Duck persona we know today.

Although they were filtered through many hands, the Duck shorts consistently exhibit themes that can be linked to Barks's authorship. Barks's conservatism and critical stance toward modernity inform many of the cartoons on which he worked. These films foreground anxieties about a loss of masculine authority and control, a dread of the feminine, and fears of technological progress. At the same time, Barks was a staunch individualist, and the cartoons also express an antiauthoritarian ethic exemplified in the nephews' struggle for freedom against Donald, and in Barks's satire of war propaganda and military discipline.

Barks had neither experience in funny-animal cartooning before coming to Disney nor any training in animation. Quitting the *Eye-Opener* was a huge gamble, for Disney had offered only a thirty-day tryout. Like all trainees in Disney animation, Barks's initial position was as an in-betweener, filling in the action between key poses drawn by the veteran animators. "You went to their art class, and you looked at their animation, and you did a few in-betweens.... At the end of the month, they picked out the ones that were likely to make the grade, and those that weren't were given their walking papers. Of the seven that went to work with my bunch, there were four of us that made it."[1]

Barks worked as an in-betweener for about six months, animating scenes for several cartoons, including the Mickey Mouse Fred Astaire dance number from *Thru the Mirror* (1936) and a scene of the Big Bad Wolf singing a parody of "Schnitzelbank" while basting the piggies in the *Three Little Wolves* (1936).[2] Barks also animated a scene of Donald fighting an eagle from *Alpine Climbers* (1936), his only known animation on a Donald Duck cartoon. What survives of Barks's in-betweening is often livelier and more charming than the extremes drawn by seasoned animators, yet he found the work tedious. He explained, "I was a *plot* man.... I wanted to see movement from one situation to another rather than movement revolving endlessly within one situation."[3] Rather than animating microscopic changes of mood and motion in a series of drawings, Barks wanted to communicate ideas in a single sketch. Even at this stage he was predisposed to the comic book method of telling stories. As he recalled, "[T]hat's one of the things that handicapped me. I don't think I visualized stuff in action like I should have. I could work out the plots, the timing on gags, but all the individual action that was to depict that gag on the screen was something that was over my head."[4] Barks also felt that his days as an in-betweener were numbered as a result of his defective hearing: "In-betweeners needed to confer at times with assistant animators, I couldn't do that by telephone, and the resultant awkwardness made me pretty much of a nuisance. I could see the axe was poised, and set about making myself so valuable as a gag man that my shortcomings would be overlooked. The gags saved my neck."[5]

In hopes of being transferred out of in-betweening, Barks began submitting gags to the *Donald Duck* newspaper strip and the cartoon story department. In 1936, the studio staff was invited to contribute gags for a cartoon that would eventually be known as *Modern Inventions* (1937):

> We were trying to think of things that Donald could invent or that he could get involved in. I happened to come up with the thought of a barber chair that would automatically clip hair. And Donald, being a precocious character, messed up the machinery by trying to get his coin back. I had no idea how the gag would be used. I just created a situation in which Donald got into this barber chair and messed up the machinery: it flipped him upside down and gave him a haircut on the wrong end. I also included the little gag about the shoeshine apparatus being down where his feet would be, so he got a shoeshine on his beak. Walt saw it, liked it, and paid me fifty dollars for the gag and suggested that I should be put into the story department.[6]

Although Mickey did not appear in them, the two previous films starring the duck, *Donald and Pluto* (1936) and *Don Donald* (1937), had been released as Mickey Mouse cartoons. *Modern Inventions* was initially conceived as a film starring Mickey, with Donald as part of the cast, apparently because Disney thought that Donald did not yet carry the name recognition to be the solo attraction of a cartoon. *Modern Inventions* changed all that, making Donald a star and launching a series of Duck shorts. A Barks gag—his first to be animated—made the cartoon possible.

After Walt had given *Modern Inventions* the go-ahead, Jack King was brought over from Warner Bros. to direct the new Donald Duck series. At this time Barks had his first conference with Disney: "He was in the building and just dropped in to see how Jack King and I were progressing. He stayed for about an hour and seemed quite enthusiastic about the situations we'd developed for Donald. He and King were long-time friends from the early days of animation."[7]

An expert storyman in his own right, Disney made a significant contribution to the cartoon. Barks recalled, "He suggested that the barber chair be a very talkative machine, like some human barbers."[8] Walt also soothed some of Barks's anxieties about the sequence: "Jack King and I were scared to death we were getting too risqué with this gag. But Walt said, 'Oh, no! Part his hair right down the middle and by all means use hot towels to make him glow.' The towel gag was one of my original jokes, but I only wanted enough heat to make the duck uncomfortable. But Walt wanted his fanny to be glowing red. He could see the visual possibilities."[9]

Not only did the barber chair joke become the climax of the cartoon, it was "the gag that caused Walt and the others to think they could get enough material to make a picture on that subject."[10] The cartoon initially was to have been called *Mickey's Inventions* and would have starred Mickey and Donald. But Mickey had become an idealized hero who could not sustain the comic abuse that Donald might, and in the next few years, many films that began as Mickey cartoons would end up starring Donald, who displaced his predecessor in popularity.

After finishing *Modern Inventions*, Barks was "put in a little room and told to think up another story."[11] He decided to create a tale from an abandoned plot idea in which Mickey was an intrepid Mountie on the trail of Black Pete. Minnie was the love interest, and the humor was provided by the antics of Mickey's horse, Tanglefoot. Barks drew more than four hundred story sketches, including alternative chase sequences through the frozen badlands. However, the film was never taken beyond the exploratory storyboards. *Northwest Mounted* is a fascinating document showing Barks as a novice still learning the rudiments of story construction. At this time he was still a gag man with no experience writing continuity, a fact that explains much of the story's unevenness: while it contained some imaginative gags, it lacked plot and character development, and some of the action violated Disney's rules of plausibility. Barks explained, "I was new to cartoon comedy, having seen only a few cartoons up to that time. . . . I didn't know how much of a character's actions should be justified or made logical, or whether any sort of inkwell trick was acceptable. Mickey and Black Pete were new to me. I assumed they could do *anything* as long as it translated into amusing action."[12]

Barks continued, "My ideas were pretty wild and too illogical for Walt's taste, so he had me put into a story room with Harry Reeves, who had much experience in what could and couldn't be used in animation comedy."[13] Reeves had gotten into animation by a fluke. In 1929, he had been a barker in front of movie theaters, trying to entice passersby to come inside. One day at a promotion for a Tarzan film, a live monkey got loose, and Reeves chased him around the movie marquee. As Reeves scrambled up the marquee to capture the monkey, three animators from the nearby Felix the Cat studio asked when the cartoon would be shown. Always a go-getter, Reeves let the monkey go and immediately talked himself into a job in animation. Working with the seasoned storyman helped Barks refine his humor and bring it into conformity with the requirements of Disney animation.

The collaborative nature of animation raises the question of how much Barks may be said to be the author of the Donald Duck films. As he described the process, "There were usually two guys to a unit. They did most of the work. But they would call in other fellows for conferences, or to help them out. Once a story was presented to the other storymen, then a whole bunch of guys would work on it."[14] After Disney approved the story, it would pass through more hands—animators, in-betweeners, background artists, and other gag men. Nevertheless, Barks and Reeves bore primary responsibility for the story, and because they wrote in pictures, their work influenced the film's final look: "It was natural for animators to follow storyboard drawings fairly closely," Barks explained. "After all, the whole theme of the gags and the idiosyncrasies of the action were planned and staged and partially timed on the storyboards."[15]

Barks and Reeves also had a major hand in shaping the duck's personality. In the Mickey shorts, Donald had been a prankster who upset the staid Mickey's attempts to organize such activities as a band concert, a fire drill, or a magic act. In effect, Donald played a rebellious child to Mickey's parent and was already known for his apoplectic temper. His screen image was epitomized in a fighting stance, with fists cocked and beak sputtering incomprehensible insults. Observed Barks, "Up to *Modern Inventions*, Donald had been a firebrand and a rather silly character. Jack King and I made him a mischievous, sly-looking son of a gun. We made him a more well-rounded character that could be used in more situations."[16]

In his first work on the Donald cartoons, Barks searched for a comic foil with whom to pair the irascible duck. An established formula in the Mickey cartoons had been to team the mouse with a rambunctious animal—at various times, Mickey was saddled with a parrot, an elephant, and a boxing kangaroo.[17] In their first collaboration, Barks and Reeves followed suit. *Donald's Ostrich* (1937) features a bird named Hortense who is delivered to a whistle-stop where Donald is stationmaster. The gags deal with Donald's frustrations caused by Hortense's voracious appetite. When he leaves her unattended, she swallows balloons, an accordion, and a radio. These objects give her the hiccups, causing the radio to change stations and the ostrich to act out the broadcasts. The film climaxes with Hortense chasing Donald around the station as she mimics an auto race. When they crash together into a pile of baggage, she pops up in the wreckage to give the trapped duck a kiss.

Hortense functions as a kind of out-of-control child, and Donald as a controlling parent. The cartoon was designed to appeal to an audience of children who enjoyed seeing adult authority put to rout. But another kind of humor is also at play: Hortense repeatedly antagonizes Donald by kissing him. With her swivel hips, sexy eyelashes, smothering love, and bottomless appetite, she represents a stereotype of the devouring female who threatens male systems of authority and control, a type of misogynist humor typical of Disney animation of this period.

This anxiety about female engulfment occurs in all patriarchal societies but was exacerbated by social changes that occurred in the nineteenth century. As Max Horkheimer and other social theorists have noted, the family has been the transmitter of orientation to authority in most modern societies.[18] However, the nature of this orientation changes with the structure of authority in the economic sphere. In America, men have traditionally defined their identity in terms of their competence, status, and power in the work world and as breadwinners who support their wives and children. Since the nineteenth century, however, masculine authority in the workplace and the home has steadily eroded. A decentralized economy of small enterprises and independent professions has been replaced by a bureaucratized workplace and monopolistic economy, making men's work seem less like a sphere where they could realize independence and autonomy and more like being a cog in a machine.[19] With the growth of corporate capitalism during this period, fathers became less involved in family life as they left home to become wage earners. As fathers became more dependent on wages and the vagaries of the market and subordinate to the authority of capitalists and managers, the material basis of their authority in the family became eroded.

As discussed in chapter 1, the 1920s and 1930s saw an even greater diminution of masculine identity. Women's attainment of the vote and access to a previously male-dominated public sphere and the rise of the sexual freedom and independence of the flapper challenged Victorian ideals of feminine domesticity and gentility. In the 1930s, half of all college students were women, and one-third of all employed Americans were female. The widespread unemployment caused by the Great Depression further undermined traditional notions of masculinity. Never before had American men suffered such a massive shock to their ability to prove their manhood as breadwinners.

Michael Kimmel points out that "mocking fatherly incompetence became a boom industry" in popular culture between the two world wars.[20] Chick Young's comic strip, *Blondie*, featured Dagwood Bumstead as the archetypal bumbling father, tyrannized by his boss, frustrated by his domestic responsibilities, and a model of paternal incompetence in comparison to his levelheaded wife. Likewise, Clarence Days's play (and later film and TV series), *Life with Father* (1936), portrayed the patriarch as a blustering despot whose bark was worse than his bite. Women became scapegoats for and the perceived cause of the decline in male authority. Female power was looked on as dominance over males rather than as a movement toward gender equality. "Feminism really spells Masculinism," argued *Fortune* writer Anthony Ludovici in 1927. "Exposure to the vicissitudes and asperities of the struggle for existence brings about the combative, predatory, and latent male side of female nature, and represses its dependent, loving and sequacious side."[21]

Both scholarly and popular culture sought to ward off the development of feminized males and masculinized females. In 1936, psychologists created the "M-F scale," which measured gendered behaviors and attitudes and gave parents information by which to plot their children's "masculinity" and "femininity" and the effectiveness of gender socialization. The mother was seen as a threat to the development of a son's ability to develop into an appropriately developed male. J. B. Watson, founder of behaviorism, wrote a chapter of his book, *The Psychological Care of Infant and Child* (1928), on "The Dangers of Too Much Love." He criticized mothers for "showering love" on their children, claiming that it destroyed their independence and mental health. "Mother love is a dangerous instinct," he declared, arguing for the need to separate mothers and sons and treat boys differently from girls. "Never hug [boys] and kiss them and never let them sit on your lap," he admonished mothers.[22]

According to historian Gilman Ostrander, during the Depression and war years, American society underwent a major shift "from a paternal faith in the wisdom of age and experience to a filiarchal faith in the promise of youth and innovation."[23] The rise of a filiarchy, or rule of the young, was epitomized in the mass media's emphasis since the 1920s on the young as embodiments of modernity—the flapper, flaming youth, movie celebrities, and fashion icons in advertising.

These developments inflected American popular culture during the 1930s and 1940s and formed the background of the Donald Duck shorts. In 1937, Barks and Reeves received a memo from the story department asking them to introduce three nephews into the Duck series. Barks remembered that he and Reeves received only a "nephew idea" and had to "develop most of the business by batting ideas back and forth. We thought, 'How is Donald going to get the nephews?' Well, the doorbell rings and there they are—they've got a note from Donald's sister and have come to spend the day."[24]

Donald's nephews would become permanent fixtures in the Duck shorts and function as Donald's surrogate offspring. In this all-male family, the female/mother is effaced. Donald becomes the sole domestic authority, thereby eliminating the threat of emasculation by maternal power. At the same time, the cartoons mocked the patriarchal image of the authoritarian father. Donald becomes an antihero whose incompetence is the source of his problems. Acting in loco parentis, Donald often behaves like a petty tyrant—one with fascist tendencies, it has been claimed.[25] He is a product of the nuclear family in the age of capitalism, when the father, enslaved by the factory or corporate system, wreaks his revenge and the little authority he can command on the only underlings he has: his nephews. He was a "bully–ragging whiner and a belly-aching loser," in Barks's words.

Because sons' rebellions against their fathers might appear too subversive, comic strip convention had dictated that their animus be displaced onto conflicts with paternal surrogates. Thus, Hans and Fritz could blow up and otherwise torture the Captain, the father figure in Rudolph Dirks's *Katzenjammer Kids*, because he was only a boarder living with the family. In this way, a child audience could delight in witnessing the flouting of male authority but not overtly challenge the sanctity of paternal power. The Disney Studio adopted a form of this displaced father-son rivalry, pitting nephews against uncles.[26] Mickey had been plagued by unruly children in *Orphan's Benefit* and in *Mickey's Nightmare*, in which he married Minnie in a dream sequence. In 1932, Disney asked Floyd Gottfredson to introduce two nephews, modeled on those in *Orphan's Benefit*, into the Mickey Mouse Sunday page. That first appearance of Morty and Ferdy Fieldmouse was inked by Al Taliaferro, later artist on the Donald Duck strip, so it was no coincidence that he came up with the idea of giving Donald some offspring. Gottfredson recalled, "When Al introduced the duck nephews, he did it emulating the three nephews in *Happy Hooligan* that [F. W.] Opper had done. Hooligan had three little nephews that were all identical."[27] Dana Coty, a gag man who later sold story ideas to Barks for the comics, came up with the euphonious names Huey, Dewey, and Louie, with the names taken from Huey Long, governor of and later senator from Louisiana; Thomas Dewey, governor of New York and subsequently a presidential candidate; and Louis Schmitt, an animator at the Disney Studio in the 1930s and 1940s.

The ducklings first appeared in Taliaferro's *Silly Symphonies* Sunday page on October 17, 1937, but the cartoon that would feature them was already in production early that year. Barks and Reeves's first concept was to make the boys "real little hellions." Barks explained, "The idea that they were to be mischievous came out of Mickey's nephews.... They were brought up according to Dr. Spock, so they thought they could get away with anything."[28]

The 1930s and war years marked a major alteration in child-rearing practices. A significant shift occurred from the strict discipline and adherence to schedules advocated by previous behaviorist approaches to more attention to the child's emotions and "natural" development. In a world slipping from Depression into war, child guidance experts offered parents "the promise of the 'secure child' in a 'world of change.'"[29] In an overview of western theories of child rearing, Daniel Beakman concludes, "If we can judge from its books, the 1940s during the war and in the years immediately afterwards may be described as the most permissive time in child care."[30] Permissive child rearing doubly undermined paternal dominance by ceding more autonomy to children and by enshrining child guidance professionals as the fundamental authorities on child rearing.

Reflecting Barks's traditionalist philosophy, *Donald's Nephews* (1938) spoofs the modern philosophy of permissive child rearing, which taught that parents must not restrain or punish their offspring for fear of stifling them. Donald's attempt to follow the advice of a child training book by soothing and manipulating his charges is met by escalating abuse: they pummel him with croquet balls, douse him with water balloons, and spike his sandwich with hot pepper. After they triumphantly depart, Donald tears his copy of *Modern Child Training* to shreds in frustration.

The youngsters had caused apprehension from the beginning. According to Barks, "Most of us guys in the duck unit felt the introduction of three nephews would hamper the development of Donald's character as it was then being channeled. We couldn't see that it would lead to a sort of duck dynasty completely divorced from the Mickey Mouse influence. I recall some comments about it being too early in Don's career to clutter him with a family."[31] The animators also had misgivings about the hellion image and thought the nephews were too violent to be continuing characters. Recalled Barks, "Harry [Reeves] and I realized that the character of the nephews in their first appearance would quickly become tiresome to audiences. We set out to make them more interesting and acceptable by broadening their characters."[32]

Good Scouts (1938), the nephews' next cartoon, shows how Barks and Reeves solved the problem. The cartoon satirizes the impotent patriarch as would-be despot. Donald is an overzealous scoutmaster who marches his young charges like a drill sergeant. In this film, however, the nephews do not play vicious tricks but earnestly try to follow their uncle's commands. Donald's arrogance and obtuseness, not the nephews' rebelliousness, set him up for a fall. "You kids can't do anything!" he jeers as the nephews struggle to erect a tent. When his own makeshift shelter threatens to fly apart, the boys try to warn him, but to no avail. Paternal authority is made to appear bumbling and incompetent instead of merely being flouted, and the boys, once Donald's tormentors, have become his rescuers.

Here we catch the beginnings of the Junior Woodchucks, the scout troop that would appear in Barks's comic books fourteen years later. By the time he wrote those stories, however, the artist had transformed his satire of parental authority into a parody of the scouts as a paramilitary organization obsessed with war games and merit badges. In addition, the comics trade on a role reversal in which ultracompetent children find clever ways of saving their befuddled elders. The Good Scouts, after making futile attempts to save Donald from a geyser and a bear, retire uncaring to bed. Only in the comics would Barks fully develop the image of the child who was more adult than the adult.

The Hockey Champ (1939) added a new dimension to the parent-child relationship. Once again, Donald arrogantly claims superiority over the boys, this time as a hockey player. He is so confident that he offers to play them blindfolded and proves an easy prey for their tricks. This formula of competition in which the boys best their uncle plays on a fantasy rooted in the Oedipal rivalry between fathers and sons in which sons not only challenge their father's authority but supersede him in power and competence. The theme would become a mainstay of Barks's early ten-pagers in *Walt Disney's Comics and Stories*. Unraveling the notion that fathers had absolute sway over their children, Barks and Reeves converted the ducklings into a unit. The boys would strategize against their uncle, act in unison, complete each other's sentences, even look identical, giving them the collective power with which to defeat a larger, more powerful adult.

Barks drew most of the story sketches for *Hockey Champ*, specializing in action scenes. No other set of storyboards shows so well his mastery of motion gags and physical humor. He helped transform Donald from a squat, awkward-looking fowl into an elastic character with great squash and stretch, key elements in dynamic action. His drawings often gave precise indications of the direction and kinds of movement a character should make. He used multiple poses of characters within storyboards to show animators how the characters would look in different stages of an action. In one drawing, the duck shows off his skating prowess by twirling so fast that his muffler unfurls; the next sketch shows him spinning in reverse, with the muffler wrapping back around his neck. The latter also contains a second figure of Donald off to one side, as if the duck had just watched himself perform. Other storymen rarely used such multiple poses, and the technique allowed Barks almost to animate a scene by himself.

Hockey Champ also shows Barks's mastery of caricature, as Donald mimics skating star Sonja Henie. To parody the female athlete, Barks exaggerated Donald's eyelashes and drew him performing fluttery pirouettes, even giving the duck feminine hand gestures.[33] Most of these touches unfortunately did not make it into the final cartoon, where Donald appears more as a puffy-face yokel. The rest of the time, however, the animators chose to follow Barks's storyboards. As testimony to Barks's skill, the animators adhered more closely to his sketches than to those of other storymen: when the animators departed from Barks's art, the film was often inferior to the original conception.[34]

Besides presiding at the birth of the nephews, Barks had a major hand in creating another member of the Duck family, Cousin Gus. In October 1937, Disney's staff received the outline for a cartoon, *Interior Decorators*, with a plot revolving around Donald's attempts to renovate an old mansion, hindered by a bumbling new assistant, a goose tentatively named Gus. Gags, the outline suggested, could arise from a contrast between the two personalities: while Donald was a firebrand, Gus would be "a slow-thinking fellow who never loses his temper and can do things in his own tricky manner which annoy Don at first—but then make him wonder how the goose did them. So Don tries to imitate the goose, with disastrous results." [35]

This formula derived from Stan Laurel's use of what he called "white magic" in his films with Oliver Hardy. [36] *Interior Decorators* is modeled on comedies such as *The Music Box* (1932), which featured Laurel and Hardy as bumbling piano movers. Donald was cast as Hardy to Gus's Laurel, repeatedly falling victim to the goose's stupidity. Donald's subsequent ire would get the same response that Laurel gave to Hardy's rage: quizzical looks and bewildered head-scratching. Barks worked on the key sequences and sketched many of the storyboards. In one of his gags, Gus asks for food, and an angry Donald offers him a can of paint. To Donald's chagrin, the voracious goose mixes the paint into a soup and gobbles it down, even eating the can. The drawings are humorous and would have animated well, but a coherent plot never emerged, and Disney scrapped the film.

Disney animation is famed for basing its humor on personality, and storymen are constantly on the lookout for something unique, often visually distinctive, about their characters. In Gus's case, the writers concocted a "funny waddle" and a "goofy" way of shaking hands, but neither feature made the character stand out. When they had a second try at animating Gus, Barks's eating gag—the one bit of story material salvaged from *Interior Decorators*—crystallized the goose's image. In *Donald's Cousin Gus* (1939), the goose is no longer Donald's helper but a moocher eating the duck out of house and home. Barks and Reeves wrote the story, and Barks drew most of the storyboards. Gus's appetite not only provided a running gag to tie sequences together but helped define his look. "Harry and I never really visualized Gus until we'd been using him in eating gags several times," Barks recalled. "Then we assumed he would have to be fat." [37]

In Barks's hands, Cousin Gus acquired style and charm. Instead of being just a bloated nuisance, he became deft and imaginative in his eating habits, shuffling slices of bread and bologna like playing cards. In another gag, he cleverly steals a pea by sucking it into a teapot. Such unstoppable greed gives Gus a kind of strength. He is always able to outmaneuver Donald and snap up the food his cousin tries to protect. Gus's voracious appetite had a political point as well. Depression films often sought scapegoats for the nation's economic ills.[38] Hollywood films blamed social disintegration on shysters and unscrupulous businessmen and cast the slum environment as the cause of juvenile delinquency. At the time of *Cousin Gus*'s release, the public was still experiencing the effects of the Great Depression, and the image of the moocher had great cachet, serving to displace popular animus against the failing economic system onto individual greed. Though Gus never returned to the screen, he became an established second banana in the comics. As early as 1938, Taliaferro included Gus in his Donald Duck comic strip, but Gus did not became a permanent member of the Duck clan until 1950, when he surfaced in Barks's stories as a hired hand on Grandma Duck's farm.[39]

Gus was an insignificant character in the comics, but he played an important role in Barks's creation of other secondary characters in his stories. While working on *Interior Decorators*, the artist had drawn two versions of Gus. One, a pear-shaped goose sporting a derby hat à la Stan Laurel, prefigured the screen Gus, but the other version was an anomaly. Tall and skinny with a short beak, he looked more like an elongated duck. Like his rounder counterpart, this Gus wore a vest, although a small straw hat atop a mop of unruly hair replaced the derby. Though this look was discarded, it left a strong impression on Barks, for it later became the visual inspiration for one of his most famous characters, the gawky inventor, Gyro Gearloose.

Desert Prospectors, another unproduced short starring Gus, was equally important as a harbinger of Barks's comic book work. In this story, Gus and Donald are stranded in a sun-baked desert, where they encounter a capricious laughing spring. Drawing on Donald's image as a loser, Barks gave Gus the ability effortlessly to capture the precious water, while Donald's attempts to get a drink are frustrated. Thus, Gus remained a comic foil to the unlucky Donald but without the eating gags. Disney did not like this departure from the goose's earlier persona, and the picture was scrapped. Once again, a germ of an idea stuck in Barks's mind. Years later, the idea of a lucky foil for Donald blossomed into another cousin, the insufferably fortunate Gladstone Gander.

In collaboration with Reeves, Barks was also responsible for creating Donald's girlfriend, Daisy Duck. A prototype called Donna had appeared in *Don Donald* in 1937; she had the hot temper and squawky voice that made her a female double of Donald, but the storymen never intended her for his sweetheart. She was just another foil, a coquettish senorita in a plot where Donald played the caballero. "Donna Duck was invented and incorporated into the story *Don Donald* before I came to the studio," Barks explained. "I never associated that fiery Latin senorita with the more American-type Daisy Duck that came along later." [40]

The first true prototype of Daisy grew out of Barks's fondness for drawing sexy females, a holdover from his days on the *Calgary Eye-Opener*. In a mirage sequence for an unproduced Donald short, *Lost Prospectors*, Donald sees a group of Daisy look-alikes lolling seductively around a swimming pool. All have the curved eyelashes, pert hair ribbons, and high-heeled shoes that would later characterize Daisy, and one is even manipulative and huffy, anticipating her personality. However, unlike Daisy, she is a seductress, "beckoning flirtatiously and tantalizing Donald by mixing a drink in front of him." But the striking visual similarities suggest that this Lorelei duck inspired the costume and look of Donald's girlfriend.

Daisy first appeared as the duck's hot date in a 1940 Barks-Reeves cartoon. "*Mr. Duck Steps Out* was about ballroom dancing and seemed to us coarse duck men to be a subject more suited to Mickey's type of stagecraft," Barks commented. "As for gags, I may have concocted some wild routine or two of antigravity flips and spins, but overall the animators, not the storymen, were the people who injected humor into such terpsichore. None of us older duck men knew what was hip in the dances of the day, and we had to call in younger talent such as Ford Banes to tell us what the ever-changing new steps were all about." [41]

Daisy is the only major female character to appear in the cartoons Barks wrote, and he used her only once. The storymen likely resisted the idea of introducing women into the all-male preserve of the Duck shorts, but Barks denied this: "I had nothing against Daisy appearing in Donald Duck cartoons. If business could be invented that would make her role funny and interesting, she was as welcome as sunshine. Seriously though, neither Daisy nor Minnie were basically funny. We wasted little time try-ing to include such females in the rough-and-tumble heroics of cartoon humor." [42] Of course, what made these characters less interesting was the misogynist assumption that women must be delicate and sedate. Daisy's persona reflects the gendered division of labor at the studio, where the great majority of story artists and animators were men, while the less creative jobs of inking and painting went to women. [43] Even in her screen debut, Daisy is a subordinate character, functioning only as a prize to be won in a competition between males. *Mr. Duck* is less about a battle of the sexes than the Oedipal rivalry between fathers and sons and who will end up with the honor of being Daisy's dance partner.

In comics, Daisy also was a slow starter, with only a walk-on part in her first appearance. Barks admitted that he delayed using her because he "still regarded her as a diluting influence." [44] In 1945, however, she appeared in a cartoon entitled *Cured Duck*, demanding that Donald con-trol his temper. That year Barks also wrote a ten-pager that may well have been inspired by the cartoon (*WDC&S* #64 [January 1946]). Thereafter Daisy began to appear more regularly in both films and comics, finding a niche in the postwar era after women were called on to relinquish their jobs in factories and munitions plants and a cult of domesticity had been installed.

In 1939, Harry Reeves became head of the Disney Studio's story depart-ment, leaving Barks without a partner. That same year a young animator named Jack Hannah transferred into the department. Though Hannah had come to the studio two years before Barks, both men had joined the crew hired to work on *Modern Inventions* and the subsequent line of Donald shorts. Hannah ended up animating many stories Barks helped write, including *Donald's Nephews, Donald's Cousin Gus*, and *Mr. Duck Steps Out*. When the storymen moved to the new studio in Burbank, the company announced that Barks and Hannah would become a new story unit, working exclusively for Jack King.

This changed the relationship between Barks and his partner, since both were now experienced Duck men. Reeves had been Barks's men-tor; Hannah became his collaborator. Functioning more as equals, each had much to teach the other. Hannah felt that Barks was "older and more grown-up. He was more than just a gag man. He was interested in the overall theme and made sure that the gags helped develop the story and weren't just thrown in for an easy laugh." [45] Hannah also influenced Barks: "He knew nothing about writing stories," Barks recalled; "however, he knew a lot about technique and how those stories could be put into animation. He knew about music and timing and all those things, and I didn't. I could think of gags and a funny situation for Donald, but . . . techniques . . . went over my head. So . . . [t]he two of us together made a good team. And we produced a number of good shorts." [46]

The new partnership also changed the type of gags in the Donald cartoons. Reeves was known for his terrible temper and habit of becoming red in the face when angered: "Harry was a fireball," Barks observed. "He was full of nervous energy and on the go all the time, while Jack Hannah was a relaxed sort of fellow who could sit at the coffee bar for half an hour and never miss the time he'd spent. Jack Hannah's gags were more gentle. Harry just thought in terms of violent action." [47] Hannah also had an important influence on Barks's visual style: "I was the type of storyman that whipped out very rough sketches at great speed," Barks recalled. "My forte was to get something visual up on the board and to get a continuity going. Once a gag was well set and accepted, Harry Reeves or Chuck Couch or Jack Hannah would do most of the cleaned-up drawings that we'd show to Walt." [48] Hannah's habit of making finished, shaded drawings rubbed off on his partner, and Barks's storyboards took on a more polished look, especially in key scenes, although his initial concept sketches were still whipped off quickly.

At this time Barks's visual style began to coalesce. His drawings of Donald for *Fire Chief* (1940) bear a remarkable resemblance to his comic book duck of the late 1940s, with a long bill, pie-cut eyes, and a supple, expressive body. Background details of the type that would later appear in the comics crop up, like the satiric Napoleonic portrait of fire chief Donald hanging by his head. *Fire Chief* reprises themes from earlier films such as *Good Scouts*, showing Donald as an arrogant authority figure who tries to impress his nephews and ends up causing one disaster after another.

At the same time, the film breaks new ground by portraying Donald at work. Barks's rural background and years of jobs as a laborer caused him to know the "perversities of beasts, machines and nature," and these themes found their way into the Duck cartoons.[49] Many of the Barks-Hannah collaborations do not include the nephews, focusing instead on Donald's attempt to master a particular task, with ornery animals causing him trouble. In *Window Cleaners* (1940), he traps himself on a scaffold when an angry bee attacks him. *Old MacDonald Duck* (1941) shows a fly making a mockery of Donald's efforts to milk a cow, and a donkey resists being shod in *The Village Smithy* (1942).[50]

Not all the cartoons built on the mastery formula involve work or even animals. Barks was a would-be inventor whose favorite reading was *Popular Mechanics*. His fondness for mechanical gags had surfaced in his first cartoon, *Modern Inventions*, and a number of his later shorts satirize the way in which everyday mechanical devices can thwart and humiliate people. *Donald's Vacation* (1940), for example, shows the duck trying to master an "E-Z" folding chair and becoming more entangled each time he tries to straighten it out. *Early to Bed* (1941) involves a fold-down bed that refuses to stay put until Donald finally nails it down. These films emphasize the duck's determination, not just his temper. Though diminutive, he will tackle enormous odds and become positively obsessive in trying to bend technology to his will.

Barks's concerns about technology have a deep resonance in American culture. Since the late nineteenth century, notes Richard Pells, American writers have expressed ambivalence about the advance of science and technology, wondering whether it promised a new millennium or a menace to humanity's survival.[51] Throughout the Progressive era, claims Pells, these doubts lay submerged beneath a liberal conviction that scientific methods could effectively be applied to the solution of social problems. But World War I demonstrated technology's destructive uses, reviving public anxieties about overmechanization. In the 1920s and 1930s, an intense debate arouse about the dangers of dehumanization by science and technology. Writing about America in the 1930s, Pells notes, "Many of the decade's efforts to understand and deal with science centered around the symbol of the machine. Unable to decide whether it represented the most sophisticated achievement of the modern mind or a supreme expression of evil, writers sought to assess the machine's impact on the economy, on literature, and on man's capacity to sustain a rational life."[52]

The 1920s also saw a dramatic increase in the standardization of all aspects of American life as a result of mass production and consumption and the growth of image-based advertising. As Siegfried Gideon points out, mechanization invaded everyday life around 1920 and took possession of the domestic sphere, including the kitchen, bathroom, and household appliances: "In the time of full mechanization, more appliances grew into household necessities than had been introduced in the whole preceding century."[53] The mechanization and mass production of food also led to a dramatic increase in the demand for processed foods.

Robert and Helen Lynd's famous sociological study of the effects of modernization in the 1920s, *Middletown*, described the effects of modernization on the town of Muncie, Indiana. Using 1890 as a baseline in which the American pioneer spirit finally gave way to industrialization, the Lynds described the impact of mass production, electricity, radio and film, advertising, and the automobile in transforming life in Middle America. The Lynds saw modernization as destroying traditional neighborhoods and communities, isolating and alienating people from each other, and giving people an increasing sense of being at the mercy of external forces they could not understand and over which they had little control. The average (male) American no longer took pride of craftsmanship in a job that demanded little of his personality; large offices and factories made the work process more regimented, monotonous, and impersonal; and the weekly paycheck along with the ability to spend it during leisure time was the sole compensation for an otherwise alienated existence.

Leisure time and consumption were also unsatisfying and destabilizing: according to Pells, "On the one hand, the automobile, the radio, and the movies contributed to the disintegration of family and class solidarity by making leisure largely an individual pursuit. On the other hand, the mass media tended to standardize habits, attitudes and values, absorbing the citizen in an increasingly homogenized nation."[54] As a result, people could no longer easily feel themselves part of an identifiable region or community.

Barks's cartoons satirized the ironies and contradictions of America's passage to modernity. In *Modern Inventions*, he parodied the notion of automation as an ideal of unlimited progress. Instead of fulfilling its promise of making life more comfortable and convenient by increasing efficiency through eliminating labor, the machine ends up mastering its master. The cartoon utilizes a running gag in which the robot butler tries to enforce politeness on Donald by asking for his hat. Donald rebels by producing ever more novel chapeaus, which, to his chagrin, the butler also claims. Intended as Donald's servant, the butler has become a despot and the cause of the duck's eruption into a state of blustering rage at the end of the film.

The cartoon features a number of Rube Goldberg devices in which simple tasks become overmechanized and demean Donald by flying out of his control. He becomes a victim of his desire to be pampered and fed milk like a child. A toy rattle jabs him in the eyes, and the robot nurse-maid squirts him in the face with a bottle of milk and sticks him with a safety pin while diapering him. Barks's gag of the automated barber chair is the coup de grâce in Donald's humiliation. It literally inverts the functions for which it has been designed, giving him a haircut on his rump and a shoeshine on his beak. Becoming an impersonal device that does not respond to "human" commands, the robot barber is totally oblivious to Donald's discomfort, mimicking the chatter of a live barber and mocking the duck's helpless frustration.

Donald's trials result from the fact that he cheats the automated barber by getting his coin back, messing up the works and causing the machine to go berserk. As in other Duck cartoons, Donald deserves the punishment he gets because of his mischievousness and stupidity. In the culture industry chapter of *Dialectic of Enlightenment*, Max Horkheimer and Theodor Adorno interpret this formula as evidence of a masochistic ethic in the Duck cartoons: "Donald Duck in the cartoons, like the unfortunate in real-life, gets his beating so that viewers can get used to the same treatment."[55] Sadistic pleasures are mobilized not to encourage rebellion against forces of social domination but to elicit a form of schadenfreude that makes us internalize our abuse and adapt to the forces that enslave us. However, while this masochistic element is present in the Duck films, the cartoons also contain oppositional elements: they question the effects of technological progress and assert the need to rebel against authority.

Literary critic Walter Benjamin has described the "shock" effect that modern life introduced into the human sensorium.[56] Nowhere was this transformation more evident than in the emerging commercial culture of America. In the 1920s, advertising leaders heralded a new society transforming itself according to a breathless tempo: "What an age," gasped a columnist for *Advertising and Selling*. "Photographs by radio, machines that think. Lights that pierce fog . . . vending machines to replace salesmen. . . . [T]he list of modern marvels is practically endless." Everything now had to be done quick, observed another advertising writer: "Quick lunches at soda fountains . . . quick cooking recipes . . . quick tabloid newspapers . . . quick-service filling stations."[57] The new mass media of film and radio, which first became a fully commercial medium for advertising in the 1930s, created the specter of a country whose masses could be swayed overnight by the latest fads and fashions.

As a purveyor of mass entertainment, radio is a constant cause of disruption and dislocation and an emblem of the shock of modern life in the Duck cartoons. Radio transmitted the new ethic of speed to which the body must respond and which disrupts traditional and organic life, as in *Donald's Ostrich*, where Hortense wreaks havoc on the rural post office where Donald is stationmaster by acting out the programs on the radio she has swallowed, climaxing in her frantic dash around the station house when she mimics a car race. And in *Mr. Duck Steps Out*, the popping corn Donald swallows causes his body to erupt in violent tics and spasms, parodying the way jitterbugs danced to swing music on the radio.

The most important of Barks's cartoons featuring radio is *The Plastics Inventor* (1944), a satire of the duplicity of how-to programs. But the cartoon also implicitly critiques the way in which a flood of cheap, inferior, mass-produced goods, symbolized by the dominance of plastic in commercial items, has displaced the more durable, handcrafted goods of an earlier artisanal culture. Donald is cast as a gullible listener who imbibes, tout court, the facile slogans of the *Plastics Hour* announcer, Professor Butterfield, on how to "bake an airplane out of junk."

The cartoon reveals fears about the breakdown of masculine identity and its "pollution" by feminization. Donald is domesticated, adopting woman's traditional role as cook. Building a plane typically involves the "masculine" processes of industrial production; here Donald uses "feminine" skills to build a plastic aircraft. He cooks the plastic in a vat, pours the liquid onto the griddle, and bakes the plane's parts, cutting them out of the "dough" with a cookie cutter. When the plane starts to fall apart on its initial test run, Donald's homemade plastic helmet dissolves into a woman's braids, mocking his loss of masculine potency and control by again feminizing him. Like *Modern Inventions, The Plastics Inventor* satirizes America's confidence in unlimited technological progress. The professor's voice is cheery and upbeat, claiming that "this little number will do anything." At first the professor's confidence seems warranted: Donald's plane climbs like a "rocket" and dives like a "comet." But the professor forgets to tell Donald "one thing"—that the plane melts in water— and a rain burst immediately starts dissolving the ship, driving Donald into a hysterical panic.

"Don't get caught with your pants down!" Butterfield warns, as the plane's landing gear sags and breaks off, his voice mocking Donald's emasculation. As Donald gets stuck in the dissolving plastic, Butterfield comments in an ironic double entendre, "If you just keep flying plastic planes, you'll be in the dough." Fortuitously, the mass of plastic billows into a parachute, but Donald is suspended from it and dangles helplessly in air, his body pulled by strings of dough as if he were a marionette. Instead of conquering nature, Donald has become the plaything of his own technology. He lands in a plastic pie formed from the plane's debris and, in a fairy tale pun that serves to further infantilize him, blackbirds fly out of it as the enraged duck pops his head out of the crust and sprinkles water on the plastic radio, dissolving it and muting the announcer's voice.

Popular culture has often depicted work as oppressive and technology as alienating, as in Charlie Chaplin's famous satire on the assembly line, *Modern Times*. While Barks's cartoons address our frustration with work and machines, they omit the industrial system itself, making no reference to factories, assembly lines, or the regimentation of the labor force.[58] In this regard they follow the studio's prohibition on dealing with topical or political themes. With the exception of two films, *Timber* (1941) and *Bellboy Donald* (1942), no bosses appear in Barks's cartoons: Donald is either self-employed (*Window Cleaners*), an independent farmer (*Old MacDonald Duck*), or in charge with no higher-ups (*Fire Chief*). In the same way, the machines that frustrate him are usually simple gadgets in his domestic life.

These elisions spell an oversimplified account of the relationship between humanity and nature. As Horkheimer and Adorno demonstrate in *Dialectic of the Enlightenment*, humanity's project of dominating nature through technological conquest and instrumental reason has resulted in a repression of instinctual needs. Horkheimer used the phrase "the revolt of nature" to suggest that such instinctual renunciation would result in violent outbreaks of persistently repressed desires. As William Leiss notes, the concept of "the revolt of nature" can also be applied to the domination of the natural environment: it suggests that there cannot be a limitless exploitation of the external world without damaging natural ecosystems.[59] In representing the resistance of animals and insects to Donald's attempts to master (them and) his surroundings, Barks's stories allude to the antagonism between humanity and nature implied in the attempt to master it. However, the films personalize this relationship, portraying it as merely a duel between Donald and other species in which nature is never harmed and, indeed, in which nature dominates Donald, rather than the reverse. As a result, the narrative occludes the industrial context and its devastation of the natural world.

The Golden Eggs (1941) offers a glimpse at what Barks's films both alluded to and effaced. On learning of a boom in the price of eggs, farmer Donald manipulates his chickens by speeding up production. However, when he tries to make off with a huge basket of "liquid gold," he is prevented by a formidable rooster, an apt symbol of nature's resistance to human domination. The plot hints at labor relations and the wartime inflation of food prices but displaces these processes onto the conflict between a farm owner and his animals. Labor and assembly line speed-up thus function as "structuring absences," an absent center around which the plot revolves but which is ultimately repressed.[60] No direct reference is made to capitalism, though Donald is punished for his greed: after escaping from the rooster, he falls into his basket of eggs, emerging with two large yolks over his eyes. So he gets his gold, but in an ironic fashion that mocks his profiteering and studiously avoids castigating capitalists.

Truant Officer Donald (1941) offers a similarly obsessive duck pitted once more against the nephews. The cartoon breaks new ground, however, in portraying Donald as a tyrannical cop and the boys as his defenseless victims. While they want to enjoy a summer swim, he takes gleeful delight in treating them as criminals. He bags them like fish, imprisons them in his paddy wagon, batters his way into their clubhouse, and finally tries to smoke them out. The boys retaliate by turning his strong-arm tactics against him: they plant three roasted chickens in their bed to make it look as if Donald has killed them.

"Harry Reeves hated that sequence," Hannah recalled. "He thought it was too gruesome, and Carl and I really had to fight for it. Later, when the cartoon was previewed, it got a big laugh, so we were proven right."[61] But the nephews carry their revenge too far, making their uncle suffer with a hoax in which one of them poses as an angel. Donald reasserts control by marching them off to school, but his fixation on capturing the kids has blinded him to the fact that school is closed for the summer. So the nephews' struggle for freedom is vindicated, and the child again triumphs over the repressive patriarch.[62]

Their rebellion is even more justified in *Donald's Snow Fight* (1942). Again Donald is the aggressor, destroying the nephews' snowman out of spite and assailing the boys from the bridge of his ice battleship. He has become a power-hungry military leader swaggering about in an admiral's hat, an emblem used in the Duck cartoons to satirize deluded authority.[63] His attack on the fort is relentless, and one of Barks's drawings shows the nephews battered and bruised, although the film tones down their injuries. Again a political issue is displaced onto a domestic context, so that the Duck family war becomes a metaphor for the allied victory. Watching this mock battle, spectators could identify with the little man defending his home territory, a common theme in American war propaganda.

But deeper, more psychological tensions are at work here. Because they allegorize conflicts between parents and children, Barks's stories evince a degree of realism not commonly found in other cartoons, where characters are usually unrelated. The Duck cartoons allow for the expression of a large degree of hostility that may be assumed to exist between fathers and sons under the institution of patriarchy but that would not be morally permissible to express in real life. However, sons' rebellion against their fathers and the extreme violence they inflict on one another in the cartoons are muted by displacing conflicts onto battles between an uncle and his nephews. In this way, sons could revolt against fathers and fathers inflict abuse on sons without disturbing the mantle of paternal authority. Barks's cartoons thus depict a fantasy in which paternal authority can be dismembered yet simultaneously left sacrosanct.

The introduction of Black Pete into the Duck shorts changed Donald's role yet again. Earlier films had featured conflicts between parents and children displaced onto uncle-nephew conflicts. In most cases, the audience sympathized with the children, delighting in their rebellion against unreasonable parental authority. Now the battles would be between adults. Pete had been an unregenerate villain in the Mickey shorts, but he also had a comic side. His bullying manner and irascibility made him much like Donald. In the later years of the Depression, Black Pete began to be cast as an oppressive authority figure. *Moving Day* (1936) featured him as a heartless sheriff trying to evict Mickey, Donald, and Goofy, while in *The Riveter* (1940), he played a belligerent foreman. Confronted with a larger, nastier version of himself, Donald reverted to the role of sympathetic little guy, once occupied by his nephews, and Pete became the authority figure who had to take the fall at the end of the cartoon.

Probably inspired by Barks's experiences as a logger, *Timber* (1941) was the first Barks-Hannah collaboration to feature both Donald and Pete, and it shows the formula they evolved for dealing with the characters in tandem. Pete (in this case, Pierre) is the tough owner of a lumber camp who makes Donald work off a stolen dinner. Donald is a free spirit, like the nephews, who is suddenly and brutally forced to labor. The duck resists until Pete threatens him with an ax; then he sets to work, wreaking havoc by not knowing the proper way to fell trees. Because the injuries he causes his boss are unintended, Donald gains in sympathy while Pete becomes the subject of the comic tableau shots that characterize his punishment in earlier films.[64] Oppressive labor conditions move from a Depression context into a wartime one as Donald grouses, "I might as well be in a concentration camp!"

At this time, Barks was chafing under Jack King's direction. Barks felt that King's "ideas seemed a little old-fashioned" and that he "always "played it safe," failing to allow innovations in his cartoons.[65] As an example of King's timorousness, Barks cited a sequence from *Timber* in which Donald is stealing food off Pierre's table until he catches on and hands a lighted stick of dynamite to the unsuspecting duck. "We wanted an ominous, low-key drumming, if not complete silence," as Donald picks up the dynamite, Barks noted, so that "the silence would build up to a tremendous explosion."[66] However, King wanted the action timed to a musical beat, which Barks and Hannah felt spoiled the scene's drama. In addition, Barks felt that King's action was often "too slow" and needed more change of pace.

The most common vehicle for the Pete-Donald battles is the army film, in which Donald portrays a hapless private and Pete his gruff sergeant. These films confront the new stresses imposed on Americans by military regimentation during World War II. "The audience took to them immediately," said Hannah, "because it was a natural thing for the duck to try to live up to the big guy, but he would only take it so long and would reverse the thing and end up getting the best of the situation with Pete."[67]

Donald Gets Drafted (1942), a parody of boot camp and the induction process, was the first film to employ this formula. Barks was a pacifist who was highly critical of the coming war: "The war was a very unpopular subject with me.... I had seen one generation of young men marched off to war—World War I—and I was stupid enough that I wanted to get into it, but I was a little too young. And then comes this Second World

War, and I had learned my lesson in the meantime. When I saw how little we had accomplished with World War I, I thought, why in the devil kill off another whole generation of young men to accomplish the same result?"[68]

These sentiments color the humor in *Donald Gets Drafted*. Barks satirized the falseness of American military propaganda in a series of mock recruiting posters, all of which survive unchanged in the film. One, captioned, "Everybody is pals in the army!" shows a smiling general welcoming new troops. Another depicts a private being served breakfast in bed by his sergeant, while an ad for the Army Air Corps sports a sexy drum majorette. In front of the induction office, Donald sees another poster showing pretty hostesses walking arm in arm with a soldier. All the while, an advertising jingle plays in the background: "The army's not the army anymore! It's better than it's ever been before!" The song deconstructs recruiting propaganda that implies that the army is a place where rank does not matter and where bevies of women will swoon over any man in uniform.

The reality is far less enticing. Donald is pushed through his physical, invaded by instruments, and finally has his rump stamped "O.K." as if he were a side of beef. Although he signed on to be a flier like the glamorous men in the posters, he ends up in the infantry under the command of Sergeant Pete. Donald's incompetence as a soldier provokes a brutal response from Pete, allowing Barks to parody military discipline. Donald is now in the position of the nephews, with Pete as the bullying authority. Donald eventually is thrown into the brig and forced to peel mounds of potatoes, giving the lie to the upbeat recruiting propaganda. Pete is punished after a fashion by getting his backside peppered with bullets. His treatment reflects the widespread resentment of army regimentation felt by both soldiers and civilians as the country mobilized for war.

Barks's last Duck film, *The Plastics Inventor*, was released in September 1944, but *Trombone Trouble* (1944) was the last for which he drew storyboards. This cartoon takes the Pete-Donald battles into a civilian context, with Pete portraying the duck's ornery horn-playing neighbor. His music disturbs not only Donald but the gods Jupiter and Vulcan, who give Donald a shot of superpower with which to punish the noisemaker.

Donald goes wild, baring large, pointed teeth and crying, "Power! Power! Power!" When a terrified Pete falls over a cliff and extends his hand for help, the duck jolts him with a shot of electricity. The film ends with the gods congratulating themselves—until Donald picks up the trombone.

Originally titled *Superduck*, the cartoon was initially intended to be a satire of Superman. However, it has more portentous implications. When this short was written, America was heavily involved in the war effort, and some were beginning to have second thoughts about the destructive power being unleashed to win the conflict. Barks projected these anxieties onto Donald. Initially a plucky little guy defending himself against a larger opponent, he becomes as malicious as Pete. Watching the battle, Jupiter says to Vulcan, "Methinks our little man is a foul fighter." *Trombone Trouble* calls into question the link between might and virtue that was being forged by the American propaganda machine.

By 1938 Barks had achieved proficiency as a storyman. However, he felt the need for a change. Because a backlog of Duck shorts had been produced, Barks got his chance. He was assigned to work as a gag man on *Bambi*, collaborating for a time with Chuck Couch and Ken Hultgren. However, Barks's drawings were too cartoony for the naturalistic style of *Bambi*. "Maybe it was six months I was on that," he said. "I don't think we produced one single thing that ever appeared in the movie."[69] Barks would have preferred to remain on *Bambi*: "Life was such a dream over there on the Bambi unit," he recalled. "You could work for a week and never produce anything and still get your paycheck." The features were also considered more prestigious than the Duck shorts. "I felt that I was in with the guys who were really producing the future," he commented.[70] He protested being returned to work on the Duck films, but to no avail.

A story artist as seasoned as Barks and one with his sense of irony could have made significant contributions to the feature films. But he had wearied of storyboarding. "The years I spent in the Disney Studio were toilsome, grinding, and unhappy," he admitted nearly a half century later.[71] By nature a solitary worker and isolated further by his partial deafness, he had never enjoyed Disney's collaborative approach: "Every one of those little shorts was put out by a committee. . . . Of course, we called them teams—'the Duck team'—but it was a conglomeration of a whole bunch of guys' ideas all put together and then sort of molded by two or three guys into a sensible story. The life had all been beaten out of it by the time it finally reached the film. Now in my work all alone, I managed to preserve that spontaneity in my stories; they were like the first sketches in an artist's work. They had bounce to them."[72]

Barks was also very sensitive about criticism of his work: "I didn't like the pressure and the fact that there were so many straw-bosses looking over your shoulder to see how you were doing, criticizing your work all the time. I can't take criticism," Barks admitted.[73] Chuck Couch, who worked with Barks and Reeves in the Duck unit, recalled that Barks reacted to criticism in a manner not unlike the way Donald erupted on the screen.

In addition, the studio was rapidly being converted into a war plant. In 1943, 94 percent of Disney's films were produced for the military.[74] Barks remembered, "It was when they were starting to put badges on everybody, and we were going to have to check in at the gate every morning, and we couldn't have any gasoline to drive anywhere. You were just going to be locked in there for the duration, and I just didn't think I wanted to be locked into that place for the duration." Barks also resented the subject matter of the wartime films. "We were working on one about medicine, and the way germs invade the body. They were getting lined up for some war picture on gun barrels, or something like that. I couldn't see myself getting tied up with that sort of thing."[75] The final straw was something unexpected. In May 1940, the Disney Studio moved into new quarters in Burbank, and its air-conditioning upset Barks's sinuses so much that he was forced to undergo a painful operation. He felt that a move to the drier climate of San Jacinto, east of Los Angeles, would offer a respite from his allergies.

Barks left the studio on November 6, 1942, and moved with Clara to rural San Jacinto to set up a chicken farm, planning to use the money from the chicken ranch to support him while he broke into comics. Barks felt that comics were the perfect medium, allowing him to work at home and exercise more control over his production. Before he left Disney, he wrote to Western Publishing that he would be available for full-time comic book work: "I took a big gamble," he recalled. "I hoped that I could get on with Western Publishing doing these familiar ducks. Otherwise, I was going to be stuck with having to develop something myself and see if I could sell it" to a publisher.[76] But before he could start working on his own strips, Western asked him to illustrate a ten-page Donald Duck story for *Walt Disney's Comics and Stories* (#31 [April 1943]). Western would keep him busy writing and drawing the Disney ducks for the next twenty-four years and even into his retirement. However, his work in animation proved to be an invaluable source of inspiration, suggesting gags, characters, and plot lines for years to come.

FROM BURBANK
TO DUCKBURG

The creation of Donald Duck is tied to the man who would be his
voice for more than fifty years, Clarence "Ducky" Nash. Nash
had been a well-known entertainer on the Chautauqua circuit
(traveling tent show), playing a mandolin and performing animal and bird
imitations. His specialty was an imitation of a baby goat reciting "Mary
Had a Little Lamb." Nash had heard that Disney was looking for people
to do animal sounds for his cartoons. One day, on his way to work, Nash
stopped at the Disney Studio on an impulse and was interviewed by animation director Wilfred Jackson. In the middle of Nash's recitation of his
baby goat imitation, Jackson secretly switched on the intercom to Disney's
office, and Walt came down. Disney had already heard Nash perform on
the radio and was interested in auditioning him. After Nash finished,
he quacked like a duck. Walt looked at Jackson and said, "That's our
talking duck! That's the voice we've been looking for!" A star was born.[1]

According to Nash, Disney invented important aspects of Donald's
personality, such as his volatile temper and infectious laugh. It was also
"Disney's idea to have Donald dressed up in a sailor suit," Nash claimed,
because "Donald is a duck and ducks are associated with water. Therefore
it seemed only natural to have Donald dressed as a sailor." Disney also

wanted "Donald's birthday to be Friday the 13th—March 13th to be exact!"—forever tying him to that unlucky number.[2]

Donald Duck first appeared as a bit player in the 1934 Silly Symphonies cartoon *The Wise Little Hen* and quickly became the bad boy of Disney cartoons. With his second appearance, in *Orphan's Benefit* (1935), Donald was already noted for what was to become his trademark: an explosive temper.

Despite a conspicuous lack of talent, Donald was driven to assert his ego and to master his surroundings, whether this meant hogging the limelight at Mickey's band concert or succeeding at so basic an activity as making waffles. Whereas Mickey worked steadily, even agonizingly, to achieve his goals, Donald's rashness, combined with the general perversity of fate, doomed him to wasted effort and perpetual frustration. Like other film comedians, his humor derived from being an inveterate loser.

In his early ten-page tales for *Walt Disney's Comics and Stories*, Barks drew heavily on Donald's screen image and on the warring relationship between him and the nephews that had been established in animation. "I felt that Western wanted something very much like what they saw in the movies," Barks explained, "and I didn't know how far I could go at the time, taking the duck away from his own backyard."[3] Like the cartoons, Barks's first stories portrayed explosive conflicts between Donald and the nephews as they competed murderously at skiing, skating, kite making, swimming, and even bill collecting. As in the cartoons, Donald would usually lose these bouts, often through bungling attempts to rig the contests in his favor.

The early stories also have the feel of cartoons and are constructed like animation storyboards, with six large drawings on each page rather than the eight panels that became standard fare in most comics during the 1940s and 1950s. At this time, Barks used dialogue sparingly, keeping the story simple and subordinate to his visual images. Like animated shorts, stories devolve on a string of sight gags with the focus on action and movement and center on mayhem and the physical abuse that Donald and the kids heap on each other. Humor tends to be slapstick, with little narrative complexity or plot development.

Barks's working methods at this time reflected his dependence on his training in animation. After he thought of a situation for the ducks to get into, he started thinking up gags that might fit that situation. "First, I just jotted down a bunch of gags that would come to my mind. Then, I started hooking the gags together, and pretty soon I'd have a sort of a little synopsis. From that I'd break it down into a longer synopsis, make a mark every two or three lines and think, 'well, that will make one page, and this'll make another page.' By the time I'd get to the bottom of my synopsis, I'd know whether I was going to have enough material." Then Barks broke the story down into panels, created the dialogue, and roughed in the pictures: "That's when the gags really begin to pop into the story—when I'm breaking it down into panels. I would begin thinking of all kinds of different new things because each panel would suggest something that might happen in the panel just a little later, or a page or two later." [4] As he progressed, he would try to "end each page, especially the latter part of the story, with a little zinger that would carry the reader forward. . . . [T]hat's the way we learned to do it at the Disney Studio [while] working on the short subjects." [5] The narrative rhythm of Barks's early ten-page stories thus quite deliberately evoked the look and feel of an animated cartoon. In fact, Barks even stuck his pages side by side onto a large Celotex board, as in animation storyboarding, so that he could look at the whole story. Standing back from his drawings, he would discard or change various elements, tightening and polishing the final result.

Many of the animated cartoons inspired Barks's early stories. The lifeguard story in *Walt Disney's Comics and Stories* #33 (1943) derives from *Sea Scouts* (1939), "The Duck in the Iron Pants" (*WDC&S* #41 [1944]) from *Donald's Snow Fight* (1942), and the race to Pumkinburg (*WDC&S* #54 [1945]) from *Hockey Champ* (1939). Even some later tales originated in the shorts: for example, the truant officer story in *Walt Disney's Comics and Stories* #100 (1949) was inspired by *Truant Officer Donald* (1941), and Donald's stint as a volunteer fireman (*WDC&S* #86 [1947]) derives from *Fire Chief* (1940).

Although Barks's early work had its basis in animation, it also radically departs from it. Cartoons stress action and the details of movement rather than character complexity or plot development. Comic books, conversely, are a hybrid form that combines the use of extensive dialogue and well-developed plots characteristic of written literature with the visuals of the graphic arts. As a result, they are called graphic narratives. Rather than extending action and movement, comic book panels compress movement into single panels, leaving what is left out to be suggested. As Barks put it, "You have just one drawing; the climatic moment. That's the secret of the action."[6]

According to Clarence Nash, "The writers always kept the Duck dialogue to a minimum [in animation] because sentences would have to be short to be understandable if said in Donald's quacking voice."[7] In contrast, as a partly written medium, the comics emphasized dialogue. Making Donald a speaking character gave him the opportunity to be more human and to emphasize thought—and reflection—as major elements of the storyline. This was key in Barks's stories, which foregrounded the way characters undermined their actions through egoism, self-delusion, and hubris.

From the beginning, Barks intuitively grasped the differences between the two media. The third ten-pager he wrote was inspired by yet also radically departs from the cartoon *Sea Scouts*. The cartoon bases its humor on Donald as a petty tyrant who is the inept commander of a boat with the nephews as his crew. The story culminates with a frenetic battle between Donald and a shark who has knocked off the duck's admiral's hat. Other than showing the absurdity of Donald's arrogance, no point is made.

Because this was too thin a reed on which to string a comic plot, Barks added a girl to his story, introducing a more nuanced storyline. As in many of Barks's ten-page stories, Donald represents the alienated Everyman seeking some form of recognition in a society that denies him any feelings of self-worth. Declaring his desire to prove his bravery, he immediately receives the opportunity with the appearance of a shark that threatens the nephews. This is one of the many coincidences on which Barks plays in the story, giving it a richly complex and ambiguous texture. Donald bravely swims toward the shark to rescue the kids but then sees its enormous mouth up close and flees in terror, stopping to protect himself by hiding behind his surfboard. He becomes a hero only by chance—and by dint of an unheroic act—when the shark knocks himself out by hitting Donald's board.

But Donald's defeat of the beast affords him no recognition. When he claims to have bested it with his "bare hands," the stuck-up duck girl on the beach whom he seeks to impress thinks that he is a "boastful phony." The story foregrounds the unpredictable nature of the cosmos and the tenuous dividing line separating appearance and reality. When the kids try to help by buying a shark carcass and staging a fake rescue, it finalizes the girl's judgment that Donald is indeed a phony. Just then, however, what appears to be a real shark menaces her, and Barks draws its head looming over her to emphasize the danger. After Donald battles the shark to save her, she rewards him with a kiss and invites him to the dance that evening. However, unbeknownst to Donald, he has mistakenly battled the corpse of the dead shark from his previous encounter. Donald's heroism is thus paradoxical. Although his intentions were heroic, his conquest of the shark was merely a sham, making him the phony that the girl initially considered him. Barks thus pointed out the ambiguities that necessarily attend heroic acts. Such levels of irony, coincidence, and simulation were well beyond those envisioned in the animated Donald series.

In the late 1940s, Barks became increasingly aware that stories and art that were well suited to animation might not work in comic books. "You could draw just so much violent action in a comic book before it got tiresome," he explained. "Floyd Gottfredson put his finger on it one time when I was talking with him, sometime in the 1940s. He said, 'In the strip, the reader can hold it up, and he looks at it for a long, long time, but when it's on the screen, he sees it for a twenty-fourth of a second, and it's gone.' . . . I remembered what he had told me, and I toned down my action a little bit after having talked with him."[8]

At this time, Barks's stories acquired a new look. They were no longer simple adaptations of plots and gags characteristic of animation but instead utilized the full potential of the comic book medium. However, the initial breakthrough did not occur in the ten-pagers but in the Donald Duck adventure comics. In these tales, Donald remained the impulsive, explosive duck of cartoon fame but became a more complex character as Barks imbued him with the strengths and weaknesses necessary to sustain the hero of a long adventure. Donald might be brave or cowardly, lazy or resolute, but in facing danger, he and the boys became protective and helpful toward one another. "I broadened his character out very much," Barks commented. "Instead of making just a quarrelsome little guy out of him I made him a sympathetic character. He was sometimes a villain, and he was often a real good guy and at all times he was just a blundering person like the average human being, and I think that is one of the reasons people like the duck."[9]

As Donald matured, so did the nephews. Instead of mischievous troublemakers battling their uncle, they became wise little helpers struggling to save him from trouble, whether external or self-inflicted. We can see this change in *Pirate Gold* (*DD* FC #9 [1942]), the first comic book that Barks drew. "'Pirate Gold' proved to the publishers that Donald didn't have to be in constant turmoil in order to be interesting," Barks commented. "His bungling mistakes and his blissful innocence of danger and of being outrageously victimized proved just as amusing as his tantrums. He came off great in a sympathetic role, and his brattish little nephews came off equally as great as the 'brains' of the family. The comedy situation of Donald the reckless bungler getting into hopeless troubles from which he is extricated by his sharp-witted, suspicious-natured nephews was completely developed in this story, and it has carried on into many tales of high and not-so-high adventures ever since."[10]

Barks was careful, however, not to let the relationship between Donald and the boys calcify into a rigid formula. He had experienced life's randomness and perversity and imparted these qualities to his stories. Even when he allowed the nephews to be consistently wise, he confounded the reader's expectations with plot reversals. We can never tell until the last minute whether the boys' intervention will save Donald or aggravate his troubles. "I began making them into sort of smart little guys once in a while," Barks recalled, "and very clumsy little guys at other times, and always I aimed at surprise in each story so that nobody could pick up a comic book an say, 'Well, the nephews are going to behave thus and so.' They wouldn't know until they had read the story just what those little guys were going to be up to." [11]

As noted earlier, Disney comics feature no biological parents. Aunts, cousins, and nephews abound, but not fathers and mothers or even married couples. This erasure allows children to express hostility and rebelliousness toward an uncle that would not be permitted against the parent. The child can be superior to and dominate an uncle without having to confront the ambivalent emotions and Oedipal taboos surrounding the displacement of the father. Such longings had great appeal for a target audience of children. "I couldn't have the little kids get squashed or kicked around," Barks explained. "Once in a while they would get themselves in some pretty bad messes, and then Donald would have a chance to rescue them. But mostly it was the kids who rescued him. It worked out better, and it appealed to more people that way, because the readers were kids themselves. They liked to feel a little bit superior to the uncle who was strutting around." [12] The comics thus offer the child the satisfaction of reversing roles with the parent and becoming more adult than the adult.

Never encouraged by his own parents, misunderstood by his elder brother, and with little time to play like other children, Barks created in his imagination the childhood he never had. He invested the nephews with his desire to rebel against and triumph over his parents: "Every child dreams of outsmarting his parents," Barks explained, "knowing more than they do. I remember as a child thinking similarly to the way the nephews do." [13] The Duck Man's experience thus tapped into desires all children had, giving his stories a universal appeal.

The nephews' membership in the Junior Woodchucks offered Barks the perfect vehicle for his trope of child superiority. The Woodchuck organization embodies expert knowledge, resourcefulness, and moral fiber, all of which Donald lacks. The Woodchucks were inspired by the film *Good Scouts* (1938), which Barks wrote with Harry Reeves, but the idea had deeper roots in Barks's childhood desire to join the Boy Scouts: "I was never a Boy Scout, but oh, I wanted to be one when I was a kid about ten or eleven years old. But there wasn't anyplace where I could ever join the Boy Scouts. I patterned the Junior Woodchucks after the

Cub Scouts, really, the little bitsy guys ... who were supposed to be so much smarter than their older brothers."[14] In later stories, he gave the boys an almost magical power by creating the Junior Woodchucks Guidebook, an impossibly encyclopedic handbook and reference work that allows them to translate arcane languages, fight mythological beasts, and even undo the sorcery of Scrooge's archfoe, Magica de Spell.

Under patriarchal capitalism, male identity has traditionally been defined in terms of autonomy, dominance, and control. The ideal of masculinity has exemplified what R. W. Connell labels "hegemonic masculinity." A strictly hierarchical type of social relations, hegemonic masculinity is a form of the ideology of masculinism in which male self-sufficiency, toughness, competitiveness, and power define what it is "to be a man." According to Connell, any culture possesses a variety of different masculinities. Hegemonic masculinity is a particular model or definition of masculinity that has received dominance over other varieties of manhood in America and requires the "subordination of women" and "the marginalization of gay men and youth." Thus, it posits as deviant and unnatural unruly women who appear overly masculinized and "weak" or feminized males.[15]

"From the early ninetieth century until the present day," writes Michael Kimmel in his study of manhood in America, "much of men's relentless effort to prove their manhood contains the core element of homosociality. From fathers and boyhood friends to teachers, coworkers, and bosses, the evaluative eyes of other men are always upon us watching, judging."[16] This male gaze invokes a fear of being considered weak or vulnerable by other men, the ultimate fear that the male will be emasculated and feminized, dissolving the boundaries that define masculine identity by differentiating it from its gendered opposite, woman.

From the late 1880s through World War I and into the waning years of the Progressive era, Americans perceived traditional (white, middle class, Protestant) masculinity as experiencing a crisis. Many late-nineteenth-century American men felt threatened by changes in gender roles that resulted from America's transformation from a rural to an urban, industrial nation. At the heart of these fears lay the transformation of the workplace. An increasingly bureaucratized society in which men had to work as wage earners had displaced the autonomous and independent male vocations of the past, when men had been farmers or self-employed professionals rather than salaried employees in hierarchically structured corporations. The transition toward sedentary, white-collar jobs in a bureaucratized, consumer-oriented society was seen as subjecting the male to overcivilizing and feminizing forces that were unmanly. To counter this trend, organizations sought to reinvigorate traditional virility through a cult of physical strength, moral fiber, and self-reliance found in sports and outdoor-oriented activities.

The Boy Scouts was one of a number of boy-saving organizations generated during this time to counter anxieties regarding the perceived loss of masculinity and to guarantee the engendering of masculine character in a new generation of boys. The group was based on the assumption that "men believed that they faced diminishing opportunities for masculine validation in the market place, but adolescents faced immense barriers, it was thought, to the very development of masculinity."[17] The Scouts yoked the development of manhood to a nostalgic re-creation of the woodcraft and woodlore skills associated with rural, frontier life.

Barks's first story about the Woodchucks (*WDC&S* #125 [1951]) revolves around such tests of masculinity and concerns the nephews' attempts to gain merit badges for demonstrating survival skills in the snow. Barks parodies the ideal of heroism embodied in such notions of manhood. Contrary to the image of the noble St. Bernard, Donald's dog is not a valiant rescuer of snowbound travelers but deathly afraid of the cold. Donald has to chain him to the car and drag him to Frostbite Pass to test his mettle. The name Bornworthy itself constitutes an ironic comment on this most unheroic dog.[18] Heroism in Barks's universe is chancy at best, and the story depicts no valorous action. The purpose of the rescue operation holds no interest for Donald. He perverts the Woodchuck ethic, cheating to help the boys pass their test because he wants to be able to brag about having a lifesaving dog and three brigadier generals in his family.

The snobbish Woodchuck commander is little better. Though he postures impressively, he is careless about the simplest safety precautions and shouts a signal to the boys that causes an avalanche. The story exemplifies Barks's theme of child superiority. Both adults are buried in the snow, equally inept. Bornworthy comes through at the end of the story and saves five lives, but with no heroic intent: he leads the ducks home only to return to his warm fireplace. In the end, the boys earn their merit badges but do so only by treating Bornworthy's cowardice as an asset. Bornworthy remains as oblivious to the award ceremony as he was to the test, and the fact that he eats his merit badge, thinking it a cookie, ridicules the quest for such honors.

Throughout the story, Barks satirizes the Woodchucks' elitism, obsession with rank, and paramilitary discipline. Major is the lowest rank in the Woodchucks, and every trooper has a lofty title and wears quarts of medals. Though only children, they address each other as "colonel" and talk about their merit badges as if they were beginning the start of a military campaign—"war games," as Donald calls it. Parodying the mystique of military language, Barks makes a running gag of converting Woodchuck titles into unintelligible acronyms. The boys' repeated references to O.R.ST.B. (Operation Rescue Saint Bernard) give their dialogue an official air but confuse their civilian uncle, who must finally intrude on their conference to ask for an explanation. Much of the humor derives from the way the nephews take their scouting in military earnest. The nephews' infatuation with badges, medals, and titles offers a very real portrayal of the seriousness with which small children invest games and playact at being adults. But in Barks's universe, good deeds should be done for their own sake, not to earn honors.

The nephews' Woodchuck skills and moral superiority enable them to triumph where their shortsighted elders—Donald and Scrooge—invariably fail. However, at the heart of the tests of manhood they undergo lies a withering threat—a fear that haunts all masculine performance—that unless they prove their masculinity they will lose the basis of their identity and be reduced to nonexistence. Even when Donald explains to the Woodchuck commander that the nephews have not cheated and that he alone is responsible for the ruse with Bornworthy, the stern troop leader gives them only "one last chance": if they fail, they will be demoted to "mere majors—the lowest rank in the Junior Woodchucks!" They are crestfallen to be condemned, hanging their heads in shame. The reader never has to consider the possibility of their ultimate failure because the Woodchucks always succeed in the end: it would be too disconcerting in a comic addressed to children for them not to succeed and thus to be rejected by the organization they revere. Nevertheless, the story highlights the fear of failure and ridicule that attends a form of male identity in which self-esteem is continually tested and one must be proven worthy lest he be deemed unmanly.

Issues of masculinity surface overtly in the story of the Woodchucks' contest with the Chickadees, a Girl Scout group, in *Walt Disney's Comics and Stories* #181 (1955). Here, the nephews display the archetypal prepubescent fear of associating and competing with little girls. They are "insulted" by being challenged to a contest by the Chickadees and assert their virility by posing a test that only "rugged he-men can do!"— bridge building. Barks resorts to sexist stereotyping in casting the girls' leader as a butch-looking, lantern-jawed ex–Army Corps engineer. The Woodchucks are handicapped not only by lacking a leader but by having to rescue Donald twice, thus allowing the Chickadees to gain ground.

In rescuing their uncle, the nephews display the true scouting ethos. However, the Chickadee commander is an opportunist so bent on beating males that she laughs with glee at their plight and urges her charges to continue working. The contest ends in a tie, with both groups landing their bridges simultaneously. The nephews are ready to start an all-out battle with the girl troop until a high-ranking Woodchuck official shows up and magnanimously declares the contest a draw and hands out loads of medals to the Woodchucks. Their efforts and adherence to scouting ideals seem to be properly rewarded and a kind of gender equity enforced. But males are privileged throughout. The Woodchucks would clearly have won if they had not stopped twice to save their uncle and if they had had expert leadership like the Chickadees. Females are bent on dominating males, the story suggests, even at the expense of cherished ideals. As the masculinized image of the Chickadee commander suggests, women are out of place in the male world of engineering and bridge building.

Having raised the nephews to a pinnacle of wisdom and infallibility in the Woodchuck stories, Barks occasionally toned down the nephews' resourcefulness, making them just normal children in later stories. In *Walt Disney's Comics and Stories* #158 (1953), the boys seek to become Junior Woodchucks Future Farm Experts by learning beekeeping. But they thoughtlessly leave a hive of bees unattended in the backyard, and when they come home and the hive is missing, they bawl like babies. They have become schoolkids seeking an entrée to the adult world through the development of their Woodchuck skills, not members of a crack regiment performing for the pleasure of the exercise. The kids' attempt to master beekeeping first gets Donald in trouble with all of Duckburg, then lands him in the hospital. Just when he thinks that he has his boys and their nature project under control, the bees smell his cologne, go wild, and attack him. Weeks later, when the nephews' honey wins first prize at the Farmer's Fair, they run excitedly to the hospital to take him a taste of it. "Ah! We parents!" sighs Donald, swathed in bandages, "what *rich* rewards we reap!"

In the cartoons, Donald's misfortune would have been the result of a direct physical assault by the nephews. Here, however, no straightforward conflict arises: the boys keep the bees as part of their education, Donald puts up with the project as part of his parental duty, and all blunder as best they can. Nor is there any real victory. The boys' honey wins only by a fluke, impressing the judges because it tastes of cologne, and Donald's tiny reward is out of proportion to his pain. Throughout career, Barks would continually vary his characters, revealing diverse sides of the adult-child experience.

In the late 1940s, Barks's stories underwent a striking change, breaking from the parent-child formulas established in animation. Plots grew increasingly complex and convoluted, and tone became more darkly pessimistic. The postwar Donald lives in an uncertain, threatening world. While he may lose through cheating or stupidity, he cannot win simply through good efforts. Barks abandoned the stock resolutions of popular fiction in which the good end happily and the bad unhappily and strove to make his stories unpredictable. Although Barks frequently insisted that it is best to be honest and upright, his stories also reveal that morality is no guarantee of love, wealth, or success. In his words, "I was letting the story build up to a certain point in which the reader would be expecting the conventional end, and then I would fool the reader by dragging in something that was completely ridiculous, making it look plausible."[19] Many of his stories derive their humor from sudden reversals of fortune and the unpredictable effects of coincidence. Donald's schemes are often defeated by cosmic caprice or the irony of fate, with the universe seeming deliberately to manipulate events to lead him into false hopes, only to frustrate and mock his desires. In these stories, Barks constructed narratives in which there would be a six- to eight-page build-up of reader expectations, against mounting probabilities, and a crescendo that culminated in the fulfillment of readers' original expectations but in a surprising and highly ironic manner.

The story of Donald's golf game in *Walt Disney's Comics and Stories* #96 (1948) exemplifies this structure. From the outset, the reader expects Donald to lose. When the nephews trick him into thinking that he has hit a hole in one, he comes to believe that he is one of the world's greatest golfers, and we know he is in for a rude awakening. After making a sucker bet with Gladstone, Donald discovers that he really is inept, and we are convinced that the story will end in disaster.

To forestall this conclusion, the nephews help Donald cheat, and it seems possible for a moment that he may win; however, Gladstone marks the ball, and disaster again seems inevitable. Yet Barks frustrates all these expectations. Donald makes an incredibly lucky drive, and cheating no longer seems necessary. He slices the ball into a creek; it then bounces off turtle's shell, lands on a bird's back, and falls into a sand trap; finally, a gopher kicks it onto the green, an earthquake keeps it rolling, and it falls into the cup. Then, as Donald leaps for joy, the plot goes into its final reversal, and his ball is knocked out of the cup by the ball the nephews had already placed there. Our earliest expectation is fulfilled but in a surprising and highly ironic way.

Donald's defeat seems to confirm a moral stricture against cheating, yet in many ways the story prohibits any moral resolution. Though in effect he is punished for his arrogance and dishonesty, the story's most striking feature is its emphasis on the fickleness of fate, first in the outrageous trajectory of the ball, then in the final reversal. The reader remembers less Donald's punishment than how close he came to winning before fate snatched victory from him.

This is a worldview that depicts a random, morally indifferent universe, much in the vein of existential writer Albert Camus. Its pessimistic fatalism recalls postwar *films noirs* like *Out of the Past* and *Detour* whose male protagonists seem preordained to doom and destruction as a consequence of their own delusions in collaboration with cosmic forces beyond their control. As such, Barks's stories reflect a fundamental disillusionment about the prospects for male affirmation and success in American society.

The fatalism characteristic of the *noir* universe exemplifies what contemporary critics have called a crisis in postwar ideology and attendant definitions of masculinity. Social theorists writing in the 1940s and 1950s pointed to the contradictions between individualism and conformity in postwar American culture and the discrepancy between a nation grounded in frontier mythology and the domination of America by large-scale corporate bureaucracies. In *The Lonely Crowd*, for example, David Riesman et al. argue that corporate society produced a new character structure. The individualistic, "inner-directed man" of the Protestant ethic and nineteenth-century entrepreneurial capitalism had been supplanted by the "outer-directed man" of contemporary corporate society. William Whyte's *The Organization Man* argued that the corporation's demand for fealty had resulted in the displacement of individualism for a social ethic of teamwork and accommodation to the group. C. Wright Mills's *White Collar* claimed that the old American middle class had been proletarianized and had lost much of its former power and independence. Where once the middle class could have hoped for the autonomy that came with independent proprietorship, the new middle class increasingly comprised dependent employees of large corporations. The result, claimed Mills, was that rather than feeling fulfilled in their work, the new middle class was bedeviled by feelings of powerlessness, alienation, and status panic.

The bureaucratization of society had important effects on culture as well. An older, more individualistic culture was being supplanted by a homogeneous consumer society whose tastes and values were instilled by the power of advertising and the mass media. Geographic and social mobility were shattering the individual's ties to the nuclear family, local communities, and kinship groups, making people increasingly vulnerable to the media's imposition of standardized images. Formerly a society of "widely scattered little powers," America was becoming a mass society in which individuals were being manipulated by "monopoly control from powerful centers."[20]

Changes in gender roles during the war years added to a sense of male malaise. During the war, women assumed jobs formerly occupied by men, becoming truck drivers, stevedores, and welders. After the war, women were supposed to relinquish their jobs to male veterans and return to the home. However, many women refused to give up their new-found freedom and independence, creating a massive crisis in formerly naturalized definitions of masculinity and femininity. The femme fatale in *film noir* exemplified this crisis—a strong, sexually aggressive women who refused to stay in her "proper," dependent place. The power of the femme fatale enticed women because of its assertive representation of the feminine but threatened traditional codes of masculinity. Changes in the bureaucratization of society and increased corporate power were often projected onto scapegoats, especially women. Feelings of male lack and powerlessness were conflated with emerging changes in sex roles and fear of women's increasing power in the public sphere.

These tensions are invoked in the story of Donald's nightmares in *Walt Disney's Comics and Stories* #101 (1949). The comic book protagonist is typically a strong, resourceful male who fights his way through great danger, triumphing over monsters and larger-than-life villains. The Donald Duck and Uncle Scrooge adventures partake of this formula as the ducks journey to exotic locales, unearth lost civilizations, and fight bizarre menaces. The ten-page stories, however, are set in contemporary Duckburg, and this one concerns the banal problem of insomnia.

Barks demonstrates that everyday life can hold more egregious terrors than any fantasy. Donald suffers a series of horrific nightmares: he is almost eaten by voracious monsters from Mars, drives his car off a cliff, is forced to walk the plank into an ocean of sharks, and is nearly devoured by lions and wolves. But his greatest fear turns out to be something else—fear of being publicly ridiculed as unmanly, of being a sissy. Barks satirizes the hysteria that surrounds fears of being feminized by showing the absurd lengths to which Donald will go to avoid it. His doctor prescribes doing something he hates, crocheting doilies, to cure his insomnia. But Donald would rather risk death than be caught doing something "girls and old ladies do." When Daisy and her compatriots pursue him to make him speak at her tatting club, he is so eager to escape that he becomes oblivious to real dangers and drives his car over a cliff and lands in the shark farm.

However, Barks also shows that Donald's fear of the women is justified. Daisy is relentless in pursuit of Donald: she and her female compatriots hunt him down like a wild animal. Daisy's search seems sadistic and implicitly aimed at dominating and humiliating Donald. She represents a woman who is out of place, a masculinized female who acts like a hardened male troop commander, summoning "a flying squadron of companions of needlework" to surround the park in which the duck has taken refuge. Donald is forced to flee, pursued by a mob of hundreds of women. Though Donald regresses to an almost animal state in the pursuit, the real beasts are the women. Donald unintentionally adopts the doctor's cure as he is threatened by dangers even more frightening than being devoured by lions and sharks—the fear of being publicly unmanned. He becomes a hermit who would rather live in mortal danger in the lion's cage than be emasculated by Daisy and her clubwomen.

In drawing Daisy, Barks repeats the imagery he used to portray Donald's nightmares. Daisy's gaping mouth links her to the ravenous beasts of Donald's dreams, and her companion is called Mrs. Gobblechin. The zookeeper, another symbol of repression and conformity, also has a wide, toothy grin. While explaining that Donald is "cured," the zookeeper holds a baby giraffe by the throat, choking it. The zookeeper's misunderstanding of Donald's cure only reveals society's callousness. Donald would rather live in the lion's cage than be emasculated and publicly ridiculed.

This story's expression of the male's fear of being devoured by women represents what in psychoanalysis has been called the threat of the oral mother.[21] The alien monster into whose gaping maw Donald almost jumps in his nightmare (and the sharks who almost eat him) are archetypal images of the *vagina dentata*, or toothed vagina. Their sharp teeth and threat to devour him are apt symbols for the male fear of the castrating, devouring mother/female. Male perceptions of women as devouring monsters stem from what are called reengulfment fears evoked by a time when the male infant was helpless and totally dependent on his mother, who wielded the power to satisfy or frustrate his wishes and desires. The monopolization of the child-rearing role by the mother and the male child's dependence on and symbiosis with her, coupled with the exaggerated emphasis on power and autonomy as male ideals, places severe demands on the male adult, and he is plagued by fears of a return to a time when the mother was virtually omnipotent. The adult male experiences the threat of engulfment as a breakdown of masculine identity and systems of order; to defend against these anxieties he must exorcize the feminine within and subordinate and infantilize women.[22]

Women's empowerment thus may evoke in males a fear that men will lose power and autonomy, and lead to the development of misogyny. These prejudices are extended by conflating social conformity and repression with feminization, scapegoating women for social structural evils. Barks often used female stereotypes to suggest the constraints of custom and bigotry—witness the snobbish old harridans who want to jail the harmless zombie Bombie just because of his deviance (*DD* FC #328 [1949]) and the overprotective battleaxes who take over Donald's swimming pool to "protect" their young children from harm (*WDC&S* #129 [1951]).

Barks's satire acquired a new dimension in the late 1940s as he turned to parody popular fiction. Westerns, science fiction, and fairy tales have traditionally provided the raw material for many comic book genres. Barks's stories reveal a fascination with the way popular fiction holds a hypnotic power over readers and how we uncritically imbibe what mass media define as reality. Most fiction has traded on its ability to convince readers of the reality of what they consume, thereby submerging the knowledge that they are dealing with fiction. Such willing suspension of disbelief is especially important to popular fiction, which must frequently make wildly implausible characters and events seem plausible. Barks, however, displays a marked ambivalence about the fictive nature of his material. He narrates his stories as if they are real events yet simultaneously deconstructs the premises on which they are based.[23] In this way, he reveals the contradictions that lie hidden in the premises by which they—and we as readers—operate. Such stories offer paradoxical and multiple interpretations, undermining the traditional notion of narrative coherence. The result is a new type of self-reflexive comic book story that foregrounds itself as fictional discourse, allowing us to be aware of and critical towards the material we are reading. The contradictions made apparent by these stories invite us to critically examine rather than passively consume the popular formulas, myths, and stereotypes he portrays. Thus, they provide an alternative to what Bertoldt Brecht called the "culinary" approach to media consumption.

While working at the Disney Studio, Barks had been fascinated with the great popularity of Superman and had considered developing a comic book of his own featuring human characters after he quit Disney. Barks even wrote a Donald Duck cartoon, initially titled *Superduck* but released as *Trombone Trouble* (1944), lampooning the Man of Steel.[24] *Walt Disney's Comics and Stories* #107 (1949) utilizes deconstructive techniques to satirize the comic book superhero. The story opens with Donald reprimanding the nephews for wasting their time reading trashy stories about a hero called Super Snooper. After confiscating the nephews' comic book, he sends them to the pharmacy to fetch a bottle of his dyspepsia medicine. By mistake he ends up drinking a bottle of liquid isotopes and ironically acquires the superstrength he refused to credit in a comic book. "Nobody can lift these things!" he says, using one finger to hoist a steamroller parked on a child's doll. His new powers gradually beguile him into belief, much as readers simultaneously come to believe in the "reality" of what they are reading, until we enjoy unquestionably the spectacle of a once dyspeptic duck tying together the tails of two comets.

After he has the belief established, Barks begins undermining it, introducing clues that we have entered the realm of fantasy at the same time that he continues to push credibility to its limits. As Donald proceeds to leap over the moon, lifts a sunken liner from the ocean floor, and cracks open a mountain to reveal a hidden vein of gold, the panels become irregular in shape, as if bursting the structure of the rectangular comic book page. All four feats of strength are grouped in montage on the top half of one page, while Donald flies blissfully on his back in the next panel down, eyes closed as if to suggest that the panels above him are merely a daydream. In effect, the whole top of the page has become his thought balloon. Coupled with this suggestive structure is a subtle shift in tense—"I'll leap higher than the moon" rather than "I can leap higher than the moon"—implying that Donald fantasizes performing these feats in the future. Like the act of reading a comic book, they are private, interior experiences, and Barks depicts the duck performing them quite unobserved.

The next moment, Barks undermines the preceding narrative, as the isotopes wear off and Donald crashes to earth. A further disillusionment is in store when he returns home and the nephews, whom we took to be supporters of the Super Snooper myth, refuse to believe him: "He thought we didn't know that Super Snooper's stunts were impossible! No kid is that dumb!" When Donald brains himself trying to prove his strength, the boys throw their comic in the trash can: "Kids should know better than to leave fantastic stories lying around where their parents can read them!" This comments on our own gullibility in allowing Barks's story to convince us of its reality, and of superhero comics in general. We would normally take both for granted, but the comment estranges us from the naturalization of such fictions and invites us to question our assumptions.

Yet even this comment is undercut and discredited as we realize that the boys are also making a false assumption: they figure that Donald fell into a delusion brought on by reading about Super Snooper. But we know that he did briefly acquire ·superstrength from the liquid isotopes because we watched it happen. At the same time, part of what the kids say is true: such superstrength is impossible. Barks leaves the reader feeling uncomfortably ambivalent about the dividing line between fiction and reality, having unmasked his narrative without ever quite exploding it.

Barks's most self-reflexive story is that of Gyro's "think boxes" (*WDC&S* #141 [1952]), in which he deconstructs the funny-animal universe that his stories presuppose. Gyro has invented think boxes that can make animals talk and act like human beings. The boxes are, of course, a metaphor for the panels of funny-animal comics in which animals are anthropomorphized. As in "Super Snooper," Donald represents the naive reader who denies the power that comic narratives hold over their consumers. He derides the nephews for their belief in Gyro's invention and its power to humanize animals, although he is a talking and thinking animal. "Oh, that the name of Duck should ever sink so low!" he bemoans, using *Duck* as a family name, not realizing that it is also the name of a species.

To shame the nephews out of their belief in Gyro's think boxes, Donald dons a wolf's costume and threatens to eat them, treating the kids as ducks rather than children. From behind a tree steps a dogface, who trips him up. Barks lulls us into a false sense of security here, for dogfaces are standard supernumeraries in duck stories, and we have come to accept woodsmen rescuing children in tales like "Little Red Riding Hood." Even when Donald unmasks, showing that he is a duck, not a wolf, the reader is on firm ground, having seen him buy the costume a few pages earlier. But when, in a panel drawn symmetrically and placed immediately below, the woodsman pulls off his face to reveal that he is a wolf, the borders of reality begin to crumble.

To render the stories they read plausible, readers must maintain the paradoxical act of identifying with humanized animals as people while marginalizing the awareness that they are really mute beasts. In this sequence, Barks foregrounds this process and the contradictions it entails. The wolf's speech and the brief chase that follows mirror the scenes between the disguised Donald and the kids, causing us to perceive that sequence in a new light. The real wolf even looks exactly like Donald's costume, save for the rows of buttons down his chest. Because this beast is now talking and walking upright, the idea of an anthropomorphic animal suddenly appears strange, and we begin to question our previous acceptance of Donald. Barks then reverses the process and transforms Donald into an animal, revealing what he was anyway. To see the wolf tie him to a spit and roast him like poultry is profoundly disturbing. This is something that should never happen because Donald is human, not a duck, and the reader again becomes distanced from the funny-animal universe. Then Gyro reverses the think boxes, and normality is seemingly restored. But Barks disabuses us from growing too comfortable about the fictions that we consume. He confronts us with an intentional loose end: a panhandling rabbit who reminds us of the absurdity of funny-animal conventions. When Donald tells him to "Shut up!" he is asking for the impossible, because if animals ceased talking, it would be the end of the story. Which in this case it is.

Barks's most accomplished media parody appeared in a Donald Duck adventure story rather than a ten-pager. "Sheriff of Bullet Valley" (*DD* FC #199 [1948]), was a satire of B Western films. The artist had been a fan of Clarence Mulford's Hopalong Cassidy novels, and the first Hoppy film, *Hopalong Cassidy* (1935), inspired not only the plot of this Duck story but also the locale, mustachioed villain, and Donald's elongated cowboy hat.[25] Indeed, Barks even lampooned the hero's name in the story: "I saw the same trick in the picture 'Shuddering Saddles!' Stumpalong Hoppity brought the culprits to justice!" declares Donald. Barks used the story as a way of expanding Donald's character: he straddles the roles of both a benighted movie fan and a Western hero who must rise above his own limitations, attaining his greatest complexity to date as a character.

From its opening caption, "Bullet Valley" evokes a nostalgia for the Old West: "Gone now are the outlaws, the stagecoach robbers, and the cow thieves! Gone too the grim sheriffs that hunted them down!" The Old West has been superseded and the values of the frontier have become anachronistic in the contemporary era. To emphasize this, Barks drew an old six-gun covered by a spider's web, apparently in disuse for many years. Yet the fact that the gun still exists signals another possibility: that frontier values remain present in latent form, waiting only to be revived under appropriate circumstances. Barks's story is not just an elegiac tale about the passing of the West but a moral fable that concerns the redemption of frontier values in the modern era. Barks set the story in an ambiguous time frame so that it seems to take place both in the days of the Old West and in the contemporary present, indicating that frontier values can be resuscitated if they again become part of a living tradition.

The way in which Western films inculcate a confusion between myth and reality becomes the central premise of the story. Donald symbolizes the average moviegoer who unconsciously imbibes Hollywood stereotypes. When the nephews express childish excitement over the existence of rustlers in the valley, Donald winks at the reader and says condescendingly, "We're a long way from Hollywood here, boys!" Yet in the next panel, he arrogantly boasts that he can capture the rustlers because he has "seen enough Western movies to know *all* the angles!" Although unfamiliar with Western movies, the sheriff too falls into this conflation of real life and Hollywood fiction, making Donald a deputy.

"Sheriff of Bullet Valley" can be read as an allegory of postwar America and the erosion of the rural hinterland by urbanization, powerful corporations, and an expanded consumer economy spearheaded by the media. Donald represents a caricature of the postwar Everyman who manifests the effects of these developments: he can no longer distinguish reality from fantasy. In an age of mass consumerism, he has become an archconformist, copying the fantasy images he sees on the movie screen.

While Donald is a victim of the forces of modernization, Blacksnake, the villain in "Sheriff of Bullet Valley," is an incarnation of their oppressiveness. Instead of a six-gun he wields an automatic pistol, his men carry submachine guns and walkie-talkies, and he rustles cattle using an electronic branding machine. He even tries to kill Donald with a hand grenade. He exerts power over the inhabitants of the valley by virtue of greater organizational power, against which the rustic valley is helpless.

Barks satirized the mythic images of Westerns by showing the gap between fantasy and reality in Donald's continued failure to live out these images. He becomes a bigger fool with every action that he takes. Taking the intricate plots of Westerns as his guides, he decides that the sheriff is in cahoots with the rustlers and locks up an innocent rancher he believes is implicated in the plot. Then he tells the real rustler, Blacksnake McQuirt, about the rancher's hidden cattle, enabling the villain to steal them. If this were a ten-pager in *Walt Disney's Comics and Stories*, the tale might end at this point, with Donald's arrogance and foolishness causing his humiliation and disgrace. But Barks wanted to enlarge Donald's personality, allowing his nobler and more courageous (though still misguided) side to emerge. In the process, the Duck Man was able to make a fuller statement about the Western itself.

Donald is a very unheroic hero at best. Barks ridiculed the duck's pretensions by drawing him riding unperturbedly suspended in midair as he dreams of emulating his movie fantasies. Again, Donald's arrogance sets him up for a fall. Barks satirized the torrential but often bloodless violence of B Westerns in which characters pummel each other with bullets but either manage to evade injury or are anesthetically killed. In Barks's absurdist version, Donald fills Blacksnake's pants so full of lead that they fall off, and he runs away in his underwear. "That never happened in Trigger Trueshot's pictures!" Donald exclaims, surprised to find that unlike in the movies, his guns have run out of bullets.

In the finale of the fight sequence, Donald learns his lesson. He gives up trying to copy the macho heroics of Western movie stars and captures Blacksnake in his own original albeit zany fashion. He uses his lasso to turn the villain into a human yoyo. "It's not the way Rimfire Remington would do it, but it's more fun!" he declares. This resolution is more an expression of the cowboy's uniqueness as an individual than the assertion of male power as a lone, omnipotent hero. "Bullet Valley" seems to suggest that even though the media have distorted the images of the cowboy, they can still provide a worthwhile ethic if fans consciously and creatively reinterpret rather than passively consume these images. In effect, Barks's self-reflexive parodies of popular culture inscribe within themselves a new manner of reading media narratives.

This is one of the few stories in which Donald straightens himself out enough to triumph in the end. Donald rises to glory and becomes the ineffectual sheriff's ineffectual replacement: a Western movie fan has become sheriff of Bullet Valley. But Donald regresses to his movie illusions in the end, bragging about his capture of Blacksnake and his similarity to Trigger Trueshot. He abandons his role in real life to once again watch fictions on the screen: the sign on the sheriff's office door reads, "Hours: Now and Then." Bullet Valley has succumbed to the modernizing tendencies of the postwar era and gotten its own movie house, the Red Saddle Theater. Even the usually pragmatic nephews share Donald's mania for the movies. When suddenly informed of a bank robbery in progress, they placidly explain that Carson Sage is playing in *Law of the Roaring Winchesters* and that their uncle will take care of the trouble after the show. Consumerism and modern technology have come to Bullet Valley, with dubious effects on law and order.

Critics have claimed that Barks's best stories appeared during the late 1940s and early 1950s. This was also the period in which he created a pantheon of secondary characters and a town—Duckburg—for them to inhabit. Strong secondary characters were never characteristic of Disney cartoons, but Barks made them his forte. Indeed, he had a hand in creating most of the Duck family, including the nephews, for, as he remarked, he was "one of the midwives at their birth." [26] Uncle Scrooge, the most famous of Donald's relatives, provides an example of how Barks created his characters. He originated them merely as functions of the plot and as foils to Donald, without intending to use them again. But once they appeared, a pattern emerged: they stayed to become permanent members of the cast and evolved into fully developed characters in their own right—in Scrooge's case, even surpassing Donald in popularity.

"The office wanted me to do a Christmas story," Barks recalled. "Casting around, I began to think of the great Dickens Christmas story about Scrooge. Now I was just thief enough to steal some of the idea and have a rich uncle for Donald. And all the situations of the bear and of Donald having to prove his bravery grew from bringing in the uncle." [27] In "Christmas on Bear Mountain" (*DD FC* #178 [1947]), Scrooge is an arthritic miser very much in the mold of Dickens's unregenerate capitalist. We first glimpse him sitting alone in his darkened mansion, cursing those who love their fellow men. "Me, I'm different," he snarls in the next panel: "I hate everybody!" Unlike his Dickensian namesake, however, he never learns the true spirit of Christmas. Mistakenly believing Donald to be a brave man, Scrooge showers the ducks with Christmas treats, yet they remain only instruments of his pleasure and power.

In his second appearance, in "The Old Castle's Secret" (*DD* FC #189 [1948]), Barks gave Scrooge the Scottish ancestry his name implies and sent the ducks to a haunted castle to find the long-lost McDuck treasure. "He had turned out to be an interesting character in that first story," Barks explained, "so I began thinking of a way to use him again. The Old Castle established more of Scrooge's character, showed where he came from originally." [28] The story also established Scrooge as paterfamilias and the formula of Donald and the nephews as the old man's helpers, aiding him in saving or adding to his fortune.

Not until Scrooge's third appearance (*DD* FC #98 [1948]) did Barks realize that he had a "character that I could use over and over again." [29] Scrooge's financial status is now established: he is, in Donald's words, "the richest old coot in the world." "The fact that he was rich was the thing that triggered all further developments—as to just how rich," Barks explained. "I found that wealth was quite a fascinating subject. Just piles of money would appeal to a lot of people, and I gradually made him richer and richer. Then I had to develop a place where he could store the money." [30] In his early development of Scrooge, Barks played with various stereotypes of the ruthless capitalist. In *Walt Disney's Comics and Stories* #104 (1949), he is portrayed as a mean-spirited exploiter of labor. When he tries to get Donald to raise his yacht for a cheap price and his nephew calls him "dumb" for asking, Scrooge manipulates him into doing it for free as revenge and proof of his financial acumen.

The malevolent image continues in *Walt Disney's Comics and Stories* #124 (1951), in which Scrooge is an "old Shylock" who accumulates wealth through foreclosures. "Let's see," he muses as he gazes at a huge ledger in his office. "How many mortgages are due today?" His victims include a poor washerwoman in tattered clothes who is unable to pay the last nickel on her washing machine and pleads for one day's extension. "It's due today," Scrooge declares. He orders Donald to repossess the machine, making her unable to support herself and her "husband and six brothers-in-law." Donald finds a nickel and gives it to her for the payment, preserving her livelihood but subjecting himself to foreclosure because he cannot pay Scrooge the last penny on a debt.

This story exemplifies what I shall call Barks's ethic of balance. Barks's universe shuns the absolutes and dualistic oppositions such as good versus evil that are encoded into most comic book stories. Instead, his tales operate through a balance of forces in which excess of any kind tends to bring about its opposite as a natural consequence. Many of his stories hinge on the error of hubris and overreaching. As Barks put it, "'Pride goeth before a fall,' I think, was the main theme of a hell of a lot of my stories."[31] The Duck Man infrequently asserts a positive moral in his stories but rather usually implies a moral position through the negative consequences resulting when a character or group of characters create a karmic imbalance in the Barksian universe and then reap the unexpected and disastrous results. According to Barks, "My present philosophy is that no matter how bad some creed, practices, or systems may be, there is balancing evil in their opposites."[32]

Barks's stories work by satirizing excess and obsession and embrace an ethic of moderation in which extreme behavior inexorably brings about its own comeuppance. Barks followed this ethic in his own life. Asked how he was able to live so long, he replied: "Maybe it's because I enjoyed what I was doing, and I never got into any excessive fads, like food fads or drunken binges or anything that lasted any length of time. Everything I've done was in moderation."[33]

In the Shylock story, Scrooge pollutes his system by wallowing in piles of lucre so that he becomes allergic to money, forcing him, ironically, to renounce the thing that he loves most. He banishes himself to a darkened cave, living like a hermit, his solitude and cheerlessness environment mirroring his barrenness of soul. Scrooge returns to his money barn to find it as vacant of money as his life is of human warmth. Scrooge's penuriousness is countered by Donald's prodigality. He is a spendthrift who is overly charitable and squanders all the tycoon's money, giving handouts to deadbeats and wastrels. Donald too is appropriately punished: instead of working off his debt, he becomes beholden to Scrooge for the sum of his entire fortune.

This ethic is similar to what Buddhists call the "middle way."[34] They argue that human balance and harmony can be attained only through adhering to a middle ground between self-indulgence and asceticism, the two poles of excess represented by Donald and Scrooge, respectively. Donald is a creature of pure id whose impulsiveness makes him subject to every desire and frustration that capitalism can offer. No one tried harder—or failed more miserably—to attain the American dream. Uncle Scrooge achieves all that escapes Donald's grasp but is so obsessed with accumulating more and more wealth that it becomes an end in itself. Believing in thrift, hard work, and self-denial, he renounces all pleasures and comforts except those of wielding power and wallowing in his money bin, revealing the American dream as a hollow, lonely enterprise. However, he too could occasionally redeem himself. The nephews can be viewed as the ethical resolution of these opposing traits. They represent common sense and conscience in contrast to the need to consume or fetishize. As we shall see in Barks's adventure tales, the nephews' morality stems from an identification and empathy with those who are different or less fortunate, embodying Barks's ethic of tolerance, generosity, and compassion.

The Shylock story is notable for the first appearance of Scrooge's famous money swim, in which Barks translates into visual terms the old bromide about being so rich as to be "rolling in dough." Barks would later transform this money swim into a positive image of Scrooge that expressed a childlike sensuality and fun his stern work ethic otherwise denied. Here, however, it is an odious money fetish and an emblem of his acquisitiveness.

As Scrooge becomes an established character in the Duck family, he acquires menaces of his own that threaten his fortune. Two masked robbers looking suspiciously like the future Beagle Boys crack Scrooge's safe in a 1950 *Donald Duck* adventure (FC #282), "The Pixilated Parrot." However, the first time they are named and constitute a gang occurs in *Walt Disney's Comics and Stories* #134 (1951). This story represents Scrooge's first appearance as a vulnerable character rather than a prepossessing power, in danger of having his fortune stolen by the canine gang.

However, he has not yet become a sympathetic character. Barks satirizes the cliché that wealth can buy anything by having Scrooge pay Donald to do the miser's worrying; but Scrooge forgets to tell his nephew what to worry about. When Scrooge remembers, he becomes prostrated with fear at the thought of being robbed by the "terrible Beagle Boys," who have eluded the police. Great wealth brings not security but anxiety and constant defensiveness, Barks asserts.

In Barks's stories, excess begets its opposite as a counterreaction, often bringing about the result it was designed to prevent. Scrooge can't man his cannon full time and makes the mistake of installing the inept Donald's automatic cannon-firing device. Scrooge then accidentally triggers it, sending a cannonball shooting through several buildings before it rebounds out of a rubber mattress factory and breaks open his money bin. In effect, Scrooge has caused his own downfall and is responsible for bringing about what he most feared—the looting of his money by the Beagles.

Scrooge's obsessiveness is also foregrounded in the next appearance of the Beagles (*WDC&S* #135 [1951]), which marks the first appearance of Scrooge's money bin. Looking like a giant safe from its height on Killmotor Hill, the money bin dominates the city. Again, Scrooge's panic attacks and compulsive defensiveness bring about the loss of his fortune. In an apt image of overkill, Scrooge's money bin is surrounded by a moat of acid, radar, and a minefield and has walls ten feet thick. His overdoing again brings about his downfall: he mistakenly follows Donald's harebrained advice and fills the bin with water to drown the Beagles. When the liquid freezes, it cracks the bin open, and it slides down the hill onto the Beagle Boys' property, where they gleefully gather the cash with ice picks. The Beagles function as Scrooge's shadows, demonic projections of his fears that mock his obsessions. In this early period, Barks shows a marked hostility to Scrooge and to capitalists in general. In three of the stories analyzed here (*WDC&S* #124, #134, #135), Scrooge loses his entire fortune, and there is no suggestion at the end of the story that he will ever get it back.

In the January 1948 issue (*WDC&S* #88), Barks introduced another secondary character, Donald's preternaturally lucky cousin, Gladstone

Gander. Gladstone was only a plot device introduced because Barks needed "somebody that Donald would try to outdo."[35] Gladstone's fabulous luck emerged only later. His early appearances involve bragging matches that escalate and spin out of control in typical Barksian fashion. They are acerbic satires of patriarchal masculinity and the obsessive aim to prove one's manhood by dominating and demolishing a male rival.

Gladstone's first outing exemplifies this formula. He comes to take possession of Donald's house on Christmas Day after Donald has signed a contract promising to take an icy swim in Frozenbear Lake or forfeit his house. At the heart of Donald's brag is his attempt to defend his virility and prove that he is more of a man than Gladstone: "So I'm not a man because I wouldn't go swimming. . . . I'm tougher than you are any day!" he declares. But it is Duckburg's coldest day, and Donald refuses to go in. Only through the intervention of Daisy is Donald's home saved: she reminds Gladstone of his brag to drink two gallons of lemonade or relinquish his claim to Donald's home. Bloating himself with drink, he ends up having to let Donald off the hook. Although each cousin has made a fool of himself and Donald has almost lost his most prized possession, neither of them has learned his lesson, and they start a new bragging war with even more impossible boasts than before. Like most of their contests, the story ends in frustration and rancorous conflict.

These early bragging wars frequently revolve around competition for money: Gladstone bets that Donald can't hit a hole in one, Donald tries to raise five dollars for Daisy's club before his cousin can or to prove himself Uncle Scrooge's favorite relative. Exemplifying the universal scramble for the almighty dollar that characterizes American capitalism, each one is always ready to swindle and exploit the other to win. Although Donald aspires to the fast buck, he is at least willing to work for it. Gladstone, conversely, prides himself on scorning any form of labor and is one of the chief violators of Barks's apotheosis of the work ethic. Gladstone is more arrogant and indolent that than Donald ever was. In "Rival Beach-Combers" (*WDC&S* #103 [1949]), Gladstone lies on the sand, bragging about his aversion to work while hiring his cousins to search for a lost ruby for a pittance of what it is worth. For once Barks makes Donald victorious. After they find the gem, Gladstone ends up as the ducks' chauffeur, driving their new limousine because their hands are too blistered from honest labor.

Searching for a way to make him "lastingly obnoxious," Barks hit on "this lucky angle. He was the kind of a guy who got all the breaks, and poor old Donald never got anywhere."[36] In "Race to the South Seas" (*MOC* #41 [1949]), Donald races Gladstone to be the first to rescue Uncle Scrooge, believed to be shipwrecked. While mere mortals are bound by the limits of the laws of nature, Gladstone's luck gives him magical qualities: he is towed by a swordfish, carried by a whale, and lifted over a high reef by a well-timed wave. Gladstone's good luck is usually mirrored by Donald's ill fortune. When Donald tries to rescue Daisy from going over the falls when a sudden rainstorm develops at the Wildflower club picnic, they crash on the shoals below (*WDC&S* #117 [1950]). Gladstone, however, rests unperturbed atop a tree, untouched by a drop of water.

As Gladstone's luck becomes a mystique, it comes to constitute his identity, an ability on which he can always count, and his indolence becomes a source of perverse pride. He refuses to even wish for a million dollars because that would be "a form of work" (*WDC&S* #126 [1951]). When Uncle Scrooge and the ducks break into Gladstone's safe to discover the secret of his luck, they find only a lone dime (*WDC&S* #131 [1951]). "Once long ago, in a *very weak moment* I took a job!" Gladstone confesses. "I actually *worked*—I *earned* that dime! And I've been so *ashamed* of it ever since that I *hid* it in the safe and never looked at it again!" The ducks depart in silence; nothing can be said about someone who is so much an affront to the American work ethic. Gladstone reflects a legitimation crisis in American success mythology in the postwar era, when success was becoming increasingly uncoupled from virtue. He represents an inverted Calvinism in which Providence bestows good fortune on the least rather than the most worthy.

However, it was not so much Gladstone's luck but his subversion of the work ethic that made him a despicable character. "I don't think anybody likes a character who gets by with so little effort in the world," Barks explained. "They like to feel that other people have just as much of a struggle as they themselves have, and Gladstone was a fellow who would just go along, skimming all the cream out of life, without ever sweating for it." [37] While Donald has the imagination and drive to want to be rich and successful, Gladstone only lives from day to day, his only desire to prove that he can live without working. He is the only character that Donald envies and hates. "I can't stand that guy! He makes me feel so helpless!" Donald moans after witnessing his cousin's good fortune and enduring another round of his bragging (*DD* FC #256 [1949]). Donald envies and despises Gladstone so intensely because his cousin can do what Donald fervently wishes for but can never achieve: to live without working and escape alienated labor. Gladstone's ability to forgo working for a living is a projection of Donald's desire to escape his alienated existence, and his continual failure to best his cousin results from implacable forces over which he has little control.

Gladstone represents those feelings the laboring masses have traditionally reserved for those who have inherited or unearned wealth. He is an emblem of the aristocrat who believes himself above work. When he meets Donald on the golf course for their bet, he wears a straw hat and twirls a cane, emblems of the idle dandy. His name connotes rootlessness: a Gladstone is a light traveling bag. He is a narcissist and egomaniac who shows no concern for or moral responsibility toward others. He blithely abandons Donald and the kids to certain death on an iceberg, albeit at their request, because they do not want to listen to his boasting on the return trip home (*DD* FC #256 [1949]).

Gladstone is the descendant of the impudent fops and aristocratic ne'er-do-wells that populate American fiction, people who have inherited wealth and position and thumb their noses at the laboring masses. His most direct ancestor is the snob in Horatio Alger's success novels. [38] He is usually a gentleman's son or the offspring of a rich but grasping relative of the hero, envious of his skills and desirous of getting him into trouble. Lazy, arrogant, and unwilling to work because he considers it below his station, the snob is the antithesis of the Alger hero's virtues. However, in Barks's stories, Gladstone's luck occludes and displaces class and wealth as the source of the snob's power.

Barks typically refused to acknowledge an autobiographical influence in his stories but did admit to an identification with Donald: "I always felt myself to be an unlucky person like Donald, who is a victim of so many circumstances. But there isn't a person in the United States who couldn't identify with him. He is everything, he is everybody; he makes the same mistakes that we all make."[39] The emphasis on luck and fate was a constant theme in Barks's work, dating from his days in animation. He introduced the notion of Donald being an unlucky character in the 1939 cartoon *Donald's Lucky Day*. This film also permanently linked Donald with the number thirteen, later seen on everything from his auto license plate to his home address.[40] The first Donald Duck comic book story Barks both wrote and drew (*WDC&S* #32 [1943]) also featured this trope. Prefiguring the Donald-Gladstone relationship, it dealt with the way the nephews' lucky rabbit's foot always gave good luck to them but bad luck to Donald. Barks's history as a farm boy and hardscrabble laborer helps explain this fixation on luck and chance; however, the popularity of his stories indicates that these themes also resonated in readers' attitudes and perceptions.

In a study of the success myth in popular culture, Lawrence Chenoweth observes that after the Depression, a marked change occurred in attitudes toward the American dream. Although popular success writers of the 1930s implicitly stressed accidental factors, "it was not until the war that they directly acknowledged the role of fate in the outcome of a person's life."[41] This shift marked a significant mutation in Americans' attitudes toward the possibility of control over their lives. According to Chenoweth, the success myth moved away from the aspiration to thrift and hard work and toward an implicit recognition of life's fatalistic forces. The surprise attack on Pearl Harbor, the development of the atomic bomb, and the possibility of being drafted and crippled or killed made it difficult to plan for future success. Chenoweth also notes that a consumer ethos of devoting oneself to the pleasures of the moment and consumption in leisure time had been challenging the asceticism of the Protestant work ethic since the 1920s. However, rather than supplanting the tenets of the American dream, these changes marked a growing ambivalence about it. Becoming diffuse and contradictory, "the success ethic survived only to become a philosophy without substance in postwar America," claims Chenoweth.[42]

Many of Barks's stories negotiate contradictions in the American dream. "A Financial Fable" (*WDC&S* #126 [1951]) exemplifies this process. In this story, Barks creates the first positive image of Scrooge. No longer an old Shylock or exploitive capitalist, he is an emblem of the Protestant ethic. The owner of a farm, he works right alongside the ducks, who are his hired help. Donald, conversely, hates work and wishes for a million dollars for everyone so that they can live a life of leisure and fun rather than toil. These positions stake out contradictions in the tenets of the American dream and the way in which alienation in the workplace and a consumer ethos of immediate gratification were undermining the Protestant ethic, which demanded hard work, thrift, and the sacrifice of present pleasures for future gains. The nephews are aligned with Scrooge in this story, believing that "you have to work" if you want clothes to wear and food to eat. Representatives of adult wisdom, they chide Donald for being "too young to understand things."

The story has the structure of a fable, suggesting that one should be careful about what one wishes for, lest it come true. Donald's desire is granted when he convinces Gladstone to wish for a million dollars so that he can follow his cousin's advice to give up working and have fun. When a cyclone disperses the money from Scrooge's money bin all over the country, not only Gladstone but everyone in America becomes a millionaire. The loss of his fortune normally would make Scrooge a nervous wreck. Here he is strangely calm, as if privy to some prophetic knowledge, and tells the nephews that if they guard the crops, he will get it all back. And so he does: everyone decides to quit work and see the world, leaving Scrooge with the only food left to eat. Because of their sloth, people are forced to pay Scrooge's gouging prices (one billion for a ham, four million for an ounce of wool, etc.), and he again becomes the world's richest man.

The story attempts to link virtue and wealth and rests on several familiar premises of the American dream: that the tycoon deserves his fortune because of his labor and that the rest of humanity has earned its lowly state because of personal weaknesses—that is, lassitude and lack of discipline. Here agrarian and capitalist utopias merge as Barks associates Scrooge with the virtues of the rural past: he is a farmer who tends and sells his produce and treats his money like a crop he has nourished and brought to harvest. He even stores his money in a corncrib. Scrooge seems magically in tune with his wealth. Unlike the Beagle Boys, he can dive into a pile of hard coins without knocking himself out (*US* FC #368 [1952]). "Perhaps it is something to do with his character: often he can do things which other people can't," commented Barks. "He can go out in the desert and smell the presence of gold; other prospectors would have to dig mountains of dirt before they could find any nuggets."[43] Unlike the masses of humanity, Scrooge, atypically in this one story, knows that money is worthless and just enjoys it for a recreational swim. Once a polluting fetish, Scrooge's money swim has been converted into an expression of childlike joy and pleasure.

However, Barks's story foregrounds unresolved tensions in the success myth. Donald has the last word as he pronounces Scrooge's money swim "disgusting." It is both a comment on the miser's greed and a statement about things being "again as they were," with Donald having to toil at a low-paying job that he hates. Although the tale draws on the work ethic to justify wealth, Scrooge is depicted as a profiteer who recoups his fortune only by charging everyone in the country exorbitant prices. Economic equality and universal abundance normally would be highly desirable goals, and even the egocentric Donald is willing to share his good fortune with everyone. Only Donald's and the country's sloth justifies Scrooge's avarice and hoarding. But when his nephew asks him why he loves money so much even though he knows it is "worthless," Scrooge can only answer that Donald "wouldn't understand," and the miser's obsession with the accumulation of wealth goes unexplained.

In the end, the story cannot reconcile the contradictions it poses without resorting to two outrageous fantasies: first, that a tornado could evenly distribute Scrooge's fortune all over the country so that everyone could become a millionaire; and second, that great wealth would make the mass of humanity instantly indolent. Consequently, the story can be read as expressing Barks's ambivalence about the credibility of the American dream—the belief that people could become rich if they wanted to badly enough and that only sloth and lack of will power held them back.

Barks's affirmation of the success ethic in this story does not mean that he went from being anticapitalist to procapitalist in a short space of time. Indeed, two issues earlier, he wrote a story about Scrooge's greed polluting his system, using the money swim as an example of his avariciousness. Barks always believed in the American dream and the capitalist system; however, his attempt to "tell it like it is"—to be faithful to people's everyday experiences—allowed him to create multiple, often contradictory representations of American society.[44] Donald, for example, can be read as a contradictory expression of Barks's take on the "lowly workingman," as Gladstone calls the duck. Having had to work at physically demanding, dead-end jobs for years and barely making enough to survive as a comic book artist, Barks could well appreciate the plight of the worker. Donald's aversion to work can be interpreted in several ways: He can be condemned as lazy, and his habitual inability to succeed at any jobs can be read as evidence of his incompetence; conversely, he can be seen as rejecting an oppressive and alienating form of work over which he has no control and from which he makes little profit. Images of Scrooge kicking Donald in the fanny for loafing when he stops working for a minute to rest invite the latter reading.

As "Some Heir over the Rainbow" (*WDC&S* #155 [1953]) shows, what we take as fate is actually constructed by capitalist structures of power. The nephews read in a book of fairy tales about a boy who finds a pot of gold at the end of a rainbow because he has faith that he will find it. Donald dismisses such ideas as "mere ignorant superstitions." But while Scrooge is strolling the road musing about who to choose as his heir, he overhears the ducks' conversation. He decides to stage a competition among Donald, Gladstone, and the nephews to determine who is most worthy, hiding three pots of gold in different locations at the end of the rainbow. Donald protests that the competition is a "wild goose chase" and asks why Scrooge doesn't try to find a pot of gold himself. "I *would*," replies Scrooge, "but I've already found *my* pot of gold—long ago! Each person is entitled to only *one* pot!"

The relatives find their pots and spend them in ways indicative of their individual characters. Donald the spendthrift and archconsumer buys an expensive limousine and goes in debt for a thousand dollars. Not needing the gold because of his fabulous luck, Gladstone hides his pot in a tree hollow. The nephews finance an old sailor on a hunt for buried treasure, spending all their pot on a speculation. Scrooge judges his relatives' worthiness by capitalist standards: who has made a profit with the money. Believing that the nephews are victims of a scam, only Gladstone appears to be worthy because only he has not lost any money. "What an *awful* injustice for the world!" Scrooge exclaims. But, at the last moment, the old mariner turns up with a chest of coins and jewels, the kids' share in what was a successful treasure hunt.

In this story, Barks reveals that what is deemed fate by the characters in his drama is really governed by those in control of the levers of power and wealth in capitalist America. Scrooge decides who will get money, the standards by which they are deemed worthy to obtain it, and how much they will receive. Moreover, this structure operates, like ideology and social relations under capitalism, in ways of which all the agents except for Scrooge are unconscious. The story thus reverses the reification of market relations under capitalism, showing them to be not the laws of an inexorable fate but social relations that are humanly chosen and therefore changeable.

The message of this tale is to have faith, to follow our dreams—more specifically, the American dream. Those who have faith, like the nephews, succeed; those who lack faith, like Donald, do not. Barks believed that capitalism functions best when people put money into circulation so that wealth is distributed throughout society to create jobs, services, and goods for the many. Because the nephews give their fortune to a poor old mariner and wealth is shared by all rather than being hoarded by a few who are already wealthy, like Scrooge, the nephews seem to deserve to be their uncle's heirs. Merit thus seems to go hand in hand with the possession of faith. However, the narrative shows that success ultimately depends on the will of the wealthy and being in conformity with their decisions and values. The story thus again reveals capitalism's contradictions.

An earlier story, (*WDC&S* #144 [1953]), reveals the mechanisms behind capitalist power, showing that Scrooge's fortune stems from his monopolization of the economy, not just hard work. Scrooge has accumulated so much money that even the steel walls of his money bin will burst if he tries to add to its mass. Being unable to bear parting with a penny, Scrooge ironically must hire the spendthrift Donald to go on a shopping spree, buying the most expensive items he can: a luxurious limousine with ermine seat covers, boiled bosoms of Caledonia Chickadees at Ye Olde Gype Inn, and silver trinkets designed to fleece tourists at an Indian reservation. Barks's effete and euphonious names signify the profligacy involved in such transactions. However, the money comes back to Scrooge in the end because he owns all the businesses that Donald patronizes. Capitalist power is a self-replicating structure, the story implies, in which surplus value always accrues to the most wealthy and powerful.

Chance has always been a corrosive element and vulnerability to disaster a constant in human affairs. But the rise of an unregulated capitalist economy accented a heightened sense of anarchy and unpredictability in human life. Gladstone's luck, Donald's failures, and Scrooge's magical affinity for money work by effacing the socioeconomic structure, attributing to coincidence or fate the effects of an unequal economy. As Lucien Goldmann notes, the effects of this structure seem to operate as uncontrollable events beyond our knowledge or control because of our lack of consciousness of them. He describes "classical liberal society" as possessing "no conscious regulation of production and consumption at any level. In such a society, of course, production is regulated . . . but this regulation operates in an implicit way, outside the consciousness of individuals, imposing itself on them as the impersonal action of an outside force." [45] In the mythology of the American dream, the worker's failure results from personal flaws, not social structures. Thus, even during the Great Depression, when almost a quarter of the population was out of work, men blamed themselves rather than the economic system for their inability to work for a living. [46]

Barks also believed in this individualist ideology. He admitted in a conversation with David Kunzle that Kunzle's characterization of him as an exploited worker rang true. His top rate for art and scripts was $45.50 per page, received during the last two years that he worked. Although his comics were the best-selling in America and had made millions for Disney and Western Publishing, he received only the "median rate" for an artist. Western tried to discourage him from recognizing his value to the company by withholding fan mail except for the occasional reader complaint, never telling him about the phenomenal success of his books. "I never got a swelled head over hearing that *WDC&S* was selling millions of copies," Barks commented. "Besides, Alice Cobb, one of the editors, told me that my work wasn't selling those comics—it was Walt Disney's name over the titles."[47]

It is thus understandable that Barks tended to blame himself for his lack of pay. "The fact that you painted me as an exploited worker doesn't hurt my feelings a bit," Barks told Kunzle. "I would have been exploited under the Russian system or the Castro system as well. My big trouble was in my lack of aggressiveness. Never could convince myself that I was writing and drawing anything that deserved a premium paycheck."[48] Barks never blamed the economic system for his low pay or lack of credit, echoing the individualist assumptions of the success myth. "The economic system is such that a guy that has any ability can make something of that ability, and I just didn't have the ability, so I was where I was, I accepted that."[49]

Nevertheless, Barks continually harbored a desire for more money and for some recognition of his work. The Duck Man often stated in interviews that he had no trouble with the fact that he was unknown to the readers of his stories, acknowledging that in the Disney comics empire, no one received credit except Walt. However, he would occasionally admit being disappointed in not being allowed to sign his stories. "You ask about the anonymity of being a sharecropper on old Marse Disney's animal farm," Barks replied to a fan. "Well I've grown used to it, although there are times when I regret that some particularly good story or drawing doesn't bear my name in pulsating letters."[50] From time to time, he would even sneak his signature or other means of identification into his stories, but these attempts were always discovered and removed by Western before they were published.[51] The Duck Man tinkered with the idea of developing a comic strip with human characters in the event of a collapse of Western Publishing but "trashed the whole pile of drawings and notes because the stuff seemed too much like a humanized version of my duck formulas."[52] He was too busy chronicling the adventures of the ducks to have the time to develop a comic strip of his own.

Wealth and luck are not the only elements of the American dream. A third axis of the success myth derives from America's fascination with technology. In the western tradition, success meant that man had to dominate a recalcitrant nature and make it do his bidding. Gyro Gearloose, Barks's daffy inventor, exemplifies this impulse. His first appearance is a cameo: he tries to churn butter by riding a pogo stick (*WDC&S* #140 [1952]), and his only function in the story is to confirm Gladstone's luck by providing him with two free items on his shopping list—a quart of cream and a pogo stick. "Every cartoonist . . . had a crazy inventor at some time in his strip," Barks explained. "I was in need of a crazy inventor . . . so I created Gyro."[53] Gyro's constant companion was a tiny lightbulb that never had any dialogue in the stories. "I created his helper because much of the time I had Gyro working all alone on some goofy machine. I put the little guy in to fill up the corners of the panels. I treated him as a complete nobody; not even Gyro noticed that he was around."[54]

Gyro's dizziness was noticeable from his first appearance. His baggy clothes, big feet, and mop of hair protruding from his small hat gave him the clownlike look of an oversized Harpo Marx. His size was a problem: "I only figured on using him once in a very great while, so I just made him a big awkward-looking chicken. If I had known that I was going to have to do a book of Gyro stories, I would have made him about the same size as Donald or Uncle Scrooge, so that he could have been handled much easier. . . . [I]t was difficult to work him in the same panels with the ducks."[55]

Gyro invents for the sheer joy of exercising his creativity but fails to assess the implications of his devices. He creates inventions that are miraculous but have little practical use: think boxes to make animals talk, trained worms that make fishing poles obsolete, and a "hydraulic ramjet peanut butter spreader." Gyro grew out of Barks's fascination with technology. "I'm kind of an inventor at heart," Barks confessed. "I can think of all kinds of crazy inventions. I would go broke if I ever tried to patent all the things I think of."[56] Mechanical gags had been Barks's forte since the automatic barber chair he created for *Modern Inventions* (1937) that launched his career as a Duck artist. Although many of his mechanical devices are far-fetched, Barks always took great care to make them seem mechanically operable. Indeed, one of his devices had its use in real life. In 1964, a Danish scientist, Karl Kroyer, raised a sunken ship by filling its ballast hold full of polystyrene balls. Kroyer was inspired by a 1949 Barks story, "Billions to Sneeze At" (*WDC&S* #104), in which Donald raises Scrooge's yacht by filling its hold with ping-pong balls. When Kroyer tried to patent the process, he was denied on the grounds that a description of it had already been published.[57]

The dilemmas posed by Gyro's creation of oddball inventions are apparent in *Walt Disney's Comics and Stories* #153 [1953]. Donald is determined to win the fishing derby at Mudhen Lake but is unable to catch anything. He initially rejects the nephews' suggestion that he needs specialized worms to improve his catch, objecting that this would make the "worm more important than the fisherman." However, he succumbs to Gyro's new invention of a breed of worms that act as teams that pull in the fish, making "fishing poles *obsolete!*" To Gyro, the ability to invent such a magical device is its own reward, and he does not think of the ends to which his creations are put. Unable to land old Bombasto, the lake's king bass, Donald decides to win the fishing contest by using Gyro's trained worms. But he ignores Gyro's warning that it is dangerous to use more than a dozen teams at a time. He unleashes fifty teams of worms and, like the sorcerer's apprentice, they spin out of control and threaten to catch all the fish in the lake, provoking the ire of the other fishermen.

Barks's story implies that how a technology is used determines whether it will have good or bad effects. Donald's rashness superficially seems to cause the problem, but the tale implicitly points to a larger problem in the nature of technology itself. Gyro fails to consider the ends of the technology he uses and its potential costs: that it would eliminate fishermen and thus the craft and pleasure of fishing itself. At the end of the story, he has not learned his lesson, telling the irate fishermen, "If any of you boys want *more* worms, I'll have a new batch hatched off at daylight tomorrow!" His failure to take responsibility for the problem leads Donald and the other fishermen to chase him angrily with clubs.

Gyro's invention exemplifies what philosopher Max Horkheimer has called instrumental rationality, a form of reason that is declared incapable of determining the ends of life and contents itself only with determining the reasonability of technical means.[58] As a result, means are fetishized, becoming ends in themselves, and the costs and need for them are ignored. Efficiency and the ability to make a device become more important than any considerations about whether such technology is necessary or desirable. This reductionistic type of rationality promotes what critics have called an autonomous technology that spins out of human direction and control, turning on its makers.[59]

In "Monsterville" (*GG* FC 1184 [1961]). Barks satirized the idea of a technological utopia.[60] The daffy inventor bemoans the lack of efficiency in Duckburg and the way it "needlessly wastes *energy*." He proposes that the city council tear down the old Duckburg and reshape it into a futuristic new city according to his guidelines. The new city is placed under a dome so that the weather is totally controlled; filters on factories' smokestacks eliminate all air pollution; and people slide to work along ramps instead of walking. Donald gets to sleep twenty-three hours a day because his factory has been automated so that he only has to do ten minutes of button pushing, and Scrooge's electronic brain makes all of his deals for him.

But there is trouble in paradise. Scrooge is furious because he has made so much money he cannot get inside his money bin to swim in his loot and unhappy because he no longer has the fun of making big deals, and Gyro has been replaced by an automatic inventor, which he angrily smashes because his greatest joy is his work. When Gyro discovers how bored and lazy people have become, he sabotages his machine and people rediscover the joys of walking. Barks's story satirizes capitalism's instrumentalist, technocratic ethic and the compulsive form of rationalizing efficiency that forgets to consider the ends of human life. In consumer ideology, work is toil, so leisure is viewed as the place of true freedom and happiness. But Barks's tale shows that joy in work is one of humanity's most important pleasures and that human effort is necessary to maintain vitality and happiness. At the same time, even this joy can become obsessive and must be moderated: although Duckburg officials have forbidden him from creating any more "wild" devices, Gyro cannot resist inventing a car that looks "normal" that he can fly when "nobody is looking!"

Of the cast of secondary characters on which Barks drew for his dramatis personae, only Daisy Duck was a holdover from animation. As discussed earlier, even as a storyman, Barks had a problematic relationship with Daisy. Because she was a female, he considered her unsuitable for the rough-and-tumble antics in the Donald animated shorts. Indeed, Barks was so unsympathetic to Daisy that he never acknowledged creating her even though he and Harry Reeves had invented her for the 1940 film *Mr. Duck Steps Out* and Barks drew the first prototype of her in the unproduced short *Desert Prospectors*. His comments about Daisy are decidedly uncharitable. "Rattlebrains like Daisy Duck are the curse of the earth!" he groused to an Italian interviewer.[61] When Barks began writing Daisy into comic book stories, he used her only sparingly, believing that she was still a "diluting influence." Unlike other the members of the Duck clan, Daisy had few abilities of her own. She did not posses Scrooge's affinity for money, Gladstone's luck, Gyro's technical genius, or even Donald's ill fortune. Rather, she was defined primarily as a projection of male desires and anxieties, and we see her primarily through Donald's eyes.

In Barks's stories, Daisy exhibits the traditional female roles of being courted, placated, and rescued. In the story of the daisy hunt (*WDC&S* #117 [1950]), for example, he used her to satirize patriarchal traditions of chivalry and romance. At the spring picnic of the Duckburg Wildflower Club, a man must earn the right to ask a woman to lunch by finding a daisy for her. Barks lampooned the absurdity of this male ritual in the first panel, showing the picnickers fighting, catching hay fever from a flower, stabbing themselves on a cactus, and manifesting their bravery by being treed by a rabbit. Barks draws puns on flowers throughout the story to mock the masculine heroics that demand noble bravery from males and passivity from females, who are the objects of the male's romantic quest.

As usual, Donald is jinxed in his attempt to find a flower for his girl and is repeatedly doomed by Gladstone's luck. When a flash flood occurs, Donald, always trying to play the chivalrous male, rescues Daisy from the safety of Gladstone's gondola only to have her swept over a waterfall. As Donald and one of the nephews fish Daisy out of the water, she screams, "To think we came out here to pick flowers, and all this had to happen!" Although Daisy berates Donald for his failures, she incites him to such absurd quests and is one of the prime enforcers of male roles. If males violate the norms of masculinity, she throws tantrums and attacks, unaware that the definition of manhood she upholds has provoked their bad behavior: "You disgraceful ruffians—look at you! I'll have *neither* of you for a partner! I'll eat with the first *gentleman* that finds me a daisy!" In a formula Barks would repeat several times, Daisy rejects both Donald and Gladstone, preferring the company of the nephews.

Barks's stories operate by invoking separate gendered spheres. Males are engaged in demanding forms of labor or go off on exciting adventures, while women are concerned primarily with romance, fashion, and beauty and are confined to the domestic sphere. When characters cross gender boundaries, it is considered transgressive and threatening to males. The sexy seductress Madame Triple-X and the sorceress Magica de Spell, who play power games with the males, are more interesting than the proper "lady" Daisy, but are also more dangerous and cast as villains. Conversely, when the male is coerced into crossing gender boundaries and adopting "feminine" behavior, he is considered emasculated and his identity threatened. In *Walt Disney's Comics and Stories* #213 (1958), for example, Donald is terrified of having to help Daisy with spring cleaning and flees like a wanted man. The nephews help Daisy track him down with the help of the Woodchucks' Official Bloodhound, making his first appearance. When Donald jumps off a high diving platform to escape the indefatigable dog, Daisy catches him in a net and forces him to beat rugs, inflicting "man's inglorious defeat." As in the nightmare story, this tale can be read in different ways. Donald's hysterical terror at having to do housework and the story's mock melodramatic tone ridicule yet simultaneously play upon male anxieties at being feminized.

These fears ultimately derive from the terror of being dominated by women.[62] When Daisy invites Donald to a box-lunch social, for example, she engraves on her invitation the acronym "T.I.N.A.I.—I.A.C."—"This is not an invitation—*It's a Command!*" Although both sexes in reality are compelled to act out roles and conventions defined by patriarchal society, Barks's stories omit the view that females, like males, are oppressed by sexist conventions and are unable to express their competence and power without evoking male anxiety.

By creating a set of secondary characters and a city for them to inhabit, Barks had a means of spinning off a virtually infinite number of stories that had remarkable variety. Comics writers might call this the invention of a Duck universe. However, Barks was elusive about whether such a universe existed. In interviews he both stated that "there never *was* a Barks universe" and acknowledged that his art had the *stylistic consistency* that defined a "Duck universe."[63] Indeed, his universe differs markedly from those produced by other comics writers, including contemporary authors of Disney comics. Unlike them, Barks never tried to create a coherent, unified worldview for his stories. Rather, his tales encompass a clash of worldviews and cultural discourses. "My view of my Duck universe was that of a blind man feeling his way through a borderless maze," the artist commented. "My idea of its limits kept changing and expanding."[64]

Barks's tales are what Umberto Eco calls "open texts," polysemic narratives that resist definitive resolutions of conflicts and do not attempt to close off alternative meanings in favor of monological readings.[65] In Barks's fiction, characters' attributes are primarily plot driven, determined by how they function in particular stories, and are ambiguous, fluid, and continually open to revision. Thus, Scrooge went from being an old miser in the first story to an unscrupulous Shylock to a daring adventurer in his own book and ultimately to a villain again in the Junior Woodchuck tales. He could be condemned for being an amoral capitalist and eulogized as a hardworking, self-made man. Indeed, he could change from one story to the next, depending on what the plot required; he could have traits like an addiction to nutmeg (*US* #39 [1962]) or chronic memory loss (*US* #495 [1953]) that popped up once but were never mentioned again. Barks also introduced an element of unpredictability into tales about Gladstone's luck. Despite his cousin's egregious good fortune, Donald bests Gladstone in a surprising number of adventure stories in which male rivalry was not the predominant theme. In "Luck of the North" (*DD* FC #256 [1949]), for example, Gladstone lays claim to an ancient Viking ship that the ducks have discovered and leaves them abandoned on an iceberg. Nevertheless, they discover a rare Viking map much more valuable than the treasures Gladstone has recovered and end up ahead.[66]

The Duck Man also resisted uniform readings of his characters by intentionally refusing to give them fully developed, coherent biographies similar to those of real people. While he created an origin tale in which Scrooge made his fortune by striking it rich in the Klondike, Barks also created contradictory stories that revealed that Scrooge's fortune derived from the magical power of an ancient Arabian hourglass (*DD* FC #291 [1950]) or the possession of the first dime he ever earned (*US* #46 [1963]). Despite the fact that Barks wrote stories about him for almost thirty years, Scrooge has only the faintest biography, and only tiny tidbits are known about McDuck's childhood in Scotland or his early days in America.[67] Likewise, we know nothing about Donald's past and have only the vaguest information about the nephews' mother or their origins.

Unlike many contemporary comics, Barks's stories have no continuity. Each one is independent and must stand on its own. Barks preferred this type of narrative structure, called the episodic format:

> All of these characters were strangers to me . . . and, when I was developing these characters, I remember having thoughts like, "Should I mention something about a previous story that had taken place?" And always I discarded that idea because I felt there's nothing worse in picking up a comic book on the stand and starting to read and finding that you are reading something that is continued from some earlier issue that you don't have and have no means of getting. . . . I felt that each story had to be a complete story in itself, and whatever introduction of a character that took place, it was just an incidental part of the story. If I used that character again, he was just introduced in the part he was going to play in that story, not on the strength of what he had been in the past.[68]

Thus, when he introduced the Beagle Boys, they were presented as if they had always been part of the Duck universe, and their past is never explained.

Like Scrooge, Duckburg too changes from story to story and had contradictory sets of characteristics. This gives it a location that could not logically exist: "The town of Duckburg was a real strange place. It was on an ocean, it was near a lake, and it was out in the plains and close to tremendous mountains and a black forest and all of that. It had snow in the winter—terrific snows—and all these palm trees and so on. It was really a strange place. It's always very close to the desert. [Donald] would leave Duckburg and go right out into the Mojave Desert, just a short ride."[69] Barks mentioned the exact location of Duckburg in only one story ("The Gilded Man," *DD* FC #422 [1952]): the mythical state of Calisota, a contraction of two places where Barks had spent much of his life, California and Minnesota. Scrooge's money bin was also ambiguous, located high on Killmotor Hill, in Scrooge's office building in downtown Duckburg, and on a bare lot in the city.

Barks also had trouble keeping Donald consistent with the look of the animation duck. "I never could follow the model sheets," Barks confessed, and he wasn't even able "to keep the ducks consistent" with the model sheets he drew.[70] The screen Donald had been more of a duck, with "rubbery legs" and a distinctive waddle. In the comics, Barks drew him taller and more straight-legged to make him more human in appearance and action. However, the artist's visual style varied not only from year to year but from comic to comic, sometimes even changing within the same story. In the late 1940s, for example, he began drawing Donald with a long bill. "About [1949] somebody came up to me at Disney Studios," Barks recalled. "One of the women up the road was an inker at Disney, and I think that she was the one that told me that 'The word is out all over the studio that you draw that beak too long.'"[71] So Barks started shortening the ducks' bills to bring them into conformity with the animation Donald. But there was a struggle between Western Publishing and the Disney newspaper division that supervised the comics and had to approve the comic art.

One of Barks's editors at this time was Chase Craig, who was responsible for showing Western's comic art directly to Walt Disney for approval.
Disney later became too busy to perform this function and told Craig
to stop, but the comic strip division thought that Barks's ducks should
look more like Al Taliaferro's Donald in the newspapers. Craig felt that
comparisons of Barks's Donald and the animation duck were unfair, and
in 1950, at Western's direction, Barks prepared a model sheet called the
"Magazine Comics Duck."[72] Craig got Walt Disney himself to approve
the model sheet, and Barks subsequently was permitted to draw the ducks
in his own singular way. Barks never knew that Disney was reading his
stories, but Walt's intervention was crucial in protecting Barks's autonomy as a comic book artist.[73] Disney came to have great faith in Western,
especially after several popular Disney-owned characters including Uncle
Scrooge originated in the company's comics. Walt made several unsuccessful efforts to buy Western and retained a special affinity for his association with the publisher. In the 1950s, when he needed money to finance
Disneyland, much of the initial funding came from Western.

Barks's resistance to a uniform Duck universe even carried over into
retirement. He disagreed with attempts of other writers, including Don
Rosa, Barks's heir apparent as the scripter of Uncle Scrooge comics, to
develop fully fleshed-out biographies for his characters and a coherent
family tree. Barks wrote to Rosa, "I think it best if you avoid any mention
of Don's sister Thelma (or Dumbella whatever!). The public is not going
to die of jitters if her mysterious appearance and disappearance is never
explained. However, if you feel that you have to legitimize the nephews
by giving her a plausible name and responsible husband, do it your way.
Disney stories forbid your making her a pimp's wife who got pregnant
while working in brothels in Kansas City."[74]

For Barks, the ducks and other animals that peopled his stories were
fictional characters rather than real people and could change from plot to
plot as the situation required. "On the problems that arise in explaining
the family tree in stories dealing with Gladstone and others, why get into
such a predicament?" Barks asked Rosa. "The ducks and mice and Pegleg
Petes of Disney's menagerie are all fairy tale creatures. To humanize

them to the extent of explaining their parental origins detracts from their mystique."[75] By creating a fluid, pluralistic universe that lay open to many possibilities rather than forcing his cosmos to congeal into a static totality, Barks allowed himself an enormous degree of flexibility, giving his imagination free rein. Varying his plots so that readers' expectations would be continually thrown off guard, he created a variegated, unpredictable world in which the audience was never quite certain about what to expect next, undermining the illusions of a fixed, unified subjectivity and sense of mastery that informed most comic books.

AMERICAN GOTHIC

arks's debut as a comic book writer occurred with a little-known story, "Pluto Saves the Ship" (Large Feature #7 [1942]), which he wrote in his spare evenings with two coworkers from the Disney Studio. "My experience working with Jack Hannah and Nick George . . . convinced me the comic book method of presenting stories was not too difficult to be mastered." The comic, Barks recalled, was "designed to take advantage of the wartime jitters. [W]e three did the final draft in rough sketch form in my den room in North Hollywood. The post–Pearl Harbor blackouts were in effect, and we had all the window blinds closed and taped shut. It was hot and stuffy, and we consumed many beers. The story shows the effects."[1]

"Donald Duck Finds Pirate Gold" (FC #9 [1942]), was the first comic book story that Barks drew and the first Donald Duck adventure.[2] Until 1942, when "Pirate Gold" was published, Disney comics had been largely reprints of newspaper comic strips. Floyd Gottfredson's Mickey Mouse comic strip adventures were serialized in monthly installments. However, Donald Duck comic strips had been self-contained gag strips, and no Donald Duck adventure stories existed for publishers to reprint. By the late 1930s and early 1940s, Donald Duck had surpassed Mickey Mouse as Disney's most popular cartoon character, creating a pressing need for Western Publishing to produce new stories about the duck.

In 1942, Western editor Oscar Lebeck came to the Disney Studio in search of a story on which to base a full-length Donald Duck comic book. The discarded ideas for animated films through which he looked included "Morgan's Ghost," written by Homer Brightman and Harry Reeves. It consisted of twelve hundred storyboard drawings and needed to be condensed into a coherent narrative. The story starred Mickey, Donald, and Goofy in search of the treasure of Morgan the Pirate. Lebeck contacted John Rose, head of the story department, and asked who would be able to draw it. Rose recommended Barks and Hannah, who had been working as a team on the Donald Duck cartoons for the past two years. Bob Karp, writer of the Donald Duck comic strip, received the job of turning the storyboards into a written script. Barks explained, "When we began, we were given four or five pages of script, while Bob was working on other pages. I took a couple of pages, and Jack took a couple, and by the time we got those done, there was much more of the script done, and we had a little talk together as to which we enjoyed or felt either of us could draw better than the other. We decided that I would take most of the outdoor scenes, and he would take the indoor ones. Jack had a wide knowledge of perspective and liked to do shadow effects and furniture."[3]

"Pirate Gold" was Dell's first originally drawn funny-animal adventure. The precedent for combining humor and adventure in one story had been set in silent films like Charlie Chaplin's *The Gold Rush* and Buster Keaton's *The General*. Gottfredson applied the formula to the funny-animal genre in the Mickey Mouse adventures: "When you look at my later stories in comic books," Barks explained, "you'll see that I was trying to follow the format Floyd Gottfredson established of having Mickey and the other guys involved in funny situations at the same time that they were having serious problems, and they solved their serious problems by funny means."[4]

But the final comic showed its debt more to animation than to comic strips: nearly half the pages were wordless. The focus was on visual action, with panels drawn three rows to a page rather than the standard four.

"That's why there's so little dialogue in 'Pirate Gold,'" Barks commented. "Bob took it from the storyboards. In animation they wanted things moving on the screen: they didn't want characters in held positions moving their lips."[5] Barks claimed that he and Hannah based their drawings on Karp's script and never saw any of the storyboards. However, details of the comic are so close to the animation drawings that it seems likely that Barks did see them.[6] The comic book set a pattern for a plethora of cartoon character adventures to follow featuring Western's lineup of cartoon stars, including Bugs Bunny, Porky Pig, Andy Panda, and others.

In Barks's adventure tales, Donald remained the impulsive, hotheaded duck of the cartoons but became a more complex character as Barks endowed him with human strengths and weaknesses. Donald could be brave or heroic, well intentioned or power mad, all in the same story. He was a victim of his recklessness and self-delusions, transcending the simplistic good guy/bad guy formulas of most comic books.

Just as Donald matured in Barks's stories, so did the nephews. Rather than mischievous rivals and competitors fighting their uncle, they became his helpers, saving him from dangers both external and self-imposed. Like the ten-pagers, this formula had a great appeal to children because it revolved around a role reversal between parent and child, with the child proving his superiority to the adult. In "Pirate Gold," for example, the nephews discover that the old lady they are sailing with is really Black Pete in disguise and defeat him in the end. However, this role reversal was not based simply on conflicts between the generations, as in the early ten-pagers; rather, the adventures manifested the ways in which parents and children had to unite to defeat a common menace. "Children turned their skills and resources not to defeating the parent," as in the ten-page stories, explains Mike Barrier, "but to saving his life, and in so doing, proved that they were indeed 'men'—that is mature and responsible."[7]

Barks had only been writing and drawing the Donald Duck ten-page stories for several months when Western contacted him about doing a second Donald Duck adventure comic. "The Mummy's Ring" (*DD* FC #29 [1943]), was the first Donald Duck adventure that Barks both wrote and drew. Because of his inexperience in writing full-length adventure stories, editor Eleanor Packer asked him to submit a script in advance. Barks recalled, "She wanted some big changes made in the way the priests in the temple accepted the ducks and the unwrapping of the mummy . . . so I worked it up the way she wanted it and sent it in again. She read the two of them together and sent back my script and said that one was best after all, so go ahead and use it. I don't remember the specific changes, but they took the suspense out of the script: the climaxes came in the wrong places. She didn't have the sense of timing I had picked up in my animation work. My stuff had crackle to it; hers didn't."[8] Barks never again sent a script in for approval until the more timorous days of the 1960s.

The Duck Man's stories during this period show a marked fascination with the Gothic. According to Barks, "The Mummy's Ring," for example, "was prompted by an archeological item I read at the time [1943] about mummies and the ancient custom of providing food for the deceased."[9] The story was also inspired by the 1932 Boris Karloff horror film *The Mummy*. The image of the mummy had been reconfigured in a second cycle of mummy films, sans Karloff, that began with the *Mummy's Hand* in 1940 and again made the mummy a hot item in American pop culture. This film marked an important departure from the original. Where the first film was primarily a story of perverted love, these films stressed the Egyptians' revenge against foreigners, which had been a subtext in the first film, thereby playing on widespread xenophobic anxieties at a time when America was girding itself for war and the Far East seemed not only exotic but dangerous.

Barks's story encodes these fears of foreigners, revolving around the ducks' attempts to rescue Huey, who has been accidentally locked into a sarcophagus and taken to the Bey's palace in Egypt. The Bey is a tyrannical Hitler-like figure who wants to purge his nation of modern values and return it to its ancient roots. He "takes what he wants with threats of starting a war," a custodian tells Donald. When the ducks encounter the Bey in person, Barks depicts him in snarling close-up, announcing that the ducks have despoiled the resting place of his ancestors and threatening to bury Huey in the sarcophagus in which he is imprisoned.

Barks was a recluse and a homebody. Like many of his readers, he was an armchair adventurer and had not visited the places about which he wrote: "I've traveled nowhere, seen few movies or plays, read few books (e.g. Zane Grey's and Perry Mason's)."[10] He gave careful attention to developing realistic backgrounds because he had always wanted to do straight adventure comics. This required researching locales in the *Encyclopedia Britannica* and *National Geographic*. "I used to rob [from] the *Geographic*. It is one of my best reference sources. . . . It just wouldn't have seemed right to say that the ducks were in Egypt and then draw a bunch of squiggles across a page and make the kids think that that was Egypt."[11]

"The Mummy's Ring" was a breakthrough for Barks. He invested the story with a sense of historical authenticity by basing his drawings for Egyptian buildings, clothing, and artifacts on photographs from *National Geographic*.[12] The museum and palace sequences are peppered with accurate Egyptian designs and motifs. Barks was so meticulous in rendering the ambiance of Egypt's ancient past that he drew pyramids and statues in shadows, as in the *Geographic* photographs. Barks's synthesis of realistically drawn settings and fantasy-based cartoon characters created a unique, hybrid art form. The realistic backgrounds and ambience of his stories invited readers to fully identify with the ducks' plight as quasi-human figures undergoing the same travails readers might experience. At the same time, the characters' status as cartoon animals who talked and acted like humans made them parodies of human foibles and follies.

However, Barks had not yet mastered the fusion of these two styles. He often failed to integrate background detail within a scene, and those visuals remained just an excuse for sightseeing. Barks invokes a tourist gaze by making Egyptian monuments into exotic spectacles that are the most prominent elements in panels and aligns our vision with that of the ducks as they stare at them. The carefully shaded pyramids and colossi stand out from the rest of the art because the backgrounds are simply drawn and lack texture. As a consequence, these artifacts function as picture postcards, insufficiently contributing to the narrative.

Barks also had not yet achieved the delicate balance between melodrama and comedy he would invoke in his best adventures. The story lacks a feeling of real horror, and the slapstick humor undermines any sustained Gothic ambiance. Although the plot seems motivated by the threat of Huey's premature burial and what appears to be a living mummy, the details never coalesce into a coherent narrative. "My locales and plot ideas came mostly from looking at pictures in the *Geographic*," Barks admitted, "and thinking that is the kind of place I'd like to draw—also the boats and temples and the pyramids. So I made up a story to give me an excuse to use all that scenery."[13] The ending is also contrived, lacking Barks's characteristic irony: not only is the mummy revealed to be Black Pete in disguise, but the murderous king suddenly turns benevolent, coddling Huey on his knee and rewarding the ducks with a chest of jewels for returning the sacred ring. "The Mummy's Ring" was the first Barks story about the "far away and long ago," as he put it; not until later in the decade would his art fully mature.

Barks's stories underwent a noticeable shift during the late war and postwar years. Breaking from the simple, straightforward adventure tales that preceded them, they became dark, complex narratives, many of them horror stories. Two stories, "The Firebug" and "The Terror of the River" (*DD* FC #108 [1945]), mark this transition. Unlike "Pirate Gold," these stories do not deal with a quest for treasure; there is no rescue of a family member, as in "The Mummy's Ring"; and they do not present an imaginary society of little people such as the Gneezles (*DD* FC #62 [1944]). Rather, as Donald Ault points out, "The Firebug" and "The Terror of the River" feature apocalyptic themes about psychotic Americans who wreak havoc on their country.[14]

"The Firebug" was inspired by a Donald Duck short, *Fire Chief Donald* (1940), written by Barks and Jack Hannah, in which Donald is an overzealous fireman who accidentally burns up his fire truck and incinerates his firehouse. In "The Firebug" Barks invoked an image of Donald so outré that it would have been prohibited in a Disney cartoon. He is a pyromaniac with a demonic love of building fires. A bump on the head releases unconscious, aggressive drives that Donald would never express in his normal state. Before his fall, he exclaims, "I hate to start fires! If people could do without fires they would be better off!" But after his fall,

Donald's personality is inverted: "Ah! a beyootiful fire! I love to build fires! I'm going to build fires everywhere!" In a panel shot through his fireplace, we see Donald engulfed in flames, a maniacal gleam in his eye as he stares at the blaze.

As noted earlier, Barks was a pacifist who opposed America's entrée into World War II. This story reflects his concern. Donald is an Everyman who symbolizes the destructive potential Barks saw when humanity's aggressive urges were unleashed during wartime. Donald is so consumed by his mania to mold fires into aesthetically pleasing structures that he is blind to their destructive potential. Throughout the first part of the story, we believe that he might be unleashing a string of blazing infernos that threaten to burn down the city. However, Donald's designs are being appropriated by the real pyromaniac, who turns out to be a police officer in disguise. Ault suggests that a parallel exists between the destructive pyromaniac's relationship to Donald and the atomic bomb designers' relationship to the physicists whose creative research made the Bomb possible. Donald, like the physicists, is blind to the destructive implications of his actions.

While Ault's parallel between the physicists and Donald seems initially a possibility, the atomic bomb analogy breaks down because Barks wrote "The Firebug" several weeks before the dropping of atomic bombs on Hiroshima and Nagasaki. Rather, the story evokes the ethical dilemmas brought about by changes in military techniques and qualms about the bombing of cities and civilian populations, a reversal of policies of which the Bomb was both an expression and a culmination. The story's indexing of fears about the destruction of Duckburg by arson is paralleled by the Allied firebombing of Japan. Although the firebombing was quickly eclipsed by the greater threat of nuclear holocaust, it was so memorable that Barks referred to a napalm attack decades later in an *Uncle Scrooge* comic book (FC #386 [1952]).

The United States did not start bombing civilians until World War II. Before the war, the United States was committed to precision bombing—that is, to the avoidance of civilian targets—although military strategists had for many years contemplated long-range bombing as a new way to win wars. As early as 1926, U.S. bombing doctrine defined itself as "a method of imposing will by terrorizing the whole population."[15] In 1941, U.S. Army Air Force General Henry "Hap" Arnold asserted that bombing would reduce large cities to the point of surrender and that the "will of a nation" was now an objective. British firebombing of Hamburg and Dresden in 1942 suggested the viability of the new military strategy, and massive American firebombing of Tokyo killed 100,000 civilians, setting the precedent for Hiroshima and Nagasaki. Thus began a new era of attacking civilian targets, with a military strategy of using bombs as weapons of terror against civilians. Where male soldiers had previously died to protect women and children, now women and children would perish to protect soldiers (the precise argument that would be made in defense of dropping the atomic bomb on Japan).

Barks's story expresses an ambivalence about the morality of authorities who would order such actions. The policeman is both a figure of law and order and a psychotic terrorist, and the two are indistinguishable. In this scenario, the state is both a representative of law and order and an insane force laying waste to cities and victimizing innocent civilians in an attempt to destroy military targets. (The pyromaniac attacks natural resources such as oil and coal and a seaport.) "The Firebug" has a graphic style reminiscent of 1940s *film noir*. Barks drew Donald and the city in dark shadows and gave the story a claustrophobic feel by using twelve panels to a page rather than the usual eight. "I had to do some stories like that because of the paper shortage," Barks explained.[16]

Several of Barks's stories satirized the notion that the evils in human nature could be easily surmounted through schemas of reform. Humanity was not perfectible, and utopias such as the peaceful kingdom of Tralla La (*US* #6 [1954]) were bound to fail (see chapter 5). In the conclusion to "The Firebug," Barks satirizes the liberal therapeutic ethic that proposed that criminals should be cured through psychiatry rather than punished. Just as the judge sentences "Benzine Bazoony," the real firebug, a doctor stands up and proclaims that he can cure him with a "simple operation" costing only "$365—plus tax." The facility and cheapness of such a panacea and the bathetic cheer from a bystander reveal the doctor to be a quack and his remedy a sham. Barks's satire culminates when Donald, whom the judge has just exonerated and praised for capturing the real pyromaniac, builds a fire in his wastebasket and burns the courthouse down. Barks thus reveals to readers the intractability of the dark forces that existed not only in society's lawbreakers but in average men like Donald.

Barks's editors objected to the last two panels because Donald set fire to the judge's wastebasket and wound up in jail. "They couldn't have a Disney character behind bars," Barks commented.[17] So the editors had the last two panels redrawn to show that the whole story had been Donald's bad dream, effectively erasing Barks's satire of the dark psychosocial forces released during wartime.

"Terror of the River" was the first story Barks wrote after the end of World War II. The tale was inspired by an unproduced Disney cartoon, *Prehistoric Mickey*, in which Mickey, Donald, and Goofy encounter a serpent on the high seas.[18] However, the comic book story reveals how Barks both drew on and transcended his sources in Disney animation. The serpent proves to be a machine; the real monster is a psychotic submariner. In creating an insane villain, Barks invoked a kind of horror atypical for a Disney comic book. But the creation of a crazed submariner was in part an attempt to avoid censorship: "I knew that I could not put in much violence. . . . I felt that if I made the Scarer totally nutty, it would get by the editors a great deal more easily than if I made him murderous. I created a guy that didn't leave any bad taste in people's mouths, didn't cause children any nightmares afterward."[19] The story drew on wartime anxieties about submarine attacks: It envisages the potential invasion of America and depicts images of mass destruction, scenes familiar to the public from wartime newsreels and newspapers. Barks's tale implies that even the Mississippi, America's heartland, was not safe from attack.

However, Barks's story differs from most wartime comics, radically subverting their premises. It reverses the axis of patriotism and xenophobia that pitted American good guys against brutal foreigners, exploring the dangers of the psychic and social forces unleashed by the war. The real danger is not attack by an enemy power, Barks suggests, but invasion by a psychotic American. Barks's serpent turns out only to be a machine: the real monster is a sadistic bully who takes glee in terrifying those above.

The character of the Scarer condensed some of the intense psychological forces unleashed in Americans during the war. "Few remember that the prospect of the World War II veterans' demobilization and reintegration was a cause of widespread concern, indeed alarm, long before V-J Day," writes historian Donald Gerber. The vet was a psychologically troubling figure in many postwar films, including *The Best Years of Our Lives* and *In a Lonely Place*, which starred Humphrey Bogart as a potentially murderous Hollywood scriptwriter and war veteran. "On the one hand," writes Gerber, "the veteran's heroism and sacrifices are celebrated and memorialized and debts of gratitude, both symbolic and material, are paid to him. On the other hand, the veteran also inspired anxiety and fear and is seen as a threat to social order and political stability."[20] In 1945 and 1946, as various governmental and professional experts prepared Americans to receive millions of men returning home, the discourse surrounding the veteran problem cast doubt on the mental stability of every demobilized man. "Every veteran was seen as a potential 'mental case,' even if he showed no symptoms," writes Gerber.[21] These fears of the psycho vet turned out to be exaggerated but began to call into question the definitions of aggression and hypermasculinity the war had mobilized. The vet was viewed as embodying "an excess of masculinity, a brutal killing machine set loose on the streets, or as a 'paucity' of masculinity—a shell shocked bundle of nerves" unable to maintain the responsibility of holding a job and being the family's chief breadwinner.[22]

Although Barks carefully avoided any references to the actual conflagration, "Terror of the River" implicitly explores the crisis in masculinity invoked by the war and expresses his fears about the aggressions unleashed by global violence. The story shows that the Scarer's delight in terrifying others is a means of disavowing his own anxieties. When the nephews threaten his sub and it fills with water, the Scarer becomes terrified, and when his sub's controls jam, he has a nervous breakdown, becoming catatonic with terror. The Scarer's toughness, aggression, and need for dominance—qualities of patriarchal masculinity encouraged by governments waging war—rest on a denial of his vulnerability and soft-ness. Barks's story exposes the same fears on a social and political level: government assertions of dominance are bought only at the expense of masking fears about falling from power—that is, of having the same type of destruction that we have wreaked on others turned against us. The story ends with Donald and the kids having conquered the Scarer and being given the "serpent" as a new houseboat. The ducks sail away to the tune of "Anchors Away," the Navy anthem, played by a brass band. The apocalyptic destruction conjured up by submarine attacks seems safely contained by American military power. But the preceding events cast doubt on whether such destructive impulses, once unleashed, can so eas-ily be domesticated.

In the mid-1940s, Donald Duck reached the pinnacle of his popular-ity, starring in his first cartoon features, *Saludos Amigos* (1943) and *The Three Caballeros* (1945). Although Barks did not like the latter film, he was sufficiently impressed with them that he set two Donald Duck adventures in Latin America, "Volcano Valley" (*DD* FC #147 [1947]) and "Lost in the Andes" (*DD* FC #223 [1949]). "I realized that it was a popular subject at the time," Barks recalled, "and that Disney would love to have me use that locale, because they were patting the Latin Americans on the head, trying to be pals and get access to show their films in South America. They'd lost the whole European market during the war."[23]

Between 1941 and 1943, Walt Disney, his wife, and a group of Disney artists made three U.S.-government-backed trips to Latin America to gather material for films. The Latin American films had both a political and economic rationale. U.S. officials feared Nazi penetration into Latin America and wanted to shore up the American presence there and to cement ties with political allies in the region. This demand for American hemispheric unity intensified with the coming of the Cold War and conflict with the Soviet Union, a former ally. Moreover, U.S. corporations had a foothold in Latin America and feared nationalization and expro-priation. During this period, the United States financed the European recovery and came to see itself as the defender of the "free world" against the other great superpower, the Soviet Union.

This posture represented a major shift in American attitudes toward intervention. After World War I, Americans felt betrayed by President Woodrow Wilson's claim that the United States had entered the war not for reasons of economic interest but to "make the world safe for democracy." U.S. citizens came to believe that their country's involvement in the war had been a mischievous conspiracy by munitions manufacturers and bankers. Consequently, pollsters during the Depression found that only 26 percent of respondents approved of U.S. intervention in foreign affairs.[24] Yet as revealed in *Casablanca* and other wartime films, a commitment to intervention became the norm in the 1940s. By 1945, 81 percent of survey respondents supported the United Nations and America's global commitments. Yet some conservative groups opposed America's new foreign policy. A wave of neoisolationism led by Republican Senator Robert Taft swept the country in 1946, giving the party a big win in that year's congressional campaigns.

Barks's "Volcano Valley" references this context. Set in the fictional village of Volcanovia, the story was inspired by the "Little Pedro" sequence in *Saludos Amigos*, in which a baby airplane makes a terrifying flight over the Andes during a storm to deliver the mail. In the film, Disney artists caricatured Aconcagua, the highest mountain in the Western Hemisphere, by giving its snow-filled crags the visage of a scowling monster. The sequence inspired Donald's precipitous flight to Volcanovia, during which his pilot, Pablo Mañana, takes a siesta in midjourney to his village, narrowly missing one mountain crag after another. Barks even mimicked Aconcagua's glowering face, transferring it to Old Ferocio, Volcanovia's volatile giant volcano.

The threatening geography was an index of a parallel threat to the United States. "I was with the America First type of guys," Barks commented. "We despised the darned war and what caused it, and our reasons for getting into it seemed so unjust, so I didn't have a feeling of wanting to cooperate a hell of a lot with it."[25] "Volcano Valley" plays upon these neoisolationist sentiments. Donald mistakenly buys an army bomber, then sells it to Major Mañana, "Volcanovia's favorite son." From the start, Barks portrays Volcanovia as an impoverished country that drains American resources. Donald sells a plane worth millions for what he thinks is a good price, three hundred thousand pezoozies, which turns out to be equivalent to only three dollars. Donald foolishly offers to pay for the gas on Pablo's return flight, which turns out to be so expensive that Donald must sell his car to pay his debt. The military connotations of a major buying a bomber for his country satirize the U.S. involvement in providing arms to foreign countries as a bad deal undermined by inflated currency and poverty.

The story evokes a paranoia based on popular stereotypes of Latin Americans. In Volcanovia, no one works, and the citizens continually take siestas. The only activity is that of its continually erupting volcanoes. These geological formations range from baby mounds to the gigantic Old Ferocio, which threatens to destroy the entire nation at any moment. Engulfed by the eruptions around them, the natives are blind to their danger. The volcano is a metaphor for Latin America's penchant for revolution and political violence.[26] These stereotypes suggest an oxymoronic image of Latin America as simultaneously slothful and tempestuous, politically unstable as a consequence of periodic revolutions and the inability to govern itself.

The ducks are trapped in Volcanovia and cannot leave. Permission to depart depends on Donald performing a great service to its people and being proclaimed a national hero. However, his attempts to do so only result in his offending Volcanovia's president and being declared a national menace. The conclusion evokes anxieties that American intervention in foreign affairs can easily backfire, leaving America not only drained of its wealth but persecuted for "meddling" in the affairs of a "more primitive" people. However, Barks mitigates the stereotypes on which this satire rests, suggesting that Americans are just as bigoted as other nations. A kangaroo court sentences Donald to hard labor, but the vote that convicts him comes from another North American, a Texan who is so biased that he would believe Donald innocent only if he came from the same state. Moreover, the jailer who comes to take Donald to the "salt mines," a reference to Russian totalitarianism, sympathizes with the duck's plight yet is powerless to help him. Prejudice and corruption lie on both sides of the border.

Freed by a propitious earthquake, Donald continues his attempt to become a national hero but ends up destroying the country. When Old Ferocio begins to erupt, Donald tells Pablo to stuff the volcano with baskets filled with corn. By supreme irony, the would-be hero becomes a national menace. The country becomes inundated with popcorn, which piles up to the tops of the smoldering volcanoes, making it unlikely that any townspeople could have survived. As Donald Ault suggests, the apocalyptic ending is an apt metaphor for the American bombing of Japan and the popcorn a symbol of nuclear fallout. But the ridiculous image Barks constructs deflects from the horrific nightmare. Trying to become the heroic savior of other nations, the story asserts, may not only condemn America to becoming a pariah but ironically even cause the destruction of the very people we set out to save.

From the first, Americans sensed that the atomic bomb had revolutionized life, ushering in a new, more anxious age. In her study of postwar Bomb culture, *Dr. Strangelove's America*, Margot Henriksen convincingly argues that the birth of the Bomb precipitated a fragmentation in American life and a fissure in American culture. Official culture was triumphalist and saw the Bomb as a sign of American power, material progress, and technological superiority—a sign that God was on our side. Conversely, the Bomb and the Cold War consensus that supported it provoked a culture of dissent and disillusionment with American values and institutions.[27] This alienation from the American mainstream is evident in the images of corruption, pessimism, and paranoia in *films noirs* of this period. But even such mainstream films as *The Best Years of Our Lives* and Frank Capra's *It's a Wonderful Life* registered a sense of trauma and disaffection. According to Henriksen, these two cultures coexisted throughout the postwar era, culminating in the rebellious youth cultures of the 1960s.

Comic books utilized multiple strategies for representing the Bomb and the potential for nuclear holocaust. Some authors fully depicted the horrors of nuclear devastation. In *Captain Marvel Adventures* #66 (1946), for example, the television station WHIZ showed scenes of American cities destroyed by an A-bomb from an unknown foreign power. However, these stark scenes were sanitized in the story's conclusion, which revealed that the televised images were just dramatizations designed to warn the audience about the folly of nuclear war. As long as America retained a monopoly on the Bomb, American comics emphasized the threat that the Other Side might invent nuclear weapons, eliding the dangers in U.S. possession of a doomsday device.[28] Comics often domesticated the bomb, disavowing its horrendous effects. Fawcett Comics utilized a mushroom cloud to advertise its comic book titles and touted the "safe" use of nuclear energy in *Captain Marvel Adventures*.[29] Conversely, some comic books for older readers, such as EC's *Weird Science-Fantasy*, carried antiwar messages that depicted the horrendous effects of nuclear war and debunked the ideal that such wars were winnable.[30]

Barks's stories of the 1940s and early 1950s reveal a fascination with the Bomb. Although Western Publishing prohibited him from drawing any overt scenes of nuclear devastation in his comics, many of his stories contain references to the Bomb and carry an antiwar ethos. Barks's first story dealing with the topic, "Donald Duck's Atom Bomb," appeared in a 1947 Cheerios giveaway comic. Donald is a mad scientist who invents a bomb that goes "fut" instead of "boom." The Cold War had not yet become common coin, and the villain of the story, Professor Sleezy, is an aristocratic, Nazi-like spy who steals Donald's invention. However, Barks was not a nationalist. He was equally contemptuous of American scientists' moral blindness and of Nazi militarism. Professor Mollicule's coke-bottle spectacles and wizened neck are emblems of his myopia and head-in-the clouds intellect. Professor Mollicule is power-mad and oblivious to the destructive consequences of creating nuclear weapons: "Whole cities could be crumbled by an explosion that goes 'fut' instead of 'boom!'" he exults. After Donald has decided to give up his avocation as bomb maker for something more lucrative, Mollicule demurs, "Think of the money, the fame!"

However, Barks domesticates the terrors of nuclear weapons, turning the story into a screwball comedy of a war between the sexes: The only effects of the bomb's "ghastly rays" are to cause the city's citizens to lose their hair. Barks again reveals his antifeminine bias and shows that the women, enraged over a diminution of their beauty, are the bomb's primary victims. A mob of enraged females chases Donald and the professor the through the streets. Indicative of Barks's cynicism about human nature, there is no moral resolution to the story. Although forgoing the role of bomb maker, Donald cashes in on the havoc he has wreaked by selling hair restorer to a long line of bald-headed victims.[31]

Although Barks avoided showing the Bomb in his tales, he came disturbingly close in a 1947 ten-pager (*WDC&S* #81). Donald finds a fake map of a lost gold mine fabricated by the nephews and, by mistake, wanders onto a missile test site. The tale was inspired by the existence of an army bombing range located seventy-five miles east of San Jacinto, where Barks lived.[32] However, the author sent the ducks all the way to New Mexico, suggesting Los Alamos, the birthplace of the atomic bomb. The story is especially frightening because it shows an airborne missile from a bird's-eye view, poised to hit the target onto which Donald has stumbled. A narration box calls it "the most awesome weapon ever made by man!" leaving little doubt that Barks was thinking of a nuclear bomb. Although Donald tries to run away from certain death, Barks draws him madly racing *toward* the panel depicting the deadly device. The graphics suggest that although we have built the Bomb to protect Americans, it poses an imminent, perhaps inescapable, danger to us. However, Barks deflects the reader from this disturbing conclusion by subverting our expectations: Donald miraculously escapes unharmed, and the explosion reveals that the bombing range, indeed, harbors gold. Barks thus sublimates and disavows the uncertainties and dangers created by the invention of the Bomb. Yet, the terrifying image of an A-bomb about to strike and the threat of our inescapable destruction remain.

The closest Barks gets to depicting a nuclear holocaust occurs in a 1950 issue of *Walt Disney's Comics and Stories* (#112). When Barks wrote this story in 1949, America was experiencing a severe case of Bomb jitters after learning that Russia had exploded a nuclear device. "Rip Van Winkle," a tale that had long fascinated him, provided Barks with a vehicle for depicting a nightmare image of a postapocalyptic America. The story has come to be known as a "drug issue" because Donald's vision is based on a hallucination induced by a broken bottle of ether. To manipulate him into going back to wintry Duckburg from the warm climate down south, the nephews perpetrate a hoax that Donald has been bitten by a Geffle Bug and slept for forty years. He awakes to behold monstrous-looking buildings and cars that are melting and people and animals walking around in pieces. "The buildings are all made of *rubber* to bend away from atomic bombs!" one nephew explains in an attempt to keep the hoax from being discovered. It is as if the city and its machines are dissolving and the citizens and their pets exploded into fragments as a consequence of the heat of atomic radiation. By showing that none of the people notice that they and their animals are walking around in pieces, Barks satirizes Americans' obliviousness to the dangers of atomic holocaust with which they live every day. Barks masks the anxiety of this nightmare by creating a surreal, drug-induced vision. As in many of his tales, Barks presented extreme anxiety-inducing images, then covered them up with a dollop of absurd humor so that they would not create nightmares for his young readers and break Western's taboos. Nonetheless, after awakening, Donald goes running home to Duckburg in terror of having another hallucinatory vision.

"Ancient Persia" (*DD* FC #275 [1950]) is Barks's most important story in which the Bomb is a subtext. It is the Duck Man's most eerie and horrific tale in which he evokes the nightmare of nuclear Armageddon without ever drawing images of an atomic blast. The central theme is self-annihilation, represented by an elixir that turns all life into dust, an appropriate image of nuclear radiation. The tale is set in the Iranian desert in the mythical city of Itsa Faka. Once a thriving society of gentle palm trees and terraced gardens that made it the nucleus of western civilization, the fertile crescent has been transformed into dust by the ravages of time. Itsa Faka harbors a strange destructive force.

Barks caricatures the despotic civilization of ancient Persia as the expression of a destructive will to power characteristic of western civilization that has culminated in the atomic age. In the opening panel, the nephews gaze chillingly at what appears to be a decayed parchment depicting a scene of ancient Mesopotamia. But we learn in the next panel that they are really looking at a strange man whom they characterize as a "mad scientist," and he is what they find so frightening. The panel exposes a metonymic link between the horror evoked by the scientist and that connoted by the image of ancient Persia. The parchment in the first panel doubles as a panel divider, eliding the spaces between the scenes of ancient times and contemporary Duckburg and suggesting the coexistence of the two places in the same time frame as well as the continuity of past and present.

At first glance, "Ancient Persia" would seem to be a variant of the Frankenstein myth. Both stories concern mad scientists obsessed with the dead and brought to self-destruction by their monomaniacal pursuit of power. Here again, Barks was influenced by Karloff's film *The Mummy*, which also concerned the resurrection of the dead. Barks's mad scientist was patterned after Karloff's cadaverous look in that film. However, the scientist in "Ancient Persia" wants not to create but to destroy life. His only interest in resurrecting the king is to learn the secret of dehydration. The only human in the story, he ironically is nameless and totally dehumanized, seeking to destroy humanity so that he "can have the whole world to be alone."

The emphasis on the destructive ends to which science can be used can be interpreted as Barks's warning about the dangers unleashed by the creation of the atomic bomb and its potential for eradicating all life on earth. Barks invokes this allegory by showing the scientist reading a book, *Up and Atom*, a humorous reference to the Bomb, as he learns the secret of dehydration. He discovers that the Persians were dehydrated through the use of radium vapor: radium is one of the key ingredients in an atomic bomb. Barks shows the vapor turning people to dust before our eyes, suggesting the effects of atomic radiation in incinerating its victims and turning them to ashes. The scenes in which the scientist and the Persians turn to dust are the most chilling in all of Barks's oeuvre, the only place where he shows people dying, a taboo. However, Barks deflects these implications by suggesting that the people are not really destroyed but are only converted to dust again and presumably are capable of resuscitation at any moment. However, such scenes of madness and oblivion remain eerie.

"Ancient Persia" is Barks's bleakest tale because it suggests the nihilistic obsession with destruction that lies at the heart of western civilization's quest for power and domination over humanity and nature. The king and the scientist function as doubles, both so consumed by power that they are possessed by a desire for self-annihilation. Like Itsa Faka, the king's name, Neverwuzza, connotes fakery and a lack of existence. The scientist's face is wizened, with concave cheeks, and he has the appearance of being mummified. His desire for unlimited power mirrors the king's arrogance and imperious manner. Both the king and the scientist reflect the nihilism of civilization's drive for conquest and ultimately death. The king is so arrogant and proud that he would rather be dehydrated than disgraced by Prince Ali Cad's jilting of the princess on their marriage day.

Cad is a physical double of Donald, again suggesting Barks's parallel between ancient and contemporary civilizations. Barks satirizes the wedding ceremony by drawing Donald, the groom, carried in on a tray like a roast pig while the princess does handstands. Barks suggests misogynistically that civilization and the family are founded on the domestication and emasculation of male power and autonomy. Cad embodies the nihilistic side of contemporary Everymen such as Donald. Although Cad escapes by pretending to be his alter ego, he decides to return to his fate rather than live in a modern world of roaring tractors, returning to the tomb and being dehydrated like his contemporaries.

Barks's later references to the Bomb take place during the burgeoning of East-West tensions during the Cold War, including the anticommunist hysteria of the House Un-American Activities Committee investigations in the late 1940s, the rise of McCarthyism (1949–54), and the Korean War (1949–52). The September 1949 news that Russia had broken the U.S. monopoly on the Bomb and tested a nuclear device surprised American leaders and the general public, who had believed Russia too backward for such a technological feat. Reacting with alarm at the news, Americans feared that the Soviet Union might use the atomic bomb on us just as we had on Japan. The hysteria of the McCarthy period was enabled by the arrest and confession of several spies for passing atomic secrets to the enemy, including the infamous 1951 trial of Julius and Ethel Rosenberg.[33]

A month after learning that Russia had entered the atomic age, Barks penned a ten-page story featuring foreign spies (*WDC&S* #114 [1949]).

Donald brags to the nephews that he is a great skier and is backed into making the precipitous journey to Codfish Cove to deliver a serum to quell an
epidemic. However, unbeknownst to him, the spies have substituted stolen
U.S. military plans for the medicine. The story both plays on and subverts
Cold War paranoia. The grinning, bearded foreign agents, who ritualisti-
cally chant "Down with America" or "Down with H'America," are such
over-the-top stereotypes that they satirize anticommunist propaganda.
Barks also subverts any good/evil polarization between the rival superpow-
ers by parodying the benevolence of the U.S. agent. The image and name
of the granite-jawed, barrel-chested Noble X. Ample both enacts and ridicules the self-righteousness of the American national security state.

In fact, this Cold War ethos is secondary to the major thrust of the
narrative, which concerns the nature of heroism. Ironically, Donald is
acclaimed a hero for reaching Codfish Cove with the serum, although the
nephews capture the spies and ensure that the hapless Donald completes
his task. In a society ruled by adults, the story suggests, children's competence goes unheralded and unrewarded while adults get all the credit.
Although Donald blusters about his triumph, the nephews and the reader
know who the true heroes are.

Barks's most important articulation of Cold War espionage occurs in
"Dangerous Disguise" (*DD* FC #308 [1951]), a spoof of spy stories. This
tale was inspired by an unproduced Disney cartoon, *Madame XX* (1940),
in which Donald is waylaid by a seductive spy, Madame XX, a sexy lady
duck modeled on contemporary screen siren Veronica Lake. "Dangerous
Disguise" is notable as Barks's greatest use of human characters. Disney
comics typically make their secondary characters into humanoid dogfaces or other animal breeds that would not clash with the zoomorphic
assumptions of the funny-animal comic that cartoon characters function
as surrogate human beings.

In this story, except for the ducks and Donald's alter ego, the spy
Donaldo El Quacko, all the characters are humans. "I somehow couldn't
visualize these master spies for all the different nations as being dogfaces or pigfaces," Barks recalled. "I visualized them as looking like they
do in the movies—suave-looking characters and beautiful girl spies."[34]

Throughout his Disney career, Barks nourished a desire to draw human characters. "My first love would have been to draw human characters—almost like Prince Valiant," he commented in a 1975 interview. "I like to draw faces and figures—I would have liked to do that in the beginning. . . . I would have drawn a thousand different faces."[35] Wanting to break away from drawing the ducks, Barks spent years trying to develop a strip with human characters; however, his work for Western kept him so busy that he never had time to develop a viable set of characters of his own.

"Dangerous Disguise" was written at a turning point in American history. In February 1950, Senator Joseph McCarthy stood on the steps of the U.S. Capitol holding a list he claimed contained the names of State Department employees who were members of the Communist Party. Newspapers all over the country carried the allegation, electrifying the nation. Although McCarthy never substantiated his claims or produced the list, the news media reported his accusations as fact, thereby launching a national panic about the dangers of communist infiltration in American life. Adding fuel to the fire, "Dangerous Disguise" was written in June 1950, at the same time that the cold war in Europe was being transformed into a hot war in Asia.

"Dangerous Disguise" is a mordant satire of the untrammeled paranoia surrounding the McCarthyite witch hunts. The story invokes a nightmare world of appearances in which nothing is as it seems and innocuous tourists cannot be distinguished from murderous spies. Even the nephews, exemplars of common sense and good judgment, fall victim to spy mania and Donald's casual suggestion that there are spies all around them. Although he would rather ogle pretty girls on the beach, Donald intercepts a message about the stolen plans of an American Q-bomb and gives in to spy hysteria. He warns his nephews, "We have to be suspicious of *everything* and *everybody*!"

The story is built on a fusion of two different graphic styles. Donald's chief antagonist, the French-accented spy Madame Triple-X, and the bathing beauties on the beach are drawn in an illustrative style reminiscent of Barks's girlie drawings for the *Calgary Eye-Opener*, while the male spies are drawn as cartoony caricatures. Madame Triple-X is a femme fatale who is both seductive and lethal, evoking the spider women of *films noirs*, who both are sexually enticing and drive men to self-destruction and death. She menaces the ducks with her stiletto, an apt symbol of castration anxiety and emasculating female power. Madame Triple-X reflects the 1940s' ambivalence toward woman's power and proper place: she combines the sexual danger of the spider woman and qualities of a wife/mother figure. When the ducks steal her bag, believing it to contain the stolen plans, it turns out only to carry her lunch, and she cheerfully fixes salami sandwiches (laced with sleeping pills) for the ducks. She later turns out to be a "good girl" in disguise, American counteragent Georgia Cornpone of the "*secret* service," suggesting the ambiguity and lability of moral definitions during the Cold War.

This duality of the good/bad, domestic/sexually dangerous woman evokes the anxieties raised by the transformation of gender roles during World War II. At that time, women left the home and worked in previously male-coded occupations while men went off to fight. After the conflict ended, women were supposed to give up their jobs to returning vets and return to the domestic sphere, but many women refused to do so, creating a crisis in gender identity. The strategies of containing women in domesticity and communism in the public sphere worked together to repress deviance and tame subversion in the postwar era, and the traumas Barks's story encodes reflect these dual forms of transgression.[36] Other spies are cast in the Cold War stereotypes familiar to the era. Madame Triple-X's counterpart is a brutish thug with Asian eyes and high cheekbones, marking him as a Russian agent who has no qualms about killing the ducks in cold blood. Barks deflects the shock of the Russian's spectacular death after he leaps out of a train window into a gaping chasm by giving it a trivial cause: one of the nephews had jabbed him in the rear with a pin. But this barely disguises the fact that the duckling has committed homicide, even if in self-defense.

Barks satirizes the Cold War universe as a lunatic regime of byzantine moves and countermoves, plots and counterplots. In a long panel he depicts an enemy spy caught by a counteragent who is in turn caught by a counter-counteragent, ad infinitum. They shoot each other in one simultaneous bang, which the naïf Donald, emblem of the unthinking citizen, thinks is a firecracker. Here the agents of East and West, good guy and bad guy, are indistinguishable, and their attempts to defeat the enemy only cancel each other out, leading to the destruction of both sides. In Barks's neoisolationist worldview, Cold War antagonisms are a fruitless but bloody game.

The story's ending amplifies the absurdity of America's fascination with domestic subversion. The ducks' attempt to thwart Madame Triple-X almost prevents her from identifying the real foreign agent, Donaldo El Quacko, another of Barks's Donald look-alikes. As the inability of distinguishing the ducks attests, it is impossible in this mad universe to tell spy from loyal citizen, subversive from patriot. The story comes to a bitter end: fearing that the dictator Brutus will sentence him to forced labor in the salt mines, Donaldo jumps out the window. Ironheelia, the name of Donaldo's country, is a thinly veiled reference to Stalinist Russia. The last panel shows a dazed, befuddled Donald slumped against a rock, too catatonic and frustrated to pay attention to the spy taking pictures of American gunboats. The best strategy, the story implies, is to develop an attitude of ironic detachment and, like Donald, to withdraw altogether from the paranoid universe of spies and subversives.

Barks's editors were not pleased with this story and published it only because it was too late to create a substitute. Barks recalled, "As soon as I took 'Dangerous Disguise' in, and Carl Buettner [Western's art editor] took a look at it, he said, 'that doesn't go good, having real humans. It takes the ducks out of their own world.'"[37] However, more was at stake in Buettner's warning than incompatible art styles. Barks had thought that he could "make more serious statements" with a human characters strip than with a funny-animal comedy.[38] His utilization of humans in "Dangerous Disguise," in effect, was an attempt to articulate more adult, sophisticated themes in his stories and to transcend the innocence of the funny-animal universe. The story may well have riled Western because of its satire of politics and foreign intrigue. Unquestionably, it had broken one of its major taboos: Although sexuality was banned in Dell comics, Barks had drawn voluptuous women with breasts.

This threat of censorship recalls Barks's restrictions when he first began his stint as a regular Duck comic book artist and was unaware that he could not draw sexy females as he had done for the *Calgary Eye-Opener*. "I got in trouble in about the second or third story that I wrote," Barks recalled. The story appeared in *Walt Disney's Comics and Stories* #33 (June 1943). According to Barks, "I had Donald as being a lifeguard, and I had this lovely duck woman.—I sure got told off about that. The guy who was the art editor at the publisher made me spend a few hours at his office just flattening the breasts of this gal."[39] Admitting that he "would love to draw" attractive women in the duck stories, Barks rarely got the chance again.

Barks felt that *The Three Caballeros*, in which Donald chases swim-suited Latinas on the beach, would allow "Dangerous Disguise" to get past his editors. In the film, Barks remembered, "Donald behaved like a real wolf. He was a lecher! He was just chasing all these pretty girls. . . . [T]hat was one of the reasons why I thought I could get away with it. But no, the comic books were for kids."[40]

Barks also broke other taboos in "Dangerous Disguise." Although he never explicitly shows people dying, this story has more deaths, including a suicide, than any other tale in Barks's oeuvre. This violated Western's dislike of death and killing. Such topics later would become explicitly forbidden as Western felt the pressure of the comics censorship movement and sought to sanitize the comics and make them safe for young readers.

Between 1941 and 1945, America emerged as the strongest nation in the world. Not only had the United States escaped fighting on its home ground while much of Europe lay in ruins, but America also possessed the most powerful weapon on earth, the atom bomb, which provided unprecedented clout in foreign affairs. The postwar era also constituted a period of unprecedented wealth and affluence, a boom time for consumer capitalism. Pundits' talk of an "American century" thus seemed not too fanciful.

By the end of the 1940s, a bipolar conflict gripped the globe. The United States became the leader of the "free world" in an internecine struggle for dominance against the Soviet Union "The effect, though not the intention," writes historian Geoffrey Hodgson, "was that America became an imperial power, of a new kind, certainly, but nevertheless as committed to intervention as it had been so recently to isolation."[41] However, Americans have been loath to recognize the scope of this new power, or its roots in American culture. "One of the central themes of American history," writes William Appleman Williams, "is that there is no American empire. Most historians will admit, if pressed, that the United States once had an empire. Then they promptly assert that it was given away. But they also speak openly of America as a world power."[42] However, as Richard Van Alstyne demonstrates, from its origins, the United States was "an *imperium*—a dominion, state or sovereignty that would expand in population and territory, and increase in strength and power."[43] A belief in American exceptionalism has erased the memory of the colonization, slavery, and resistance that constituted formative patterns in American and European history.[44]

Unlike most Uncle Scrooge tales, Barks's Donald Duck adventures are not primarily treasure hunts: many are not even adventure stories. Indeed, the genre Barks most often invoked at this time was the Gothic tale or horror story. Gothic tales typically concern psychic repression and the fragmentation of self-identity, focusing on obsession, taboo, and the irrational.[45] Gothic fiction was generated and read by a society that was becoming increasingly aware of sexual inequalities, its alienation from nature, and changes in class relations arising from the transition from feudalism to capitalism. According to David Punter, "Gothic writing emerges at a particular and definable stage in the development of class relations: we may define this as the stage when the bourgeoisie, having to all intents and purposes gained social power, began to try to understand the conditions and history of their own ascent."[46] Barks's Gothic adventure stories deal with a similar traumatic transition—the dark side of American history— conquest, colonialism, and the desire for empire that lay behind the U.S. transformation into a global superpower. His tales constitute an attempt to come to terms with the ideological contradictions evoked by America's prominence in the postwar era and foreground the imperial unconscious of American culture.

In "The Ghost of the Grotto" (*DD* FC #159 [1947]), Barks abandoned the apocalyptic imagery of the war (and immediate postwar) years and turned to the Gothic themes that preoccupy his later stories. A mystery story about a sixteenth-century "ghost's" haunting of a Caribbean fishing village, it introduces a motif that will inform many later Donald and Scrooge adventures: that western civilization's lust for conquest and empire and obsession with wealth and power invariably lead to alienation and self-disintegration. A familiar theme in Gothic fiction is the way that a protagonist's destructive psychic drives are released as a result of the repression of sexuality and estrangement from others.[47] In Mary Shelley's *Frankenstein*, for example, a scientist's inability to take up the challenges of intimacy with his fiancée leads him to reproduce himself without female agency. Barks draws on this motif by revealing that the ghost's impulse to hoard has led to the repression of his biological impulses. Like his ancestors, he cannot reproduce his line and must steal a child after fifty years to ensure the continued protection of the treasure. But not only is the ghost alienated from his biological desires, he also has cut himself off from humanity, so fearful of having his gold stolen that he has walled himself up within the grotto cave. The cave is thus a tomb, and the ghost leads an underground existence cut off from the light and life above. Deprived of even the simplest sensual pleasures, he is prohibited from experiencing love or happiness.

As *Frankenstein* shows, the resort to artificial forms of reproduction only creates monsters and grotesques. Thus, the ghost's hoarding impulse damages his own life as well as creates a misguided form of socialization that deforms himself and each succeeding generation. Each ghost teaches the child he kidnaps to think and live as he does, thereby perpetuating the bonds that have enchained him. Each child is taught that it is still living in the sixteenth century, shackled by the dead hand of the past, prohibiting freedom and maturation.

The ghost was one of Barks's most complex characters, transcending the simplistic black-and-white morality found in Disney films, superhero comics, and much adventure fiction. Like the protagonists in Gothic fiction, the ghost is a hero-villain who is both a victim of his obsessions and a threat to others. Our feeling about him undergoes a radical shift: at first he is a murderous menace who kidnaps one of the nephews, sabotages the ducks' boat, thinking that they will drown, and tries to kill Donald with his sword. But, as with Frankenstein's monster, we come to see him as a suffering as well as threatening creature, thereby making him a sympathetic figure. By the end of the story, we understand that he is a victim himself—an abducted child, not merely a kidnapper.

The ghost prefigures Uncle Scrooge, who both walls himself up within his money bin to protect his loot and can be ruthless but also self-denying. However, unlike Scrooge, the ghost's obsessive hoarding results not from greed but from an excess of loyalty and duty to his queen and to his liege lord, Sir Francis Drake. The original ghost was from the so-called Age of Exploration, during which the great European empires were built. Although Columbus and Drake are usually depicted as swashbuckling heroes, their "discovery" and colonization of the New World was accomplished only through the brutal conquest, exploitation, and extermination of native peoples.[48] Indeed, Drake and other merchant adventurers were privateers and pirates who pillaged booty from other countries. The ghost's fortune is plunder taken by the English from Spanish galleons, and his hoarding psychology reflects the avaricious drive for conquest of the nation he served, a psychology that drove those countries into internecine wars to determine who would dominate Europe.

The story's ambivalence about the ghost reflects Barks's mixed feelings about the past. The ghost is a transitional figure reflecting the decline of the aristocracy when fixed hierarchies were the norm and the rise of the bourgeoisie when a nascent capitalist ethic of profit seeking and upward mobility were undermining the aristocracy's courtly ideology of adventure.[49] Barks represents the ghost as an emblem of a transitional period in Europe, when wealth was pursued for the sake of loyalty to the Crown rather than just for personal gain. The ghost wears a suit of armor embodying the knight's chivalric ethos. Thus, he does not hoard out of avarice, like Scrooge, but keeps the booty in trust until Drake's return, following a feudal ethic of duty and self-sacrifice. In contrast, Donald, a symbol of modernity, licks his lips when he sees the gold and tries to trick the ghost out of it.

Although Donald is a hero and has saved Dewey and the village, the duck has lost the ethical principles that make him worthy of the fortune, Barks seems to say, and the ghost ends up with the gold. When the mayor honors Donald and gives him the keys to the city, he becomes enraged when he does not receive the ghost's hoard as a reward. In the modern world, self-interest and profit-seeking have displaced codes of honor, Barks's tale implies, and he emphasizes the ghost's anachronism by showing him at a fast food joint, eating hamburgers and wearing a hipster's zoot suit and pegged pants.

But Barks was not an antiquarian who believed that tradition was unequivocally superior to modernity. Donald is the ghost's double, not merely his opposite. Donald starts talking in Old English after he sees the gold, mimicking the ghost's use of *ye*. This suggests that the despite their differences, the present is an outgrowth of the past. The egoism and individualism of the modern individual are an outgrowth of the age of conquest, the story implies: Donald and the ghost have been equally deformed by their obsession with gold.

The following year, Barks wrote another Gothic tale, "The Old Castle's Secret" (*DD* FC #189 [1948]). It was Uncle Scrooge's second appearance following his introduction in "Christmas on Bear Mountain" (*DD* FC #178 [1947]). "He had turned out to be an interesting character in that first story, so I began trying to use him again," Barks recalled. "The Old Castle established more of Scrooge's character and showed where he came from originally."[50] The story was inspired by *The Haunted Castle*, a 1940 unproduced Disney cartoon starring Mickey, Goofy, and Donald that involved Mickey's purchase of a Scottish castle haunted by its ancestral owner, an invisible ghost. In Barks's story, Scrooge travels with Donald and the nephews to Dismal Downs, the McDuck family castle in Scotland, and battles an invisible ghost for the family treasure.

Scrooge is shown to be the inheritor of centuries of accumulated gluttony and greed. One ancestor died of overeating, while another, Sir Quackly, walled himself up rather than let raiders steal the family treasure and is believed to be haunting the castle. "There was an element of the horror story about that," Barks explained. "Those skeletons walled up in the walls of the old castle, that's almost in the EC Comics field."[51] To avoid problems with his editors, Barks had to modulate the representation of horror in his stories: "I knew that I couldn't put in much in the way of violence. It had to be comic violence which didn't seem to hurt anybody."[52] Although he had not received a formal list of taboos, his training in Disney animation had alerted him to the kinds of scripts that would be unacceptable. When depicting supernatural menaces that might frighten young readers, for example, Barks invariably revealed them to be only mortals by the end of the story. "I don't recall any policy" about portraying the supernatural, Barks commented, "but in Floyd Gottfredson's stories, there was always a logical explanation somewhere in there. When the Phantom Blot and all the other villains stripped off their clothes, they were just people. From these stories I got the feeling that I had better not be bringing in supernatural stuff. Besides, I wouldn't have written convincingly about the supernatural because I don't believe in that hokum."[53] Thus, the armored terror in "The Ghost of the Grotto" turns out to be merely a middle-aged man, the sea serpent in "Terror of the River" is ultimately revealed to be a submarine, and the menacing skeleton in "The Old Castle's Secret" is Diamond Dick, the jewel thief.

Besides the supernatural, Barks also knew that he was supposed to avoid drawing scenes of death or dying. "The characters frequently had to be in danger of dying in order to create suspense in a story," the Duck Man explained, "but I always dramatized the peril in such a comical way that you couldn't think back on it and get morbid." Nevertheless, Barks often trod on thin ice, as in the case of a panel showing the seemingly dead corpse of Scotty laid out on his bed. "I depended on the editors and the readers to *assume* that the old boy was faking. That story would not be acceptable in these days of timid tale-telling at Western."[54]

"Voodoo Hoodoo" (*DD* FC #238 [1949]) was inspired by Barks's reading about zombies and voodoo in newspaper articles. Donald is a victim of a curse when he receives a voodoo doll from Bombie the Zombie and must travel to Africa to have it lifted by Foola Zoola, the witch doctor who had intended it as revenge against Uncle Scrooge, who had robbed tribal lands. Understanding the story requires putting it into context.

World War II ushered two separate but interrelated developments. First was the massive increase in the power of corporate America and governmental bureaucracies. Everywhere they turned, individuals found themselves hemmed in by large organizations. As the possibility of owning one's own business or of becoming a self-employed professional declined, people were forced to become employees of large organizations. Social critics of the period claimed that members of the white-collar class that had formerly hoped to become autonomous owners and professionals were becoming proletarianized and subject to the same top-down discipline, repetitive labor, and anonymous existence that characterized factory work. These observers warned that America was becoming a nation of conformists as more and more people were subjected to bureaucratization and the homogenizing power of the mass media.

The same period also ushered in a new stage in race relations. African Americans went to war to fight a battle against Nazism and racism around the world yet continued to experience segregation in the military and racial discrimination at home. The growing awareness of the hypocrisy in American ideals spawned a new consciousness among blacks, especially the younger generation, and a more aggressive stance toward racial oppression in many spheres of American life. In 1947 Jackie Robinson became the first black man to play Major League Baseball, and jazz music, once the symbol of utopian dreams of racial pluralism and equality, became the site for new struggles over racial identity. Opposing the saccharine music and racial segregation of white swing bands, bebop emerged as a new form of jazz music with an emphasis on spontaneity, solo improvisation, and frenetic rhythm that countered the team playing and docility of wartime swing and fostered a cultural revolt against the square, white world.[55]

Barks alludes to these developments in the opening pages of the story. Donald encounters a top-hatted, tux-wearing jazz musician named Bop Bop and asks if he has seen the zombie about whom everyone is talking. The jazzman's name and eccentric image mark him as part of an underground, bohemian culture of hipster musicians. At this time, blacks were marginalized in white culture and condemned to symbolic annihilation.

Their voices were silenced in the dominant culture, which either failed to represent them or attempted to assimilate them and make them into replicas of whites. In this story, Barks breaks the silence by revealing for the first and only time that African Americans live in Duckburg. He had previously followed racial stereotypes in locating blacks in Africa or Australia and had written a ten-pager about an African "wild woman" in the circus but never before had represented blacks as regular townspeople.[56]

In making Bombie mute, Barks foregrounds blacks' lack of voice in America. Unable to speak, Bombie becomes a figure on which other characters project their fantasies, anxieties, and desires. The most glaring example occurs in Barks's parody of a radio quiz show. The garrulous announcer consistently misinterprets Bombie's silences as the correct answers to his quiz questions and as proof of the mindless zombie's "terrific intelligence." This sequence highlights the ironies and incongruities between Bombie's impoverishment and the superfluity of wealth in America. The mass media give away wheelbarrows of money just for answering trivial questions, but Americans could not face the need to ameliorate the immiseration of black (and poor white) citizens.

Barks based Bombie's image on a lurid painting from a 1942 article, "I Met a Zombie," that inspired "Voodoo Hoodoo."[57] But the cartoonist created a new image of the zombie, giving him a forlorn expression and tattered clothes that made him a sympathetic rather than menacing creature. "I was not writing for the horror comics," Barks explained, "so I wasn't going to make him a ferocious, murderous sort of person. So I made him just a harmless old zombie who wandered around: he had just this one job he had to do. He'd been at it for fifty years."[58] We see Bombie primarily through the eyes of the nephews, who are sympathetic to his plight. Barks's model sheet for the character reinforces this image, showing the artist trying to move away from the racial stereotypes typical in the popular culture of his day. An editor at Western had a staff artist replace Bombie's original vacant orbits with drooping lids and pupils because he feared that the original image would frighten children. Likewise, Western pasted over Barks's original description of Bombie as "dead," and Bop Bop describes zombies as people who "wouldn't stay done for."[59] Barks's story further domesticates zombies' image by describing them as drugged rather than reanimated corpses and the threat of zombification as that of being shrunk rather than having one's life drained away.

Barks also radically transformed the zombie mystique. In zombie films of the period, the major threat is that whites may become one of the living dead, like the blacks who menace them. However, in "Voodoo Hoodoo," the black zombie is as much a victim as his white counterpart. Bombie is an emblem of black oppression in postwar America. He is barefooted and dressed in rags, suggesting his economic impoverishment, and his mindlessness alludes to the way the underclass becomes inured to the onerous, repetitive labor it must perform to survive. The Duck Man dresses Bombie in the Napoleonic jacket of ex-slave Henry Christophe, a general in the Haitian war that overturned French colonialism.[60] Here Barks uses military dress ironically to suggest Bombie's lack of authority and place in white society. Barks's image of Bombie was also influenced by Victor Halpern's classic horror film, *White Zombie* (1932), which starred Bela Lugosi in the first American film to deal with zombies. "'Voodoo Hoodoo' grew out of the zombie nonsense that was faddish at that time," Barks recalled. "A movie I saw had flocks of zombies working tirelessly, pushing the arms of a great grinder that ground sugar cane. A zombie would lose his footing and fall into the grinder, all without blood. I became convinced that zombies do not *feel*, and I set out to preach their virtues as ideal stooges for anyone who needed a dangerous job done cheaply."[61] The image of the zombie as a metaphor for the exploited worker recalls the dialectic at work in the story.

In horror films, the Other represents those forces in the (white, male) self that are feared, disavowed, and projected onto groups that are subordinated in patriarchal capitalist society—women, racial minorities, gays, aliens, and communists, among others.[62] "Voodoo Hoodoo" embodies men's anxieties about becoming exploited, dehumanized, and emasculated by an overconformist, corporate society—in symbolic terms, that is, of becoming a zombie. Bombie is a projection of these fears, a double and mirror image of Donald's most terrifying anxieties. Not only is Bombie a mindless drudge who has no will of his own, mechanically carries out orders, and can only perform one task at a time, but he is also an impoverished black who occupies the lowest rung of the social order. Donald's fear can be interpreted as one of racialization: that he will drop in social status to the level of the black underclass and become reduced to a subhuman existence.

These fears rest on his precarious social status. Donald is a representative of the lumpen proletariat. In the ten-pagers, he lives a desultory existence, going from job to job, not knowing where the next month's rent or next day's food is coming from. His only solution is the deus ex machina of browbeating or manipulating his rich, skinflint Uncle Scrooge into giving him money, as he does in this story. When the miser buys him tickets to Africa to obtain a cure for his voodoo curse, Donald is met by the nephews and Bombie at the airport, dressed in finery, carrying the money that they have won in a wheelbarrow. Although Donald must humiliate himself to get a ticket, the nephews become rich virtually without trying. Living on the borderline alone would make him an outcast, but Donald's arrogant and obsessive pursuit of quick riches and celebrity are often so outrageous and disastrous that he is demoted to the lowest, most menial jobs or becomes a pariah. On the first page of "Voodoo Hoodoo," an upper-crust dowager gossips about the rumor that a zombie has come to town and declares, "A zombie? He should be jailed!" Her friend responds that he has not committed a crime, revealing the prejudice of her companion's statement. Just as blacks are stigmatized merely because of their color, Bombie is condemned not because he is a menace but because of his deviance from conventional norms. Commenting on the rumor that squeezing a voodoo doll has turned Donald to brass, she remarks snootily, "He hasn't far to go! He was already solid from the neck up!" Like Bombie, Donald is rejected by the Duckburg elite. The old crone's wrinkled prune face and drooping snout indicates that both he and Bombie are similar victims of intolerance.

Bombie's role as a projection of Donald's fears is most apparent in the relationship between the two. After becoming hysterical about the possibility of being shrunk to the size of a rat, Donald attempts to sleep off his fears, trying to convince himself that he had just had a bad dream. But he awakes screaming in terror when he finds Bombie standing at the foot of his bed. Bombie is graphically displayed as an extension of Donald's nightmare and an embodiment of the anxieties that aroused it. Donald's fear is that of being unmanned. He assumes the typical position of hysterical female victims in horror films. While awaiting Foola Zoola, who will shrink the duck, Donald sobs, "Daisy won't love me anymore!" revealing his fears of losing not only size but the masculine potency and attractiveness that it connotes. Donald (and Bombie) can be read as encoding Barks's fears of proletarianization as an underpaid comic book author. In a letter lamenting his economic plight after an acrimonious divorce, he referred to himself as a "zombie" who faced years more hard work to get out of debt and pay off his alimony.[63]

In a country where notions of empire were and are routinely disavowed, "Voodoo Hoodoo" is remarkable for its foregrounding of American imperialism and the way it haunts the American imagination. The story reveals that Scrooge has made part of his fortune by stealing the tribal lands of Foola Zoola and his people, building a rubber plantation there. In a number of stories, Barks emphasized the karmic imbalance created by civilization's dispossession and oppression of native people and the hostile backlash it evokes.[64] Thus, Scrooge's victimization of Foola and his tribe sets off a chain reaction that causes the chief to burn and kidnap local whites and even threatens to harm the innocent Donald, while Scrooge, the real perpetrator, ironically goes unharmed. Bombie and Donald are the real victims, the story suggests.

Barks's story has its roots in history.[65] Haitian slaves liberated themselves from French colonial domination in the nineteenth century, and Haiti became the first black republic. However, it was politically unstable. The United States occupied Haiti from 1915 to 1934. Guided by racial prejudices that Haitians were incapable of self-government, the U.S. government occupied the country, imposing martial law and a new constitution. The new puppet government lifted the constitutional prohibition against foreigners owning land, a law that had been directed against the injustices of French colonization. Haitians went from being independent landowners to peons while American business interests sought to profit by investing in the Haitian economy. In the beginning, Haitians were also conscripted into corvée labor to work on American development projects. Guerrilla uprisings and public protests against the U.S. client government and constitution and the massacring of Haitian citizens led the United States to leave the island in the mid-1930s. Barks's story never mentions the occupation, but Scrooge's imperialist tactics nevertheless replicate real-life events.

Oppressed by a system of slavery that denied their humanity, blacks uprooted from Africa and transplanted to Haiti created their own local religion based on the rites of voodoo. These beliefs created a commu-nal bond between peoples of different tribes and a secret, underground culture from which to launch their struggles for freedom. Colonialists and Christian authorities thus feared voodoo and sought to stamp it out. Zombies take their name from Jean Zombi, a slave noted for his brutal-ity during Haiti's war against the French. In the eyes of westerners, any element of African religion smacked of barbarism: voodoo was demon-ized as being founded on savagery, sorcery, and blood lust, and Haiti was portrayed as a mysterious isle of the dead. The notion of a voodoo doll used to cast spells on victims was never part of the religion but was the creation of popular fiction and American horror films.[66]

Despite Barks's attempt to create a sympathetic portrait of black oppression at home and abroad, he resorts to racial stereotypes. Bop Bop is a superstitious, cowardly character; the African natives are big-lipped and bug-eyed, speak in Negro dialect, and are venal and easily corrupted by the nephews' bribes. Moreover, Barks's characterization of Foola Zoola derives from stereotypes of the brutal savage familiar from western colo-nial history. Barks represents the chief as totally evil, with daggerlike teeth that suggest cannibalism. Although Barks portrays the natives being exploited by westerners, he never represents the struggles for freedom and independence that informed the decolonization process.

The image of the brutal savage is pivotal to the story's conclusion. The ending suggests that continued maintenance of white privilege rests on a process of divide and conquer in which rebellious blacks are contained by more passive ones. Donald bounces the inert Bombie down the hill and flattens the whole tribe of angry pursuers. Although the ducks express sorrow over using Bombie in this way, they too end up exploiting him and decide to go home and spend his money, an act we can easily forgive because he is only a mindless zombie. One of the nephews jokingly suggests the advantages of being a tireless, unfeeling drudge like Bombie, to which Donald replies "I'll take vanilla!" This suggests his choice of life and feeling over the anesthetized existence of the zombified worker. But it is a benefit gained only at the cost of repressing those dark forces that characterized Donald's precarious existence as well as those of the racial Other.

"The Magic Hourglass" (*DD* FC #291 [1950]) continues Barks's interrogation of American imperialism. The story has the sensibility of a moral fable and warns of the disastrous consequences that follow when our most cherished wish—the desire for unlimited wealth and power—is granted. It also has a contemporary reference: it satirizes the ironies and contradictions that accompanied America's rise to become the most powerful and wealthiest nation on earth in the postwar era. This new position of prominence is portrayed in the opening splash panel, which offers a panoramic view of the city and its industrial wealth. The narrative is propelled by a rivalry between Donald and the nephews: Donald brags that his uncle owns the vast business enterprises below them, while the nephews claim that Scrooge never gives him anything and likes them best. Beneath Scrooge's appearance of being a successful and honest businessman, however, Barks exposes the illicit history and unscrupulous practices on which Scrooge's empire—and, by extension, America's affluence—were built.

As the plethora of dollar signs adorning his office suggests, Scrooge can perceive the world only as a ledger of profits and losses, reducing humanity and the multiplicity of the universe to the alienated calculus of instrumental rationality. But this determination to look at objects and people only in terms of their utility leads to his downfall for, ironically, he gives away a seemingly useless hourglass only to discover that the lucky talisman was the source of all his wealth. The hourglass is a kind of fetish—what anthropologists identify as an inanimate object that is worshipped as a deity possessing magical powers. The key to the fetish is thus the overvaluation of an object. The idea of fetishism is central to Barks's cosmology, and his stories frequently satirize the way various rivals pursue with obsessive and murderous zeal what are inherently worthless objects, with disastrous consequences. When it becomes the measure of all value, even a worthless bottle cap, Barks shows us, can destroy the brotherly love of a utopian community like Tralla La and turn neighbors and friends into greedy, agonistic competitors (*US* #6 [1954]).

The idea of fetishism appears in the work of both Marx and Freud. Both thinkers use the concept to explain a refusal or blockage of consciousness in which there is "a phobic inability of the psyche, to understand a symbolic system of value, one within the social and the other within the psychoanalytic sphere."[67] The fetish object becomes a symbolic substitute for the troubling experience that the fetish masks. Fetishism creates symbolic substitutions that are defenses against traumatic perceptions. In producing goods for exchange in the market, claims Marx, fetishes come to be seen not only as having utility ("use values") but as intrinsically valuable objects having "mystical" qualities. In commodity production, the value of products is displaced from the labor that produces it and is thought to emanate from the product itself. The fetish thus disavows the unpleasant history associated with the production of commodities: the grime of the factory, workers' estrangement from their products, and, most importantly, their exploitation in creating more wealth than they receive.

For Freud, the fetish masks the traumatic discovery of the mother's lack of a phallus and the fears of castration this evokes in the young child. The object of the original desire is repressed or hidden, and an item near it (in space and time) is selected as the fetish, allowing the desire to be expressed in a safe way. Thus the sexual fetishist must eroticize nonsexual objects (shoes, fur, boots) to obtain sexual pleasure.

The Marxian and Freudian notions of fetishism can be combined if we analyze them in terms of the dual threats posed to the subject by the perceived loss of his property. Threats to wealth and property arouse fears not only of loss of wealth but also of masculine power and control, evoking anxieties of being unmanned and feminized, and losing one's identity.

Belief in the fetish is a means of psychologically acknowledging these terrors while simultaneously disavowing their sources and displacing them onto fetishized objects.

Under capitalism, claims Marx, commodity production is reified and seemingly operates autonomously, beyond people's control. Consequently, the workings of the market are attributed to mysterious forces such as fate and luck. "The Magic Hourglass" reveals that the forces of "destiny" and luck emanating from the timepiece have been responsible for Scrooge's wealth from the beginning. Because the hourglass fails to keep the exact time, the miser gives it away to the nephews, thinking it worthless. But when his enterprises begin to lose a billion dollars a minute, he realizes that the inscription on the talisman revealing its magical powers was true after all: the hourglass "was the *secret of my good luck*, but I never believed it!" he confesses.

The fetish can be seen as a social hieroglyph. Because fetishism does not involve a total denial or complete repression of a traumatic reality, it is always vulnerable to exposure. Just as the psychoanalyst interprets symptoms in terms of their origins in repressed desires and fears, so the cultural analyst can decode the collective anxieties, desires, and fantasies the fetish masks through processes of disguise, displacement, and substitution. According to Laura Mulvey, the fetish is "a ruse to distract the eye and the mind from something that needs to be covered up and this is also its weakness. The more the fetish exhibits itself, the more the presence of a traumatic past event is signified."[68] Because of the attention drawn to it, the fetish is always on the cusp of acknowledging its own processes of concealment, signaling the presence of a historical event. Thus, the hourglass's failure to keep correct time can be interpreted as a return of the repressed: since he bought the magic talisman many years ago when he was a poor cabin boy, Scrooge has denied the knowledge that it was the source of his wealth. Now his defenses have broken down.

The hourglass's magic masks the predatory business practices that are the source of Scrooge's—and America's—wealth. To keep the right time, the timepiece must be supplied with fresh red sand from the Oasis of No Issa, a legendary watering hole in Arabia. The red sand is thus the ultimate source of the hourglass's power, both symbolizing and masking the fact of America's increasing appropriation of foreign resources as a source of its expanding affluence. Scrooge's financial debacle upon losing the magic charm points to the irony that as America grew richer and more powerful, it was becoming more vulnerable and dependent on the whims of foreign nations and their rulers. The sand can be interpreted as representing the singular natural resource of Arabic countries—oil. As postwar American technology and business burgeoned, the country became increasingly dependent on petroleum and its by-products to fuel its industrial machine. Thus, the United States had to control foreign resources for its own use, while diverting control away from indigenous owners.

During this era, awareness was growing that the United States was running low on critical natural resources. A 1952 report of the President's Commission on Foreign Economic Policy described World War II as a time of "transition" for America "from a position of relative self-sufficiency to one of increasing dependence upon foreign sources of supply."[69] Before World War I, coal had been the basic raw material used in the generation of electricity, in home heating, and in making chemicals and synthetic products. But coal mining was dangerous work and destructive to the environment, and conversion into chemical by-products was difficult.

The number of petroleum-based products grew astronomically after World War II, accounting for more than six thousand individual products by the 1970s. Before World War I, America had been self-sufficient in crude oil production and as late as 1945 had even exported 4 percent of its supply. But five years later, 10 percent of domestic consumption had to be met by foreign imports; that figure grew to one-third by 1970, and demand was continuing to increase rapidly, leading to the energy crisis of the 1970s.[70]

A continuous supply of foreign oil rested on the success of American foreign policy in securing the right context for continued imports. Before the war, American oil companies had owned only 13 percent of the Middle East's oil reserves, but during the 1950s, American corporations extended their holdings all over the world so that by 1959, they controlled 64 percent of the Middle East's oil supply.[71] Meanwhile, Arab countries had become politically unstable, threatening America's continued supply of oil.

"The Magic Hourglass" was written in March 1950, during a time of troubling events. Saudi leaders insisted that Aramco, the Arab-American oil company, share its profits with the royal family on a fifty-fifty basis. Other changes beset the British Petroleum Company, which had monopolized Iranian oil. The Shah and the Iranian ruling class had siphoned off a portion of the profits, while the vast majority of the country's people lived in poverty. In 1949, the Shah was overthrown by a nationalistic leftist movement led by Mohammed Mossadegh, who nationalized the oil industry in 1951 as a means of financing a seven-year plan for internal reconstruction and land reform. In retaliation, the western nations entered a consumer cartel and boycotted Iranian oil, undermining Mossadegh's ability to finance his development program. American officials accused Mossadegh of being a communist, and a CIA-engineered coup toppled him from power in 1953 and reinstated the Shah as ruler. As a reward, the Shah gave five American oil companies 40 percent control of Iranian oil.[72]

"The Magic Hourglass" references this context. The raiders operate from an underground lair where the red sand is located, symbolically alluding to the location of Middle Eastern oil. The story constructs a struggle between good and evil sheiks, one speaking American slang, having worked for American GI's in the war, and acting friendly toward the ducks, while the other is a robber who raids caravans and seizes McDuck's hourglass.

"The Magic Hourglass" would thus seem to follow the logic of the imperialist narrative described by Ariel Dorfman and Armand Mattelart, and later by David Kunzle.[73] A binary morality has been erected in which pro-American Arabs triumph over those opposed to our interests, seeming to justify western dispossession of Third World resources. However, the story is not so simple. First, Scrooge has no moral claim to the hourglass and the wealth that it generates: the raiders are the hourglass's original owners, and Scrooge had bought it in a thief's market, indicating that he had knowingly bought stolen property. Moreover, Barks characterizes

Scrooge as a ruthless tycoon. He hires thugs to torture Donald into selling the hourglass (an act Barks euphemizes by having the thugs only tickle Donald with a feather) for the paltry sum of a quarter.

Barks's narrative also exposes and critiques the fetishism that undergirds and propels the imperialist narrative. The conclusion of the story subverts the principle of exchange value on which capitalist rationality rests. Recycling the Greek legend of Midas, Barks introduces a theme that will inform the Scrooge adventures—that money is inherently worthless and blinds us to the nature of true wealth. When everything he touches turns to riches, Donald becomes enthralled by the hourglass's magic, proclaiming, "The whole world is in our power! Riches, and more riches, here we come!" But he soon learns that life-giving water, not diamonds or gold, has ultimate value. Scrooge could be generous and offer a drink of water to the parched and prostrate ducks but instead tries to exploit them by trading the water bag for the hourglass—and untold riches. In turn, he too benefits from the talisman's magic but becomes so thirsty that he offers Donald a billion dollars and even the hourglass for a drink of water. However, Donald has learned how little gold and diamonds are worth, and gives Scrooge the bag for free. In Barks's humanistic philosophy, to thrive and be truly happy, we must overcome the limits of our egocentric desires and learn to treat others with tolerance and generosity. As Scrooge's punishment for his egoism, the ending inverts the positions of the ducks and Scrooge and invokes a form of class revenge. As part of their bargain for giving Scrooge the hourglass, Donald and the kids make the tycoon sail home in the junked ship Scrooge had given Donald, while the miser has to pay for their first-class accommodations on a luxury liner.

Perhaps Barks's ultimate statement on such themes is "The Golden Helmet" (*DD* FC #408 [1952]). The impetus for the story came from Barks's desire to draw a locale inspired by Hal Foster's *Prince Valiant* comic strip. "*Valiant* was beautifully illustrated," Barks recalled. "Each panel was a work of art. I was very much taken with one of the coastal scenes. . . . I wanted to work with the coastline, so I tried to think of what would happen to Donald to bring him up there."[74] Reading about how the Norsemen discovered America centuries before Columbus gave Barks the plot idea.

The story also reflected the crisis in Barks's life caused by a bitter divorce. The Duck Man recalled,

> The work date on the story, November of 1951, indicates that it was done at a time when my fortunes were at a very low ebb. I had just given everything I owned to my alcoholic wife in exchange for my freedom. Broke and in debt and facing years of stiff alimony at the age of 50 I chose to keep working, and I can recall one day when all the bad news struck me and I should have been heading for a bar, and instead I sat there like a zombie with a pad of paper and jotted down gags and plots and situations that seemed to pour into me from somewhere. "The Golden Helmet" must have been one of those situations.[75]

The story was one of Barks's most cynical. It examined the psychology of exploitation and conquest on which western nations had originally been founded and deconstructed the heroic myths that valorized this psychology. In the opening pages, Barks foregrounded the escapist nature of the adventure story. Donald is a museum guard who is bored by his mundane job and longs for the rugged life of the old Vikings. Donald's plight also reveals a crisis in masculinity: he must aid an effeminate "goggle-eyed nature boy" looking for the butterfly collection and then give directions to the "lace and tatting collection" to an effeminate male, an obvious gay stereotype. These encounters make him cognizant of his own feminized status: "Oh, that the race of *Man* could ever sink so *low*!" he complains dejectedly and goes up on the deck of an ancient Viking boat to "*pretend* I'm a *he-man*!"

The story has much in common with Richard Wagner's opera *Der Ring des Nibelungen*, which deals with the pursuit of a magical ring endowing its owner with unlimited power. Barks's tale revolves around a rivalry for possession of the golden helmet formerly owned by Olaf the Blue that will prove its possessor to be the owner of North America. The power-mad Azure Blue, who claims to be the last descendant of Olaf, and his unscrupulous attorney, Sharkey, set out on a sea voyage to capture the helmet. To beat them to the helmet and keep Olaf from becoming

An infinite number of secret agents and counteragents cancel each other out in a simultaneously violent act in Barks's spoof of spy stories, "Dangerous Disguise" (1951). © Disney Enterprises, Inc.

Barks's splash panel of the barroom brawl from the second Uncle Scrooge adventure, "Back to the Klondike" (1953), parodies Western films and frontier tall-tales. © Disney Enterprises, Inc.

Photo of Machu Picchu, the ancient Incan square city on which Barks modeled Plain Awful in "Lost in the Andes" (1949). Courtesy Andrew Hastings.

The ducks catch their first glimpse of the Andean square city in this splash panel from "Lost in the Andes" (1949). © Disney Enterprises, Inc.

The ducks encounter strange faux southerners from Plain Awful in this panel from "Lost in the Andes" (1949). © Disney Enterprises, Inc.

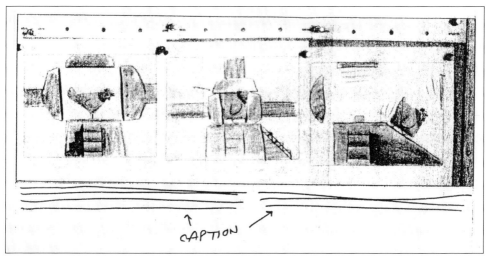

A square chicken lays a square egg in this scene from the unproduced Disney short *The Square World*. The film inspired Barks's creation of square people, chickens, and eggs in "Lost in the Andes." © Disney Enterprises, Inc.

The Barks's house at Merrill, Oregon c. 1906. From the left, Carl's parents, William and Arminta Barks, Clyde and Carl, the Barks's cook and her husband, a neighbor, and a ranch hand. On the far right is a cousin, Pinkney Barks.

Barks based Don Gaspar's rancho in "Old California" (1951) on the Estudillo Mansion in San Jacinto, California, where Barks lived. Photo © San Jacinto Historical Society; panel © Disney Enterprises, Inc.

Don Gaspar's fiesta from "Old California" (1951) depicts Barks's vision of the utopian harmony of the Californio days. © Disney Enterprises, Inc.

Barks created this drawing of the Ramona Bowl pageant for the San Jacinto Chamber of Commerce.

William F. Whittier's filter plant on Park Hill in Hemet, California, inspired Barks's creation of Uncle Scrooge's money bin, which first appeared in this splash panel (below) from *Walt Disney's Comics and Stories* #135 (1951). Photo © Robert Norman; panel © Disney Enterprises, Inc.

PRELIMINARY
STUDY FOR
BOMBIE THE
ZOMBIE

Jo Don &
Lynda
Carl Barks

Hemet founder William F. Whittier strikes a plutocratic pose, 1860s. Note the Scroogean pince-nez glasses. Photo courtesy of Mary E. Whitney.

Model sheet of Bombie the Zombie from "Voodoo Hoodoo," 1949. Western's editors added pupils to the zombie's eyes because they thought the blank orbits might frighten children.

Barks's first model sheet of Bombie the Zombie (1949). Barks made him more human and sympathetic by moving away from these stereotypical black images.

Carl Barks
1949

This lurid illustration from "I Met a Zombie!" (*American Weekly*, 1942) inspired Barks's creation of Bombie the Zombie.

Uncle Scrooge's first meeting with Glittering Goldie, from "Back to the Klondike." Goldie's fashions were inspired by the costumes Alice Faye wore in the title role of the 1940 film *Lillian Russell*. Panel © Disney Enterprises, Inc.; photo © Twentieth Century Fox.

Uncle Scrooge's famed money swim from the first Scrooge adventure, "I'm Only a Poor Old Man" (1952). © Disney Enterprises, Inc.

Gyro Gearloose tries out one of his harebrained inventions in this 1961 unpublished cover for a Gyro Gearloose comic. © Disney Enterprises, Inc.

Barks's animation drawing of Donald from the Disney cartoon *Alpine Climbers* (1936). Courtesy All-Star Auctions. © Disney Enterprises, Inc.

Gladstone Gander, the lucky loafer, always has a sadistic relationship with his unlucky cousin, Donald, as in this panel from "Luck of the North" (1949). © Disney Enterprises, Inc.

The devouring mouths of the Martian monsters, Daisy Duck, and the zookeeper signify a threat to Donald's masculinity in the nightmare story from *Walt Disney's Comics and Stories* #101 (1949). © Disney Enterprises, Inc.

Barks drew the first prototype of Daisy Duck in *Desert Prospectors*, an unproduced Disney cartoon on which Barks worked as a storyman. © Disney Enterprises, Inc.

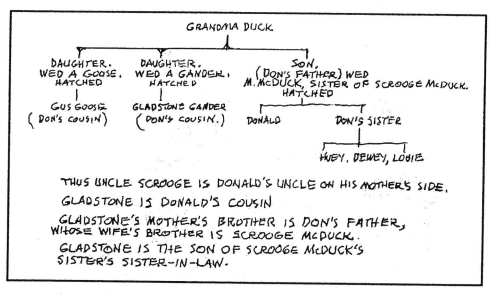

In 1991, Barks roughed out a new family tree in response to requests for clarifications about Duck family relationships from second-generation Uncle Scrooge artist Don Rosa.

This 1940 *National Geographic* photo inspired the twin colossi in the Donald Duck adventure "The Mummy's Ring." Photo © Anthony B. Stewart, *National Geographic* Image Collection; panel © Disney Enterprises, Inc.

Barks was very concerned that the backgrounds in his stories be accurate and realistic. This scene from "The Mummy's Ring" (1943) was closely modeled on the photo above.

Barks's drawings of pretty women in the *Calgary Eye-Opener* were often done in an illustrative style typical of 1920s and 1930s humor magazines.

Barks based the seacoast in the Donald Duck adventure "The Golden Helmet" (1952) on a drawing from Hal Foster's *Prince Valiant* comic strip. © King Features Syndicate; © Disney Enterprises, Inc.

The Beagle Boys were Uncle Scrooge's chief bêtes noires, interchangeable organization men who thought, sang, and danced in unison, as in this drawing from 1955. © Disney Enterprises, Inc.

This scene from Barks's Vietnam satire "Treasures of Marco Polo" (1965) features a Latin American–style guerrilla blowing up the Duckburg embassy. © Disney Enterprises, Inc.

Carl Barks and his wife, Garé, early 1970s. © Lynda Ault.

Carl Barks drawing a page from "The Old Castle's Secret." From the *Hemet News*, November 28, 1947. © Valley Studio Photo.

The sorceress Magica de Spell attempting to purloin Uncle Scrooge's first dime, from "The Unsafe Safe" (1962). © Disney Enterprises, Inc.

In the early 1950s, Barks attempted to work up a comic strip, *Pipsqueaks*, based on human characters. However, as this model sheet shows, these characters were too close to Donald and his nephews, and Barks abandoned the project.

An unpublished *Pipsqueaks* daily strip, c. 1953.

Barks drew this invitation for a 1947 barn party hosted by his neighbor, Don Currie.

Carl Barks, 1920s.

Scrooge vies with the Maharaja of Howduyoustan to determine who can build the biggest, most lavish statue of Duckburg founder Cornelius Coot (*Walt Disney's Comics and Stories* #138, 1952). Note how the statues appear to be crushing the city and are ludicrously incongruous with the remnants of Duckburg's rural life. © Disney Enterprises, Inc.

Barks drew jagged, fractured panels in scenes from "Big-Top Bedlam" (1950) to suggest the lunacy of the circus and by extension of American entertainment. Note how the panel with Donald zooming up the wire is about to collide with his image in the diagonal panel, and the jagged panel is aimed at the audience. © Disney Enterprises, Inc.

Clara Balkin, Barks's second wife and the impetus behind several of his stories, 1930s.

This panel from *Walt Disney's Comics and Stories* #112 (1950) depicts Donald's vision of Duckburg c. 1990, Barks's surrealist version of a nuclear holocaust with buildings melting and people blown into fragments. © Disney Enterprises, Inc.

Barks submitted this drawing of Snow White and the Seven Dwarfs to obtain his first job at the Disney Studio (1935). © Disney Enterprises, Inc.

A storyboard drawing featuring Donald Duck and his nephews from *Truant Officer Donald* (1941). © Disney Enterprises, Inc.

emperor of North America, Donald and the boys race to the coast of Labrador.

Barks is clearly ambivalent about the Vikings and the myth of heroic adventure that they represent. On the one hand, the story implies that they are admirable figures, and Donald becomes a contemporary embodiment of their self-sufficiency, ruggedness, and daring seamanship. After having his boat stolen by Azure, he must sail exactly like his heroes, sighting the stars rather than depending on compasses and modern navigational equipment. On the other hand, the historic Vikings were also rapacious raiders and bloodthirsty conquerors who pillaged and violently conquered other lands. Azure Blue, who claims to be their descendant, embodies the psychology of conquest they represent. But Azure is an unworthy relation. While the Vikings depended on superior fighting and navigational skills to conquer their victims, he uses knavery and the law. Coming from an acrimonious divorce in which he had lost everything, Barks was quite bitter toward lawyers. In "The Golden Helmet," lawyers manipulate the law for the advantage of the powerful and, as Sharkey's name implies, are amoral shysters. As in many Barks stories, the law is shown to be impotent in protecting people from oppression. The museum curator tells Donald that Azure is operating within the law and that they can stop him only by beating him to the helmet.

However, the story also contains a deeper satire that critiques the ideology of private ownership. According to the Code of Discovery, which justifies Azure's ownership of the continent, "Any man who discovers a new land beyond the seas shall be the owner of that land unless he claims it for his king." According to this "law," mere occupation of a piece of territory grants exclusive rights of ownership to its "discoverer." Barks's fictional law replicates the real-life assertions of ownership of the lands of the New World by European explorers such as Columbus and Drake. "The Golden Helmet" shows the arbitrary nature of such territorial claims. In hindsight we are aware that the discovery and ownership of the New World is a Eurocentric conceit. The indigenous peoples of the New World were clearly the "owners" of its lands and wealth and were already members of a thriving civilization before European explorers arrived. Barks mocks the West's claim to "own" the New World by showing how arbitrary and unstable the legal status of ownership is. The helmet unleashes a frenzy for dominance as it passes from Azure to the curator to Donald and then to Sharkey. Each claims to be Olaf's last descendent and legitimate owner of North America merely by virtue of possession of Olaf's map and helmet, rather than through any proof of lineal descent. In the words of Proudhon's famous epigram, "Property is theft."

In the West, property ownership has been characterized as providing the basis of security, privacy, and freedom on which our society depends. However, these feelings also rest on what critics such as John Christman have called a myth of property.[76] In liberal ideology, property grants an owner sovereign and exclusive rights to its disposition. Property ownership confers the "despotic dominion which one man claims and exercises over the external things of the world," according to eighteenth-century legal scholar William Blackstone, "in total exclusion of the right of any other individual in the universe."[77] However, such unmitigated power can become antisocial, so that no form of property has ever been totally free of regulation by the state, and the liberal notion of absolute property rights exists primarily as an ideal. Since the New Deal, the American state has sought to regulate the power of wealth and to redistribute wealth through progressive tax codes and welfare benefits to the needy. However, some observers still see this form of intervention as a form of interference with basic rights of ownership that should not be tampered with in the absence of an overriding social purpose. The conflict between these principles has increasingly created inconsistencies in the founding principles of private property.[78]

In liberal ideology, private property is linked to a distinction between society's public and private spheres. Property is assumed to be part of a private realm, and the distribution of wealth and productive resources in capitalist society are assumed to result from the operation of a free market. As a consequence of this division, the power of property is rendered invisible in the economy. Thus, although property may grant owners autonomy and security, the notions of sovereignty and exclusivity inherent in the concept can become oppressive for those without property, who are condemned to wage slavery. "From now on," proclaims Azure Blue, "the people of North America are my *slaves*! They'll work for me everyday of their lives with no Sundays off!!" In this way, Barks satirized the inequalities of the workplace, in which the power of employers routinely trumps the rights of workers. Behind this satire, we can glimpse Barks's experiences as a low-paid comic book artist who was "working, working all the time, and never getting far enough ahead" to take time off because he was too close to his "poverty line."[79]

As in Barks's other Gothic tales, the desire for domination is shown to be a delusion that results in self-disintegration and defeat. When the kindly old curator gets possession of the helmet, he forgoes his original intention of throwing it in the drink and declares that he will run the country for the benefit of museums and make people attend them twice a day. Donald, the nominal hero of the story who initially tried to prevent Azure's usurpation of America, also succumbs to madness, ironically becoming even more of a snake in the grass than his nemesis. He decides to own the air and make people wear meters on their chests to charge them for every breath they take. In this way, Barks reduced the liberal ideology of property to a reductio ad absurdum, ridiculing the notion that anyone should possess unrestricted ownership and control over the earth's commons, the natural environment on which all life depends.

Only the nephews ultimately provide voices of sanity in this story of vainglory and obsession. One nephew throws a fish into Sharkey's face, causing him to lose the helmet in the sea. But they too are not immune to the helmet's lure, and another nephew looks longingly at the place the helmet has disappeared, wondering if getting rid of so precious an object was a mistake. Everyone is susceptible to the allures of power, Barks's tale warns, even would-be heroes and levelheaded youths.

"Golden Helmet" is a partially self-reflexive tale that shows Donald to be living out masculine fantasies of power and adventure at the same time that we are reading an "escapist" adventure story. This opens up for questioning the conventions and pleasures that are typically naturalized in such tales. The narrative has a circular structure in which the opening events are mirrored in the end: When Donald returns to his custodial job, he has been chastened enough by his experiences to know the dangers of masculine conquest. Thus, when another effeminate male approaches and asks directions to the "embroidered lamp shades," Donald does not react in disgust as he did initially but admits to an interest in such feminine articles and offers to show the way. The would-be macho duck appears to have temporally abandoned his need to prove himself a rugged he-man and learned to accommodate his femininity.

"Trick or Treat" (*DD* #26 [1952]) was the last Barks story to appear as a regular feature in *Donald Duck* comics. In 1953 he shifted to writing the Uncle Scrooge adventures and did not have time to do both series. The story is an anomaly, a comedy in a long string of adventures. Donald selfishly hoards Halloween candies from the nephews when they call at his door, only to be forced to share his pantry with the kids by a real Halloween sorceress, Hazel the Witch. The story's slapstick humor seems most akin to the early Donald ten-pagers and holiday tales like "Christmas on Bear Mountain." Thus, it lacks the nightmarish quality and layers of irony and satire of his other Donald Duck adventures.

Part of the reason for the change is that Barks did not write the script. Western Publishing had long sought to sell its comics by tying them to holiday seasons. Barks recalled being pressured almost every year to do Christmas stories. "Christmas on Bear Mountain" had been initiated at Western's request, and the company had even given him a script for a Yuletide tale, "The Golden Christmas Tree" (*DD* FC #208 [1948]). Barks labored to make it a "robust" tale about Donald's pitched battle with a witch out to destroy the world's Christmas trees but hated the preachy ending and considered the story "just plain sop!"[80]

"Trick or Treat" was unique in having been an adaptation of a Disney cartoon of the same name. Thus, analyzing the story allows us to discern some of the differences between Barks's worldview and that of Disney animation from which it derived but remained unassimilated. The published story closely follows the cartoon: "Alice Cobb, the Western editor at the time, gave me photostats of the storyboard sketches and asked me to adapt them to a comic book version," Barks commented.[81] Donald refuses to give any candy to the nephews when they come trick-or-treating, and the story revolves around Witch Hazel's attempt to force him into giving up some of his Halloween hoard.

Barks found the Disney cartoon too bare to sustain a full-length adventure and added some elements of his own. As a result, his editors cut 10.5 pages from his story: "I departed from the movie script and added on some business with an ogre that Hazel summons. Alice Cobb deleted the extra business and didn't pay me for the unwanted pages. She was that mad."[82] However, Barks's story departs more significantly from the cartoon than he suggests. The film opens with a brief shot of a graveyard on a hill overlooking the city. The gravestones are dark and muted, giving the scene a mildly spooky flavor. Barks's opening splash is more frightening, offering a stark view of the graveyard in which the tombstones are clearly visible. Also disturbing was the Donald Duck logo, which appeared to be dripping paint—or blood. Such scenes were more akin to the horror comics that were the rage at the time than the innocent funny-animal comics produced for small children that had been Dell's trademark. Barks's editors cut the splash page and replaced it with a more innocuous sequence that focused on holiday pranks and Donald's discovery of the nephews raiding the Halloween candy in his pantry.

Barks's creation of the ogre Smorgie invoked another disturbing image. A six-armed cyclops with a derby hat and tusks, he was the most bizarre creature ever to appear in a Disney comic. With arms that stretched completely around and penetrated the inner sanctum of Donald's house, the monster had more affinity to the grotesque malleability of Plastic Man than to the ghosts and witches of the Disney cartoon. Donald gives Smorgie a stick of dynamite disguised as a candy cane, which explodes and blows him apart, an unsettling thought even though Barks was careful not to show any effects of the blast.

Despite having such scenes excised, the Duck Man imbued the published tale with charm and vitality. Hazel's feistiness redeemed what could have been a tepid comedy. Moreover, Barks invested the story with familiar themes. The central conflict is that between modern skepticism and tradition, egocentrism and generosity. Donald refuses to believe in the reality of witches, and Hazel attempts to convince him of her powers to get him to surrender his candy. When these attempts fail, Hazel uses the recalcitrant duck as a battering ram, forcing his cupboard open for the taking. In the cartoon, a large, grinning pumpkin appears and gives the audience a Halloween thrill by saying "Boo." In contrast, in Barks's story, Donald has learned from his defeat and undergoes a moral transformation. He affirms the spirit of Halloween and claims that next year, "*I'm* going to be a goblin *too!*" In a mirror image of Barks's opening splash page, we are positioned on another hill overlooking Duckburg. This time, however, we look down at the city not through the forbidding scene of a graveyard but from a hill filled with pumpkins and bales of hay. Barks's image of a pumpkin patch evokes a rural setting, tying Halloween to the fall harvest season and the ancient myths celebrating the dying and rebirth of nature that originally inspired the holiday. As Hazel flies into the moonlit sky, we can see only the trail of her path and her distant shadow, but we feel that we have glimpsed for a moment a vision alternative to an agonistic modernity in which harmony and tranquillity can momentarily exist.

"Trick or Treat" not only is Barks's last regular work on the Donald Duck one-shots but also marks the passing of the type of Gothic fiction that had preoccupied them. Barks would face increasing restrictions during the 1950s as comics became the target of a campaign to rid them of their "disreputable" elements. In the coming years, Barks would no longer write stories about sword-wielding skeletons or voodoo curses with their attendant racial stereotypes. But the critique of power and obsession would continue to inform his work, enabling him to create some of his most imaginative and memorable stories.

THE GARDEN
IN THE MACHINE

o heighten his critique of modernity, Barks invoked an imaginary world of lost races and societies. These tales encompass both satirical portraits of urban civilization and a longing for a utopian transcendence of modern life. They reflect Barks's upbringing on the rural Oregon frontier and portray isolated, agricultural communities uncontaminated by modern life and inhabited by lost races, most typically of elfin little people, who resist the ducks' encroachment into their sanctum sanctorum. These creatures tend to be insular and pacifistic, living in harmony with nature and each other. As such, they offer a striking contrast to the hierarchy, exploitation, and domination of nature characteristic of modern Duckburg.

The notion of a lost city that exists simultaneously with but unknown to contemporary urban civilization has fascinated fiction writers, religious clerics, and philosophers since the Middle Ages. At that time, many people believed that paradise still existed in some far-flung corner of the earth.[1] With imperialism at its height, popular versions of the lost city mythos became prevalent in Anglo-American popular fiction in the nineteenth century, as in the stories of H. Rider Haggard and science fiction authors such as H. G. Wells and Edgar Rice Burroughs and in film adaptations of their books. The image of the lost city also became a major theme in 1930s movie serials such as *The Phantom Empire* and *The Lost City*. Such modern fantasy writers as J. R. R. Tolkien have evolved the mythos into detailed portraits of alternative worlds.

According to Stanley Diamond, primitive societies rest on a communal economic base.[2] This is not to say that everything in such societies is owned in common. Personal property such as tools, weapons, clothes, and so forth exists. However, the material means of group survival either are held in common or are accessible to any individual and therefore need not be owned communally. As a consequence, claims Diamond, class stratification and economic exploitation as they are present in archaic and modern civilizations are absent in primitive cultures. Even when a degree of exploitation exits, as in protostates—usually through payment of tribute or labor service—it rarely results in economic ruination of one group by another. Primitive societies have no concept of economic gain: work is for pleasure or use rather than profit. In contrast to modern societies, everyone receives a guarantee of subsistence, an assurance that Paul Radin calls the "irreducible minimum," the "inalienable right" of all individuals in the community to "food, shelter, and clothing," irrespective of the amount of work contributed by them to the acquisition of the means of life.[3] No one starved unless the whole tribe was starving.

Such societies also lacked political states and their apparatuses of centralized administration, laws, and courts. Consequently, individuals possessed a high degree of personal autonomy bounded by the needs of the group. According to Radin, "If I were asked to state briefly and succinctly what are the outstanding features of aboriginal civilization, I, for one, would have no hesitation in answering that there are three; the respect for the individual, irrespective of age or sex; the amazing degree of social and political integration achieved by them; and the existence of a concept of personal security which transcends all forms and all tribal and group interests and conflicts."[4]

Barks's adventures offer a unique hybrid form combining funny animals in highly realistic settings, imaginary worlds set in authentic, historical cultures. "I always tried to tie my stories in to the locale," he explained in 1975. "It had to be grounded right on the earth of that particular scene. That is, if you're going to the Andes, it had to look like the Andes, the ways of the people, and the ways of nature and the terrain, everything had an effect on the gags and dictated the type of gags that I would use." Although he created imaginary worlds, Barks wanted to infuse them with an aura of realism and believability. "I wanted kids to be able to identify with a place that they themselves could go to, a place that was possible, that they could find in their history books."[5]

While Barks's use of realistic settings stemmed from a desire to make his stories plausible, the imaginary nature of the societies that he created derives from their symbolic and psychological dimensions. The emphasis on little people marks the tales' affinity to fairy tales. Yet Barks's stories do not possess the trappings of fairy tales: they do not deal with kings, princes, or princesses, and there is no hint of magic, a sine qua non of most fairy tales. Rather, what Barks's little people stories draw from fairy tales is their utopian dimension.

The rise of the fairy tale coincided with the decline of feudalism and the rise of a bourgeois public sphere. According to Jack Zipes, the middle class originally considered fairy tales immoral because of their implicit and explicit critique of utilitarianism and bourgeois morality. The emphasis on play, alternative forms of living, the pursuit of dreams, and striving for a golden age "challenged the rationalistic purpose and regimentation of life to produce for profit and expansion of capitalist industry."[6] Dominant bourgeois groups considered fairy tales amoral because they subverted bourgeois virtues of order, discipline, industry, modesty, and cleanliness, and these groups regarded the emphasis on imagination as harmful to children. As capitalism and bourgeois morality became more firmly established, the tales began being rewritten and watered down, becoming moralistic and didactic, and began to serve compensatory functions, soothing the public's alienation from the harshness of industrial life by retreating into a realm of pastoral innocence. Conversely, avant-garde artists and writers in the romantic movement utilized the fairy tale as a form of protest against the utilitarian ideals of the Enlightenment. Thus, many tales harbored elements of critique. According to philosopher Ernst

Bloch, "the fairy tale narrates a wish-fulfillment which is not bound only by its own time and the appeal of its content."[7] Fairy stories remain vital because of their capacity to harbor unfulfilled wishes in symbolic form and to project the possibility of their realization.

Bloch coined the word *Vor-Schein* (anticipatory illusion) to explain how fairy tales can mirror processes invoked by the imagination that depend on humanity's use of reason to carry through the wishes of fantasy. The fantastic images of such tales can estrange the reader from everyday life, providing a critical reflection on the ways that social and cultural discourses confine us within the parameters of "normal" thought and practice by opening up the possibility that what Bloch called the "little fellows" could recover power and autonomy and take control of their lives. As Alison Lurie observes, in common parlance the little people are not elves but surrogates for children and, before feminism, what we would call the "common man" or the "man on the street." Supernatural powers were claimed for the least powerful among us—that is, children and anonymous, invisible ordinary citizens. In "pixolatry," she claims, this power "was to be found not in great cities, but in out-of-the-way rural locations; in forgotten villages, isolated farmhouses, untidy patches of woods."[8] Barks's comics invoke the same protagonists and the same locales.

Bloch argued that the consciousness of a group or class does not flow directly from the material conditions of its existence. Socioeconomic developments can bring about a certain nonsynchronism in people's lives. A group of people may live in the present yet still think in terms of a previous time or behave in terms of ideas and cultural discourses of a past society. Such is the case when social development does not fully resolve the contradictions of a previous social formation. As a result, groups or classes that are marginalized or left out may feel dissatisfied, alienated, and confused and may yearn for the fulfillment of needs and desires that have been overlooked or are no longer considered meaningful or verifiable in the dominant culture. The residual ideologies and social practices that encode these wishes thus can offer alternative or oppositional critiques of the dominant culture. In Barks's stories, not the future but the past offered glimpses of (albeit imperfect) utopian alternatives to modernity.

"Mystery of the Swamp" (*DD* FC #62 [1944]), was Barks's first story about an imaginary society. He explained the story's genesis:

> I had been struggling for days, trying to think of something I could use for a long story plot. There was a whole bunch of company in the house at the time, and I never had time to really sit down and think of anything. Finally, I got to the point where I just ignored the company and did some serious thinking. All of a sudden I got to thinking of the Everglades and what sort of creatures besides alligators would he find in the Everglades. And just like that, I thought of all these weird little people, like little gnomes who lived out there. . . . So I just sat there and let the thoughts pour all over me. When I had gotten enough that I knew I had a story, I joined the party and hoisted a few drinks.[9]

Barks's imagination had been sparked by reading about the Everglades in *National Geographic*.[10] The Florida swamp's untamed environs, flotilla of small islands, and exotic birds and alligators provided the backdrop for a new kind of adventure story—a place of mystery "that no man has ever seen!" as a stranger tells Donald.

The swamp's inaccessible reaches provided a home for the Seminole Indians. In 1819 Spain ceded Florida to the United States, and settlers got the Seminoles to agree to move onto a reservation. The Americans' greed was insatiable, however, and they wanted more territory. In 1830, the settlers got the backing they wanted from President Andrew Jackson, and the U.S. Congress passed the Indian Removal Act, which forced many Indians off their lands. Many died in the march to the Indian Territory infamously known as the Trail of Tears. Only one group of Indians successfully resisted removal—the Seminoles. After a series of wars, around five hundred Seminoles remained in Florida, hiding in the alligator-infested Everglades, where white men dared not venture. Though the draining of the Everglades and the paucity of game have forced the Seminoles into closer contact with outsiders, they remain the only Indian tribe never to have signed a formal peace treaty with the U.S. government.

Donald finds the Gneezles, like the Seminoles, living cut off from the outside world and using the traditional bow and arrow. Like their Indian counterparts, the Gneezles have a long hostility toward civilization. "Go back! Go back!" calls a Gneezle guard. "Gnot for a millyun years has human creeters entered the land of the Gneezles!" Like the Seminoles, the Gneezles are undaunted by their civilized foes, and the ducks are unable to defeat the tribe despite their superior weaponry.

Barks had also been inspired by Disney's animation factory. The portfolio that won him a tryout at the Disney Studio contained two drawings based on the not-yet-completed feature *Snow White and the Seven Dwarfs*. However, while the dwarfs in that film were cute and cherubic, Barks's dwarfs are bizarre and wacky looking and include a backwoods hayseed and ethnic caricatures such as an Irish leprechaun, a Jewish elf, and a parody of Gandhi wearing only a towel. All have the bulbous noses, long beards, and strange hats that would later characterize the Gneezles.

The Gneezles' appearance and the idea of making them gnomes were partly inspired by Barks's desire to depart from Disney's dwarfs and other well-known imaginary creatures. Barks recalled, "I just tried to make them different so they'd look like fairy creatures rather than part of our human world. They had pointy ears and finny feet and wore crazy costumes. They were fairy tale creatures who lived in the area so long they had become swamp Okies."[11] The Gneezles' Okie patois, love of square dancing, and use of the bow and arrow all link them to the agricultural societies of the American frontier. They are rural rednecks, and Barks clearly sympathizes with their hostility toward and retreat from civilization; indeed, the bulbous noses he gave them were a trademark of his self-caricatures.

Barks's portrait of Gneezle Gnob, the Gneezles' city, was his first attempt at rendering an imaginary society, and he created it out of whole cloth rather than grounding it in previously existing societies. Consequently, he was unable to make the elements of his fictional world fully cohere. We are given a pastiche of details from various periods and cultures rather than a unitary world. In the crowd scene, for example, an assembly of elders wears Amish-style hats, while two guards sport Roman helmets and carry medieval halberds adorned by Indian-style feathers. Barks implies that the Gneezles have stolen this mélange of costumes and props over the centuries from groups of invaders. The effect is comic and exotic but gives us little sense of who the Gneezles are. Donald and his nephews escape from Gneezle Gnob only when the Gneezle king allows them to, and he leaves apples spiked with "fergettin' juice" so that they can recall nothing of their adventure. The land of the Gneezles thus remains only an oneiric presence like the fairy tale, an emblem of our fears of civilization and desire to escape.

Barks created his first fully realized imaginary world in "Lost in the Andes" (*DD* FC #223 [1949]). As noted in chapter 4, this story had its roots in the Disney films *Saludos Amigos* and *The Three Caballeros*, anthologies of animated shorts dealing with Latin America. Since these films were projects of the U.S. State Department's "Good Neighbor Policy" intended to encourage the two American continents, in Disney's words, to "like one another better," the films had a political purpose. They were aimed at shoring up pan-American unity as a bulwark against Fascism during World War II. They had an economic motive as well: to capitalize on Latin America's cheap, nonunion labor, the U.S. government sought to send film producers like Disney to the country to test the feasibility of setting up Hollywood film production there. Disney had his own economic rationale for the trip to Latin America: having lost most of the foreign market for his films because of the war, he saw South America as a viable new market for his cartoons.

South American scholars have been highly critical of the representations of Latins in these films. Julianne Burton-Carvajal, for example, views *The Three Caballeros* as an allegory of First World colonialism and argues that the film provides a "narrative of conquest in which the patriarchal unconscious and the imperial unconscious insidiously overlap," the most egregious example of which is the lascivious Donald's mad chase after doe-eyed Latina bathing beauties, ripe for conquest.[12] Appropriately originally titled *The Surprise Package*, the film is structured around "gifts" of Latin culture that Donald receives from his new Latin friends. Much in the same way, Disney utilized Latin culture as raw material for his films—to be repackaged, commodified, and sold to American audiences as "authentic" examples of exotic Latinness.

"Lost in the Andes" moves in an opposite direction. Barks was an antihistoricist who critiqued the First World's illusions of economic and technological progress as a model of development for underdeveloped nations. His story lays bare the dysfunctionality of the commodification of indigenous culture by American imperialism and satirizes the neocolonialist myths that legitimated it.[13]

Barks depicts three different civilizations, implicitly inviting us to draw comparisons between them. The first is modern Duckburg, a place of petty hierarchies and alienated labor. Dignity, wealth, and social status are available only to the few at the top. A fourth-assistant janitor at the local museum, Donald longs to be third-assistant janitor and to give rather than take orders. When he enthusiastically jumps at the chance to polish the museum's rare gemstones, he is ignominiously grabbed by the neck and told by the third-assistant janitor to polish a "collection of rubble" instead. Even when Donald accidentally discovers that these "stones" are really "square eggs," he receives no credit for the discovery.

Duckburg functions as an assemblage of isolated teams working separately rather than functioning harmoniously for the good of the community as a whole. A group of scientists and experts examine the rare eggs, trying to classify and categorize them by their physical properties. Barks depicts the scientists as caricatures of instrumental rationality, narrow-minded specialists so concerned with discovering what the square eggs are that they are blind to the ends to which their knowledge will be put. One has whiskers that cover most of his face; another has thick glasses and prunelike wrinkles, symbols of his myopia and desiccated humanity. Duckburg's egg barons are also morally bereft. Barks shows them salivating in anticipation of the megaprofits the square eggs will bring in solving the stacking problem. To maximize profit, the tycoons would bring all nature under their control, making eggs conform to a square shape. Satirizing the capitalists' arrogance, Barks drew them with egg-shaped bald domes that mirror the contours of the globe behind them. The farmers too are enmeshed in the mania. Rather than being close to nature, they dream of crossing square roosters with round hens, blind to the Frankensteinian implications of such tampering. The anxious look on a rooster's face indicates the deformation of nature that would result.

The expedition to Peru is structured like the museum hierarchy. Barks portrays it as a dysfunctional bureaucracy that promotes individual irresponsibility and distorts communication through its chain-of-command structure. Each of the levels sneaks a taste of the professor's omelet, which the nephews, unknown to the others, have made from square eggs. Although each one finds that it tastes rank, he passes it along to his superior, never correcting the original mistake. As a result, everyone from Donald to the professor ends up in sick bay with acute "ptomaine ptosis of the ptummy," in Barks's brilliant alliterative turn of phrase, an illness that causes the stomach to tie itself up into "square knots."

The second civilization is that of the Andean natives of contemporary Peru. Barks parodies the readiness with which they abandon their local culture to produce for the tourist trade. When Donald flashes wads of cash offering to buy any square eggs they can find, the natives crank out fakes using ice trays and a "Ward and Roebuck" cement mixer. Barks's satire shows the way in which a neocolonial system of exchange destroys indigenous cultures to make Third World subjects into avid and dependent consumers in a global capitalist market.

The third civilization Barks presents is of a pre-Columbian Inca city, Plain Awful. Aided by an old vicuna hunter, the ducks tumble through the mists of time to discover a strange square-shaped city hidden beneath the fog. "Sure is a blocky-lookin' place!" exclaims Donald. In one of his most famous splash panels, Barks drew a complete square-shaped city. Barks drew inspiration from images of the idiosyncratic stone architecture of the Inca in the *National Geographic*, especially those of the lost city of Machu Picchu (Old Mountain), which is famous for its polygonal masonry. Most of the buildings were made of granite blocks fitted together without mortar so perfectly that even the thinnest knife blade could not be forced between them.[14]

Preceded by the corrupt worlds of modern Duckburg and the contemporary native village, the square city might be expected to be a primitive utopia. And to some extent it is. The Plain Awfultonians' "southern hospitality" stands in stark contrast to Donald's demeaning treatment as fourth-assistant janitor in Duckburg. Although he is ignored for his discovery of the square eggs in that environment, the ancient Incas elevate the ducks to high positions for their discovery of the square chickens that lay the eggs that make up the natives' sustenance. "They had so little of *anything*," muses Donald after leaving the city, "yet they are the happiest people we have ever known!"

However, Barks's portrait of the Inca culture is ambivalent. Although he finds them superior to capitalist modernity, Barks rejects a romantic primitivism that elevates preindustrial cultures to the status of utopias. Plain Awful, as its name suggests, is radically flawed. It is conformist and shackled by custom. When the nephews blow round bubbles with their chewing gum, the Awfultonians threaten to consign the ducks to a lifetime of hard work in the "terrible stone quarries" as punishment for committing such sacrilege. Only when the nephews learn a trick that enables them to blow square bubbles are they freed. Barks's story implies that primitive societies have a spirit of community and generosity but are so conformist and custom-bound that they lack tolerance and freedom of expression. However, as we shall see shortly, this view stems from a conflation of primitive and archaic cultures.

Plain Awful seems at first to have always been the blocky place we see. But much of its culture has resulted from an earlier visit by another American, Professor Rhutt Betlah of the Birmingham school of English. Barks's wordplay on Clark Gable's character Rhett Butler in the classic novel and film *Gone with the Wind* refers to another insular, agricultural society, the Old South.[15] In a bizarre example of the colonizing process, much of the Awfultonians' culture results from this lone American. In a metonymic riff, Barks's story equates South America with the American South. The Awfultonians speak in southern dialect, pride themselves on their southern hospitality, and love to sing "Dixie." Their country even gets its name from the professor and dates its history by his visit. Barks's Plain Awful implicitly parodies the bigotry of the American South: because of their intolerance of difference, the natives perceive Donald as "queer-looking" even though they are square-shaped, subject the ducks to southern lynch-law justice, and threaten to make them lifetime slaves.

The shock of seeing Inca primitives as faux southerners invites a process of reader estrangement, working to defamiliarize and "make strange" to readers assumptions of neocolonialism that are embedded in Eurocentric culture, that are normalized and taken for granted. This approach invites readers to examine how Anglo-Americans have defined native culture for those in the metropolis while eliding indigenous peoples' voices. In political policies such as the Monroe Doctrine, the United States declared its supremacy in the Americas and assimilated Latin America to U.S. interests. Barks's story satirizes this cultural amnesia by making it seem ridiculous.

This estrangement process exposes what Beau Riffenbaugh calls "the myth of the explorer." The explorer had his heyday in the nineteenth and early twentieth centuries. "Men who achieved remarkable feats were more than just popular heroes," Riffenbaugh writes. "They were symbols of real and imagined nationalist and imperialist cultural greatness. Explorers, confirming as they did the heroism, romance, and adventure of empire, were a particularly celebrated genre." [16] With Social Darwinism and the western demand for the conquest of the physical world serving as ideological justification for their actions, explorers opened the way for national expansion by overcoming the challenges of the natural world, defeating "barbarism," mapping the unknown, and establishing trade. Since continued expansion provided a means of achieving or maintaining moral, racial, and national superiority, exploration came to symbolize a nation's collective cultural superiority.

Barks's satire of the western explorer is grounded in the introduction of Machu Picchu to the West. Professor Hiram Bingham from Yale University, who "discovered" the city in 1911, becomes the "Professor from Birmingham." Although other westerners and the Andeans themselves previously knew of the city, Bingham received the credit because of his exploitation of the journey in the media. [17]

Barks's tale is structured around the treasure hunt motif that characterizes the colonial adventure story. The hero typically braves native threats and gains the treasure for a song, returning to civilization in triumph. Barks subverted this ending, opting for an ironic closure. Instead of building the "new breed of super poultry" so assiduously desired by Duckburg's egg barons, farmers, and scientists, Donald mistakenly returns with two square roosters. The corporate scheme to dominate the world is derailed by a revolt of nature that ironically mocks its illusions of grandeur.

"Lost in the Andes" is considered one of the Duck Man's best stories, and Barks himself lauded it for its "technical" perfection and the fact that it was laced together by means of running gags—that is, jokes that recur throughout a story. "It was puffed up in the studio's story department as being a very good gimmick if you could get a running gag going to connect sequences," Barks recalled. "Look how the chewing gum gag holds the Andes story together." [18]

Barks's art is denser in this story than in any previous one, displaying a use of "deep focus," a term in film criticism that denotes a shot's ability to keep foreground, middle ground, and background all in clear view. Backgrounds in the story are highly defined, making the imaginary word come alive. Such high definition creates a feeling of claustrophobia in the reader, evoking fears of confinement that mirror the suffocating uniformity of Plain Awful and its square world.

Nonetheless, Barks was not satisfied with his most spectacular drawing in the story—the splash panel of the city: "I botched up my perspective a little in drawing that; I should have laid out all these squares down here by measuring points instead of from the vanishing point—see how they become diamond-shaped toward the bottom of the panels? When I was drawing it, some neighbor friend dropped in and sat there persistently talking to me, all the time that I was trying to make that big, complicated layout. And I would have to look up and answer, with my thoughts interrupted. . . .[I]t's been a problem my whole life: whenever I was up against something on which I had to use my head and do some really deep thinking, somebody would always come along and have to talk about something." [19] Yet the story marks a high point in Barks's mastery of graphic narrative and one of the medium's greatest stories.

Despite his faithful rendering of its architecture, Barks's portrait of an Inca-like civilization was anachronistic. His attraction to simple, communal societies led him to mischaracterize the Incas as a primitive social order when, in fact, they were a highly sophisticated, imperialistic culture with a far-flung empire that stretched along the Pacific coast from the equator south to Chile. Built by the Inca king Pachacuti between 1460 and 1470, Machu Picchu itself was not a poor, communal city, as Barks portrayed it, but a retreat for the Incan royal family characterized by luxury and spaciousness at a time when ordinary citizens lived in windowless, one-room huts. The hospitality and friendliness of Barks's Incan town stands in contrast to the Incan habit of conducting human sacrifices as part of religious rituals.[20] Diamond classifies the Incas as an archaic society because they possessed a protostate. Unlike primitive societies, which were protodemocratic and lacked formal governments, the Incas created a centralized, totalitarian government that controlled every aspect of subjects' lives.[21] Although the Plain Awfultonians live a life of ease and contentment, Inca stone architecture was created through slave labor, a fact alluded to, but never developed, in Barks's story when the ducks are threatened with a lifetime of toil in the stone quarries as punishment for breaking the city's taboos against depicting anything not square.

In fact, this taboo did not exist in Incan civilization, whose religion revolved around worship of the circular orb of the sun and the irregularly shaped Andes. Indeed, Machu Picchu's architecture functions as a kind of cosmic clock, the sun and constellations appearing in certain stone windows at specific times of the year. Barks got the idea for creating a world for square people, chickens, and eggs from an unproduced Disney cartoon, *The Square World*, a satire of Nazi conformity written in the 1940s. Modern conceptions of conformity as squareness, not ancient Andean religion, thus dictated the geometric shapes in his story.

Barks returned to the trope of little people living in a preindustrial utopia in "Land beneath the Ground" (*US* #13 [1956]). However, the story differs from its predecessors in situating its fairy world in a realm that is tied to and affects the everyday one. The geologic realm in literature has come to represent the psychologic, and this story deals with the repressed longings that underlie the civilized psyche.

The underground has always been a mysterious, terrifying place. In ancient Greece, it was called Hades, a shadow world where dead souls went to be washed of their memories before returning to earth. With the arrival of Christianity, the underworld became a place of evil that housed the damned, who suffered eternal punishment for their sins. The meaning of the underground shifted in the late eighteenth century, coming to signify a purely imaginary world that was somehow related to the world above.[22] In modern times, the underground has retained its connotations of menace. The word *underground* is associated with the poor, criminals, and outcasts, including political countercultures and avant-garde movements in art. It has also come to serve as a metaphor for the unconscious and the wellspring of forbidden thoughts and desires buried deep within the psyche.

Barks drew on these connotations in creating his underground kingdom. The Terries and Fermies are direct threats to Scrooge because they make earthquakes that crack open his money bin, sending all his money underground. San Jacinto, where Barks was living at the time he wrote this story, is riddled with faults, and its propensity for earthquakes was certainly in Barks's mind in inventing this story. However, Carlsbad Caverns provided the inspiration for the look of the nether realm in Barks's drawings. Photographs of a group of pisolites ("cave pearls"), round stones created by dripping water over grains of sand, provided the image of the round, rocklike creatures that inhabit the cavern floor.[23] In fact, their spherical shape became part of the earthquake motif, enabling the creatures to roll like bowling balls, smash into the cavern's pillars, and jolt the upper world.

Like Lewis Carroll's *Alice in Wonderland* (originally titled *Alice's Adventures Underground*), which satirized Victorian England, Barks's underworld both reflects and inverts surface life. Scrooge and his cash embody the civilized overground—one might say the superego. The money bin itself is a monument to the Protestant ethic, which teaches that work is toil and that pleasure must be deferred in the service of future gain. For McDuck, life is a business, and his first concern on meeting the local denizens is to ask what work they do: "Are you miners or farmers, or what?" Worst of all, the bowling-ball men reject the most basic principle of Scrooge's world: they find dollars offensive. "We all know how much money is worth!" one cries. "They try to give it away on their radio programs!"

The Terries and Fermies represent the repressed desires that undergird the Protestant ethic, fusing work and play and functioning as emblems of unalienated labor. They initially believe that getting rid of Scrooge's money would be a "lot of hard work." Then they discover that it "needn't be a job of work," transforming the task into "fun" by making it a contest. Indeed, their whole lives are devoted to work that has become play—the creation of earthquakes.

Like Barks's other imaginary creatures, the Terry Fermians espouse values from a preindustrial era. The Greek vase from the year zero they use as a trophy in their contest marks them an ancient culture, while their cowboy lingo links them to the American frontier. "Cowboy music was popular on the radio in stations in San Jacinto where I lived," Barks explained.[24] Even more than America's rural ancestors, these creatures are one with the earth, appearing like rocks when the ducks first encounter them. The Terry Fermians are also one with each other and, like Barks's portraits of other lost races, are communal beings who think, act, and look alike. In contrast to the hierarchal and exploitive Duckburg, they are eminently democratic: when Scrooge proposes a contest with the vase as prize, the underground creatures must put it to a vote of a worldwide assemblage of Terry Fermians.

At the time that Barks wrote this story, America was witnessing the upheaval of another underground. The romanticization of the juvenile delinquent in 1950s films such as *Rebel without a Cause* and the coming of the so-called Beat Generation prefigured the youth rebellions of the 1960s. Led by writers Allen Ginsberg and Jack Kerouac, the Beats advocated dropping out of the rat race to find a more spontaneous and authentic way of life. Several years later, the hippies and their guru, political philosopher Herbert Marcuse, embraced this ethic, calling for the transformation of work into play. Marcuse sought to annul Freud's equation of civilization and repression, distinguishing between "basic repression" (the degree of repression required by reality testing and social cooperation) and "surplus repression" (the "additional controls over and above those indispensable for any form of human association arising from specific institutions of domination").[25] Capitalism, claims Marcuse, operated according to the "performance principle"—that is, the almost total mobilization of the human body and mind as instruments of alienated labor rather than as a vehicle for pleasure, creative expression, and sensuous enjoyment.

The Terry Fermians can be seen as a kind of dropout, rejecting the money ethic and espousing an unalienated form of life based on the pleasure principle. Indeed, they mark the return of the repressed—the inability of civilization totally to control or even fully to sublimate instinctual needs. The earthquakes that the Terries and Fermies create jolt the surface world, an apt metaphor for the way the rejection of the work/consumer ethic was shaking up modern society. But Barks's response to the Beats was anything but sympathetic. In a 1966 story, he made the obnoxious, work-hating Gladstone Gander one of their number ("The Not-So-Ancient Mariner," *WDC&S* #312).[26]

The story's coda contrasts two viewpoints. The geology professor who visits the money bin is a rationalist who believes in material causes: he would attribute earthquakes to "gas that builds up in fissures as the earth shrinks." Scrooge, however, has seen the underground—the realm of play, imagination, and sensual pleasure that we all repress. He may not fully realize what it represents, but he recognizes its power to shake up civilized hierarchies. His final wink to the ducks (and the reader) constitutes both an acknowledgment and a dismissal of that world. We can be certain that he will not give up his asceticism, but his closing comment gives the final word to the Terry Fermians: "He shore ain't been around has he, podners?" Fantasy and imagination remain powerful expressions of utopian longings for the satisfaction of repressed needs whose reality cannot be denied.

"The Secret of Atlantis" (*US* #5 [1954]), a story about the lost continent of Atlantis, began as a ten-pager, then expanded. The initial idea came from Barks's editor, Chase Craig, who suggested "a way that Uncle Scrooge could inflate the value of a very common coin by obliterating all but one of a whole issue." [27] The Atlantis material does not begin until well into the adventure, making the story seem like two separate narratives. However, Scrooge's manipulation of the coin market in the first part is central to Barks's characterization of Atlantis.

Economists usually justify the rule of the market by arguing that it creates an equilibrium between supply and demand. However, this story can be read as revealing the way a capitalist elite may inflate the market, thereby creating an artificial scarcity. It describes how finance capital makes money by inflating markets through speculation rather than investment in productive activities by entrepreneurs, inventors, and industrialists. [28]

Barks juxtaposes this artificially created scarcity with the natural abundance of Atlantean civilization. He characterizes Atlantis as an ecotopia ruled by merpeople. They have evolved over the centuries as their continent slipped gradually into the sea, adapting to the rising waters by becoming half human and half fish. Western culture has created an image of humanity that is alienated from nature and supposed to dominate it in the name of progress. Barks's story, conversely, breaks down the traditional western opposition between nature and culture, animal and human, showing how the two can be harmoniously fused.

Atlantis itself serves as an emblem of the symbiosis that can exist between humans and nature. It possesses no machinery and fears modern technology. When the nephews point out a wrecked plane to their teacher, he recoils in terror. Rather, the city is powered by all-natural agencies. It is lit by fish, gets milk from a whale dairy, and receives electricity from electric eels. It is a completely sustainable society with no exploitation or degradation of the environment but in total harmony with it. In contrast, the king derides the surface people's "smoggy world above," echoing Barks's comments about Los Angeles. [29] In the face of such natural abundance, Atlantis views money as worthless, and the king offers to give Scrooge as many of the "rare" coins as he wants.

But like Barks's other preindustrial utopias, Atlantis is flawed. It is a restrictive society that makes the ducks prisoners and denies them freedom to leave because it fears that they will tell the surface world about the underworld's existence. Becoming a citizen is thus compulsory: "You cannot leave!" the king tells the ducks. "You must become one of us! It is the law!" The ducks are thus eager to return to the surface.

Barks most fully developed the myth of the garden in "Tralla La" (*US* #6 [1954]). The urge to withdraw from civilization and begin life anew in an unspoiled, natural landscape has been typical of the pastoral since the time of the Roman poet Virgil. The idealization of a simple, rural environment, a "virgin land" uncontaminated by the vices and bigotry of Europe, has been a core belief in American mythology. The pastoral ideal has also been associated with orientalist fantasies of Tibet as a special embodiment of spiritual harmony and enlightenment made famous in 1933 by James Hilton's novel, *Lost Horizon*, and its film adaptation four years later by Frank Capra.[30] Although Barks never read the book, he saw the film and based his story on it. So famous has the name Shangri-La become that it has become a synonym for a utopian place of peace and harmony. Barks intended his story to be a parody of the utopian vision of *Lost Horizon* and the notion of a society so pure that it was purged of all greed, selfishness, and envy.

Besieged by demands for money, Scrooge suffers a nervous breakdown. To find peace, he takes off to find the fabled land of Tralla La, where "there is no money and wealth means nothing." Barks portrays it as an uncontaminated paradise whose terraced fields and fertile crops suggest that "it is *really* a land of abundance—of milk and honey." Greeted warmly by the high lama, Scrooge is told that, "We Tralla Laians have never known greed! Friendship is the thing we value most!" However, Scrooge's visit turns this paradise into a model of the worst excesses of civilization. When he throws away a seemingly worthless bottle cap, he accidentally creates the cycle of envy, greed, and contentiousness from which he had tried to escape. "Human nature wouldn't allow them to be that good when they got up against the real nitty-gritty," Barks commented. The bottle cap inaugurates a feverish round of buying and selling, with the price of the worthless object going up astronomically. "Instead of putting it in a museum for everybody to look at," Barks explained, a villager's "wife urged him to sell it for the highest price that he could get. . . . Very quickly the profit system was going in Tralla La."[31] Barks satirizes the absurd lengths to which the natives are willing to go for the pride of owning the cap, contrasting its worthlessness with the real worth they are abandoning to possess it. One man offers Scrooge "200 pigs"; another pledges to be his "servant for forty years."

The story ends with Scrooge attempting to solve the problem by ordering a plane to dump a billion bottle caps into the village, hoping to make them so common that they would no longer be objects of contention. However, the plan backfires when the plethora of caps destroy the natives' crops and threaten to flood the city. "I wanted to do a story that had a billion of something in it," Barks explained. "I read about the appropriations that Congress makes of a billion for this, ten billion for that."[32] One can read this conclusion as an expression of Barks's misgivings about intervening in indigenous cultures with programs of massive American aid.

Barks's interpretation of the story implies that a society in which people do not take advantage of each other is only a pipe dream because of humanity's egoist nature. However, the text's construction of utopianism points to an ambiguity. The valley is corrupted not by human nature but by the arrival of representatives of civilization. The tale can be read as an allegory of the deracinating effects of western imperialism's introduction of money and a market economy into a society based on what Marx called use values (that is, the distinctive needs an object fulfills rather than the market value it has in exchange for other commodities). The story's moral seems to be that one should not ignore the value of wealth such as the bounty of nature, the value of friendship, and the happiness of a heart at peace for the sake of possessing worthless objects such as bottle caps—and, by extension, money.

Many of Barks's stories reveal a longing for a primitive, preindustrial realm free from modern cares and greed, imploring us to be critical of civilization's money fetishism. The ethic of moderation and balance voiced by the people of Shangri-La in *Lost Horizon* resonated with Barks's beliefs and must have made a significant impression on him. The people of Shangri-La seek to avoid excess of any kind, "including, if you will pardon the paradox, excess of virtue itself," explains the high lama's majordomo in the film. This philosophy of the "middle way" bears clear resemblance to Barks's ethic of moderation.

This ethos dovetails with that of the myth of the garden. According to Leo Marx, the ideal of the garden was conceived as a "middle state" contrasted both to a romanticized and nostalgic primitivism of raw nature or wilderness and to urban industrial capitalism.[33] The cultivated nature of agriculture offered an alternative to the excesses of both an untamed nature, which was equated with a hellish desert in this mythology, and to the machine technology and "satanic mills" of the factory system. Barks also deployed this type of mythos, contrasting the savage wilderness of tribes in Africa and Australia with the agricultural utopias in Tralla La and Atlantis.[34]

Barks's source material also argues for a more positive view of utopianism in this story. Rather than being inspired solely by fantasy, Barks based Tralla La on the real-life Asian province of Hunza, whose citizens were reputed to live extraordinarily long and healthy lives: "Not only the *National Geographic* had articles on the long-lived people of Hunza and the Himalayas. It was fairly common fare in the media that all us stupid stuffers of junk food and breathers of carbon monoxide were missing the good life."[35] Bordered by Tibet, China, and Afghanistan, Hunza, like Tralla La, lay in a deep valley obscured from view by the towering Himalayas and accessible only by precipitous mountain paths. Hunza boasted a communal economy and a lack of wealth and precious metals. Barks's first close-up shot of the valley, with its lush terraced fields and blossoming fruit trees, was inspired by a similar picture of Hunza in *National Geographic*, and the magazine article supplied other details for Barks's story as well.[36]

Consequently, it is not surprising that Barks later invoked Hunza in another story, this time calling the valley by its real name. In "Go Slowly Sands of Time," the paradisiacal valley of Tralla La is replaced by wind-swept slopes where a few hardy villages scratch out a meager existence. The parameters of this story are reduced to exploring the requirements for personal rather than social happiness, and the tale deals with Scrooge's desire for longevity. This focus reflects the musings of an elderly Barks about the recipe for maintaining health, happiness, and longevity. "Go

Slowly" was originally a story synopsis that Barks gave to a Danish publisher. In 1981, he worked up the idea as a prose fable for an anthology of Uncle Scrooge stories.[37]

In "Tralla La," Barks contrasts two different economies, one based on money, the other on barter and gift giving. In Marcel Mauss's classic study, *The Gift*, archaic economics are founded on the exchange of gifts. Such societies have no notions of profit and no accumulation of wealth and power; everything is given back eventually or right away, to be immediately redistributed. They are marked by "the joy of public giving; the pleasure in generous expenditure on the arts, in hospitality, and in the private and public festival, social security, the solicitude arising from reciprocity and co-operation."[38] The exchange of gifts promotes not only reciprocity and social solidarity but also reconciliation and peaceful relations. As one Bushman put it, "The worst thing is not giving presents. If people do not like each other but one gives a gift and the other must accept, this brings a peace between them. We give what we have. This is the way we live together."[39] From "Lost in the Andes" to "Tralla La" to "Old California," to which we turn next, Barks's stories about pre-industrial cultures are marked by an emphasis on generosity and giving as a means of establishing felicitous community. Christmas represents the legacy of these older, communal ways of life, and Barks's yuletide tales are distinguished by asserting the need to transcend individuals' egocentrism and the commercialization of gift giving as a way of expressing a spirit of generosity and unselfish love of others.[40]

The myth of the frontier is one of America's oldest and most cherished beliefs. The story of an expansion westward and the struggle to carve a civilization out of the wilderness has been thought to be the key to what is most significant in U.S. history. The pioneers' surge west to claim the free land that lay beyond the frontier became an integral part of the symbolism of America as a garden of the world. As Henry Nash Smith notes, the "image of this vast and constantly growing agricultural society in the interior of the continent became one of the dominant symbols of nineteenth-century America." Moreover, according to Smith, "The master symbol of the garden embraces a cluster of metaphors expressing fecundity, growth, increase, and blissful labor in the earth, all centering around the heroic figure of the idealized frontier farmer." [41] However, the myth of the garden and the ideal of the western yeoman could not be brought to fictional expression, nor could the frontier farmer be made into a viable fictional protagonist. His sedentary life and laborious calling stripped him of the glamour needed to become a frontier hero. The picturesque Wild West rather than the domesticated frontier became exploited in popular entertainment.

Barks's "In Old California" (*DD* FC #238 [1951]) solves this problem by synthesizing the garden and frontier myths. It is set in the halcyon days of the Spanish dons in pre-gold-rush California and combines a story about cowboys and ranching with the myth of the land as a paradisiacal garden. Barks first became interested in California history when he moved to Santa Rosa and entered the fifth grade. "There was a lot of California culture hooked on to us kids, even in those years. . . . That's when I started reading about it. I'd always had a desire to go along that Old Camino Real and just follow it from one mission to another and maybe make photographs and drawings of it." [42]

"Old California" was inspired by Helen Hunt Jackson's famed novel, *Ramona*. Written in 1884, the book generated four film adaptations and numerous stage productions. It is so popular that southern California hosts a reenactment each spring, making the drama the longest-running play in the United States. "Sure, I saw the *Ramona* pageant, also the film, and heard the song many times," Barks recalled. He even referred to it in his story, "partly as an introductory prop to establish the locale and historical period of the main plot, and partly to amaze my San Jacinto neighbors, few of whom knew that the duck comic books they saw on the newsstands originated in their little town." [43] The story is set in the San Jacinto area where he lived, and Barks sprinkled the tale with local references, making this one of his most authentic-looking adventures. [44]

Barks had intended to cast his story with humans rather than funny animals but was unable to because of Western's prohibition on mixing ducks and humans after "Dangerous Disguise." The 1937 film version of *Ramona* served as Barks's major reference. The story follows a young woman who is raised on the Moreno Rancho by the matriarch of the family and who falls in love with an Indian vaquero named Alessandro. Ramona discovers that she is half white and marries Alessandro, settling on his land. White settlers steal their farm. When their baby becomes ill, Alessandro takes a horse to get a doctor and is shot for horse stealing by another white settler. The story ends when Felipé, who was raised as her brother on the rancho and is in love with her, takes Ramona away.[45]

Although Ramona was a fictional character, the novel was based on a real-life incident: a Cahuilla Indian woman named Ramona Lugo married a Native American man named Juan Diego. As in the novel, he took a white man's horse in a fit of madness and was shot by the horse's owner before his wife's eyes.[46] However, Jackson named her fictional heroine Ramona before hearing of the incident, so Ramona Lubo bore no relationship to the fictional heroine. Jackson's story is a tragic tale that condemns white racism and the dispossession of Native Americans. Meant as a political tract to influence Congress, it stands as one of greatest statements of its time opposing whites' oppression of Indians.

In Barks's tale, Alessandro becomes the poor vaquero Rolando, and Ramona becomes Panchita, daughter of the grandee Don Gaspar and his wife, the Senora. The story is set in "a time of peace and happiness," Donald tells a nephew, when "there was *plenty* for everybody, and nobody wanted *much*!" Barks contrasts the open spaces and natural abundance of the Californio days with the overpopulated Los Angeles freeways, so crowded that cars cannot help crashing into one another and into the ducks. In search of some tranquillity, Donald and the nephews head off the highway, but even the hinterlands are places of restriction and confinement: we see "no camping" and "no hunting" signs posted along the route, and the old mission charges fifty cents per visitor. The ducks' first reencounter with an older, more gracious America is a stop at an Indian reservation. Rather than being savages, Donald explains, the Native Americans believed that "having *fun* was more important than fighting!" Emblems of the peace and friendliness of the period, the Indians care for the ducks when their car hits a rock and knocks them unconscious.

The story takes place in a dreamlike atmosphere, with the ducks transported back in time. Like the Indians, Don Gaspar symbolizes the friendliness and generosity of the Californios, welcoming the starving ducks to his home even though they are total strangers. The alcalde gives Donald a "small grant" of a thousand acres of land, a gesture that seems to be more his birthright than an act of charity.

Barks depicts the California frontier as a place of harmony and community, emblematized in one long panel of the fiesta. People from the neighboring ranchos, grandees and their vaqueros, and Indians and padres all gather together in friendship around the abundance of Don Gaspar's table. Barks also shows how bonds of romantic love can shatter fixed hierarchies based on arranged marriages. The Senora wants Panchita to marry the snobbish Don Porko de Lardo, Barks's first pig-faced villain, whom she does not love. But Barks depicts this as a time when even the poor vaquero Rolando can become rich and marry the boss's daughter. The struggle for their love is the emotional center of the story.

The ducks operate primarily as tourists, and we see the other characters through their eyes. We initially come to admire Rolando because a nephew links him to America's screen cowboys: "That guy is as good as Autry Mack Brown Rogers!" he exclaims about Rolando, and Donald teaches him modern songs, like those in a singing cowboy Western, with which to court Panchita. Our feelings for the star-crossed couple are guided by the ducks: when Rolando rescues Panchita from a mad bull and she shows her love for him, a nephew exudes, "Like in the movies, only nicer!" The ducks dictate the action as if they were writing the story, orchestrating events at each juncture. Because of his knowledge of history, for example, Donald sends Rolando to Sacramento to pan for gold before it is actually discovered. "Old California" is Barks's only romance: it became one of his favorite stories because of its sentimental quality. While he would end other adventures on a note of irony or disappointment, this tale concludes happily with Rolando protecting his and the ducks' fortune from claim jumpers and riding off into the sunset to marry his love.

However, Barks portrays the gold rush in ambivalent ways. The availability of great wealth enables Rolando to become rich and to marry

Panchita, but it also marks the beginning of capitalist hegemony and the enshrinement of greed and contention in a formerly agrarian paradise. Barks depicts this transition in the mob hysteria generated by the gold rush and in Donald's description of the discovery of the precious metal as the moment of California's fall from grace. The story ends with Donald and the kids returning to the rancho, now in ruins, serenading the people who have meant so much to them. Barks contrasts these onetime sightseers with the tourists of New California, who think their celebration is only a crazy stunt. We are guilty of historical amnesia, the story seems to say, and have lost our memory of the freedom and conviviality that are our heritage. Like the little people tales that embodied these desires, this story expresses utopian longings for peace, happiness, and abundance. The ducks' joyous celebration at the end offers the possibility of such a redemptive moment, however fleeting, in a more restrictive present.

To give his story historical resonance, Barks took great care to accurately depict landmarks of 1850s California, from the tiny settlement of Los Angeles and Sutter's Fort to the Californios' distinctive costumes and cowboy gear. However, Barks romanticized the overall history of the period to fit with his notion of an agrarian paradise. The narrative rests on two major occlusions. The first concerns the appropriation of Californio property by white settlers. At the end of the Mexican-American War (1846–48), the United States gained possession of California. By 1852, about 250,000 miners from around the world—the majority of them whites—had arrived in California for the gold rush. The new arrivals vastly outnumbered the Californios, and even though the rancheros had lived on their lands for generations and had been guaranteed rights to their lands by treaty, many newcomers saw those already there as foreigners. Whites condemned Spanish-speaking people as "greasers" and passed onerous laws against foreign miners. Anglos squatted on ranchos without permission or compensation to the landowners and seized land violently, chasing the Californios from their homes. In 1851 a board was set up to review the Californios' land rights, but in many cases the board ultimately stripped the rancheros of their land because they could not prove their claims or afford attorney's fees and were swindled by unscrupulous lawyers. Although a few Californios retained their property, by the 1870s the rancho system had ended.[47]

"Old California" refers to these acts of expropriation by whites but elides their racial context. Donald's land, not Don Gaspar's rancho, is stolen by the white settler, Ezry, and Ezry and his partner jump Donald's claim rather than Rolando's. Barks effaces Anglos' ruthless treatment of Latinos in California and whites' historical ascendancy in the state while offering the possibility of upward mobility for a deracialized lower class of vaqueros.

This displacement of race onto class effaces the issues of racism and fears about miscegenation that formed the heart of Jackson's story. By portraying virtually all the rancho inhabitants as Mexican, the racial hierarchies and conflicts between the Californios and their Indian workers are omitted. Consequently, the major issue becomes one of class, and it is solved by an ideology of upward mobility. In fact, however, most vaqueros were Indians who were harshly treated on the ranchos and had little opportunity for advancement. Californio society was a rigid, caste society based on racial stratification. Writes Richard Henry Dana Jr. in his eyewitness account in *Two Years before the Mast*,

> Those who are of pure Spanish blood, having never intermarried with the aborigines, have clear brunette complexions, and sometimes even as fair as English women. [The rancheros] form the upper class, intermarrying, and keeping up an exclusive system in every respect. They can be distinguished, not only by their complexion, dress, and manners, but also by their speech, for calling themselves Castilians, they are very ambitious of speaking the pure Castilian, while all Spanish is spoken in a corrupted dialect by the lower classes. From this upper class, they go down by regular shades, growing more dark and muddy, until you come to the pure Indian. . . . Generally speaking, each person's caste is decided by the quality of the blood, which shows itself, too plainly to be concealed, at first sight. Yet the least drop of Spanish blood, if it only of quadroon or octoroon, is sufficient to raise one from the position of a serf, and entitle him to wear a suit of clothes . . . and to hold property, if he can get any.[48]

Consequently, the rancho system provided those possessing Spanish blood with a relatively fluid class system that offered even those at the bottom of the social hierarchy the opportunity to obtain property, and the ranchos were noted for their hospitality and joie de vivre. Barks's utopian vision of Californio society thus had its basis in historical fact.

"The Land of the Pygmy Indians" (*US* #18 [1957]) was the final story in which Barks reprised the myth of the garden. It is one of the earliest and most powerful ecological stories in comic books, preceding the rise of a mass environmental movement in the 1970s. The story reveals the contradictions of notions of progress in capitalist modernity. Scrooge wants to leave Duckburg's smog and overpopulation and decides to buy an uninhabited wilderness preserve. At the same time, his commitment to industrial development threatens his pastoral oasis. "I'm through with it—even though I'm the guy that started all those smelly factories!" he admits. Barks uses Scrooge's inability to treat nature other than as a resource to be exploited as a running gag throughout the story. When he visits the pristine wilderness, he cannot help but see it as a source of raw material for his chemical plants, its moose as steaks to be sold by the pound, and its minerals as ores for his factories. Paradoxically, this mentality threatens to create the same environment from which he had sought to escape. Throughout the story, the nephews function as a Greek chorus, pointing out his instrumental attitude toward nature and admonishing him to "leave this country clean and free for the animals and birds!"

"The Land of the Pygmy Indians" features another lost race of little people—in this case, a band of diminutive Indians named the Peeweegahs. In this story, Barks made his fairy creatures smaller than the ducks. "That makes a slight menace out of the ducks," he explained. "They were always peewees in comparison with the villains. In order for them to become a menace, they had to come up against somebody smaller."[49] He would keep this size ratio in all the rest of his little people adventures.

Barks's story was inspired by Longfellow's famed poem, "The Song of Hiawatha" (1855), which Barks had discovered in grade school. "About the eighth grade, I had to read it and recite it in school: I thought it was a tiresome way of telling a story back then, but the meter lends itself very well to the comments of the Peeweegahs when they talk about what they're going to do."[50] Barks gave a lyrical quality to their dialogue, emulating Native Americans' singsong, mythopoeic ways of speech in Longfellow's poem.

Longfellow was the most important mid-nineteenth-century American writer to articulate the notion of the Indian as "noble savage." His poem about Hiawatha had virtually no connection, apart from the name, to the historical fifteenth-century Iroquois chief Hiawatha. Longfellow followed Henry Schoolcraft's version of a cycle of Chippewa legends, assuming, as Schoolcraft did, that the Chippewa demigod Manibozho was identical to the Iroquois statesman Hiawatha.[51] This misunderstanding of Native American history was intrinsic to the image of the noble savage. At this time the Indian as an opponent of civilization was dead but still lay heavy on American consciences. The image of the noble savage allowed writers to place the Indian in a dim, remote past that kept him outside the march of civilization. He is part of America's childhood, which it must outgrow to attain its maturity. In Longfellow's poem, Hiawatha understands the fate of the noble savage and endorses the missionaries who come, but at night he slips quietly away, traveling westward alone. He can be no part of civilization. The image of the noble savage thus allowed white Americans to romanticize guilt figures while valorizing the march to civilization as a form of inevitable progress. Thus, the image of the noble savage, then and now, legitimates the triumph of western imperialism.

However, the notion of the noble savage can be viewed more positively as containing elements of truth about the viability and accomplishments of Native Americans. The historical Hiawatha, for example, was a follower of Deganwidah, a prophet and shaman who founded the League of the Iroquois. Hiawatha was a skilled and charismatic orator who was instrumental in persuading the Iroquois peoples—the Senecas, Onondagas, Oneidas, Cayugas, and Mohawks—to stop fighting among each other and to accept Deganwidah's vision and band together as a confederacy. (The Tuscarora nation subsequently joined the Iroquois Confederacy, forming the Six Nations.)[52] The league's concept of federalism had a significant influence on America's Founding Fathers. The first person to propose a union of all the American colonies and to propose a federal model for it was reportedly an Iroquois chief, Conassatego, who suggested in 1744 that the colonists make their government into a union of all the colonies in a federal system similar to that of the League of the Iroquois. American political thinkers from Benjamin Franklin to Thomas Jefferson and Thomas Paine were heavily influenced by Native American political notions of liberty, equality, and community.[53] Barks also utilized the concept of the notion of the noble savage in positive terms, not to elegize a vanishing American but as a model of a sustainable relationship to the environment.

Barks contrasts the anthropocentric and the ecocentric ethics of the two groups. While Uncle Scrooge embodies a human-centered ethic, the Indians are avatars of a nature-based morality. Scrooge can only envision nature in terms of its utility to humans, while the Peeweegahs believe that nature is intrinsically valuable and has a right to exist independently of the way humans view it. Barks's approach also entails contrasting visions of property and property rights. When Scrooge presents his deed as proof of ownership of their land, the chief replies, "By whom was this token taken? By whose hands these written scratches? Did the *sun* from high above you sell you all these lands and waters? Did the winds that bend the pine trees? . . . [M]e no believe that such a token would be honored by the fishes, by the creatures of the forest, by the birds we call our brothers. . . . None could sign away these woodlands, none could have the *right* or reason, but the chiefs of *all* the brothers in a powwow with the seasons!"

This lyrical speech accurately reflects Native American beliefs with respect to property: that nature is sacred and comprises living beings with the same rights as people. Consequently, nature cannot be bought and sold, as in western concepts of property, which look on the land as a dead object and the flora and fauna as resources for human benefit. In tribal society, property is governed by custom and kinship agreements.[54] The territory as a whole belongs to the nation, with jurisdiction over it held in trust by the chiefs. It is inalienable, and the identity of a nation is inseparable from the land, animals, and ecosystem in which they live. In Amerindian cosmology, the Indian belongs to the land as much as the land to the tribe. When Indians made property agreements with white settlers, they were granting rights to co-use of the land, not rights to the land itself, which could not be sold.

The Peeweegahs' relationship to the environment is one of kinship, and they live in harmony with it. Barks invokes a relationship of reciprocity between the tribe and nature by showing that the Peeweegahs can communicate with the fish and animals, who will come to their aid when the Indians are threatened. When the ducks capture an Indian, he asks the fish for help, and the forest creatures work together to free him. However, Barks does not romanticize nature as monolithically benevolent. The giant sturgeon is an evil creature who eats smaller fish and destroys the Peeweegahs' canoes. When it tries to swallow Donald, he is saved by the nephews and emerges from its mouth like Jonah escaping from the biblical leviathan.

Our growing ecological awareness has transformed the nature of the pastoral. No longer can we take for granted the notion of a bountiful earth and assume its infinite permanence. We are now capable of altering and destroying nature. We have changed the global climate, polluted the air and oceans, decimated wildlife, wantonly destroyed animal and plant species, and clear cut forests. In the pastoral, wilderness—that is, wild nature— was traditionally looked on as an untenable extreme that had to be transcended, as did the city, by the humanly cultivated nature of the garden. Now, however, wilderness has become a paramount source of value and its preservation one of the sine qua nons of the survival of civilization. Barks's story echoes this change. Scrooge is hoisted on his own petard when the Peeweegahs invite him to smoke a peace pipe filled with the same noxious chemicals that he has showed them how to mine. The tale ends on a note of redemption: Scrooge proclaims that he is giving the land "back to the Indians," those from whom westerners originally had expropriated it, and the wilderness is preserved. "Land of the Pygmy Indians" was Barks's last story featuring a preindustrial culture that offered an alternative worldview to our own. Nevertheless, his Junior Woodchuck stories from the 1970s would continue to elaborate an ecological perspective.

RESURRECTING THE SELF-MADE MAN

After Western Publishing noticed that newsstand sales jumped whenever Scrooge was in the story, an editor wrote to Barks and asked him to create a one-shot *Uncle Scrooge* adventure comic (*US* FC #386 [1952]). Two more Four Color comics followed, and they were so popular that *Uncle Scrooge* became a quarterly series with the fourth issue in 1954. Over the next seventeen years, Barks wrote seventy-one adventures, with Scrooge becoming the Duck Man's most successful adventure hero.

However, giving Uncle Scrooge his own book posed a problem. The early McDuck had not been likable. In his first appearance, he behaved like his Dickensian namesake, a miser who spurned all human connection. His playful attachment to money had not yet emerged, and he seemed more interested in feeling the power he could derive from scaring his nephews and even his butler (*DD* FC #178 [1947]). In subsequent stories, Scrooge contrived to pursue power but did it through the agency of wealth, becoming a ruthless capitalist who controlled all business in Duckburg and the world. In these tales, the theft of his fortune by the Beagle Boys had seemed a well-deserved comeuppance for his avarice and delusions of control (*WDC&S* #134 [1951], #135 [1951]).

In later stories, Scrooge could be neither so harsh nor so harshly dealt with. When Western Publishing decided to feature the old duck in his own comic book, Barks felt it necessary to soften Scrooge's character and make him more attractive. The loss of his entire fortune had previously been merely a throwaway gag at the end of a ten-pager, forgotten by the beginning of the next story. But once Scrooge became a hero and star of his own title, it became a formula that if he lost his wealth, he would regain it by the end of the tale. In his first adventure story, Scrooge's loss makes him seem a vulnerable and sympathetic character. After the Beagle Boys have sabotaged his money reservoir, Scrooge is shown small and hunched over, retreating into the sunset while the nephews—and the reader—look on helplessly. Barks's decision to soften Scrooge was also a deliberate strategy to forestall censorship from Western. When collector Malcolm Willets asked Barks if the office told him to make Scrooge "more lovable," the artist replied, "No, I tried to do that myself. I kind of anticipated they would tell me that."[1]

Scrooge's popularity stemmed from the way the character negotiated tensions within the American dream in the postwar era. Americans have had a basic, almost spiritual, commitment to the principles of free enterprise, self-reliance, and the individualism of the Protestant ethic. Since the last third of the nineteenth century, this ideal has become increasingly obsolete, corresponding to an America of decentralized small enterprises. Before the Civil War, nine of every ten men owned their own farms, shops, or small crafts workshops.[2] The result was a community of equals, what Mike Walsh has called a "shirtless" democracy.[3] Since then, an increasingly urban, corporate America of salaried employees has supplanted the decentralized society of independent owners, eroding dreams of upward mobility, equality, and personal autonomy and signaling the rise of what many people deemed "wage slavery." In modern America, class background, inheritance, and connections are more important in attaining great wealth than skill or the success ethic's formula of diligence, thrift, and hard work.[4]

American comic strips reflected the decline of the entrepreneur. The builder of enterprises had been an esteemed member of comic strip society in the 1920s and 1930s but was displaced by the self-employed professional in the 1940s and 1950s and then over the next two decades by the alienated, oppressed employee who became an archetype of a mass society out of control. According to Jill Kasen, between the 1950s and 1975, "most comic residents had stumbled into an employee lifestyle that denied them autonomy, hope or self-respect."[5]

But the Protestant ethic has endured for a fundamental reason. Although hedonistic consumption promoted by business may have prevailed in the public sphere, its victory cannot alter the need for a more repressive set of values necessary to maintain economic production in the private sphere. As Daniel Bell points out, the workplace still demands the earlier virtues of diligence and sublimation, while consumers learn the opposite values: "What this abandonment of Puritanism and the Protestant ethic does, of course, is to leave capitalism with no moral or transcendental ethic. It also emphasizes the ... extraordinary contradiction within the social structure itself. On the one hand, the business corporation wants an individual to work hard, pursue a career, accept delayed gratification—to be, in the crude sense, an organization man. And yet, in its products and its advertisements, the corporation promotes pleasure, instant joy, relaxing, and letting go."[6] Thus, late capitalism requires a contradictory blend of calculating hedonism and a narcissistic personality necessary to maximize consumption, while capitalist production demands asceticism and a disciplined workforce.

Even those social theorists of the 1950s who had strongly criticized the bureaucratization of America expressed a nostalgia for the Protestant ethic and the self-made man. Barks drew on this longing in refashioning McDuck. Barks called his first Scrooge adventure "Only a Poor Old Man," but the title is misleading. On the one hand, the story makes the point that despite all his millions, Scrooge is a psychologically impoverished old man, unable to enjoy a moment's peace of mind. On the other hand, he is rich in spirit, resourceful, and self-resilient. With a lifetime of experience behind him, he can always find an extra trick or two up his sleeve. Refusing to accept defeat after the Beagles have stolen all his money, he turns on the horizon and comes back for a final match of wits with the crooks and recovers his hoard.

Flashbacks at the beginning of the story help build this more heroic image. We learn that Scrooge was once a cowpoke in Montana, a treasure hunter in the Spanish Main, and a sourdough in the Klondike gold rush. Scrooge is transformed from a "banker, industrialist, magnate and tycoon" (*WDC&S* #104 [1949]) into a prospector. It seems now that he has amassed his fortune not by usury or dirty tricks but by hard work. "Froze my fingers to the bone digging nuggets out of the creeks!" he tells his nephews. "And I brought a fortune *out*, instead of spending it in the honkytonks!" As he speaks, the panel art shows a determined, gun-toting young Scrooge stalking past a group of ruffians outside the casinos of Dawson. His stinginess has become thrift, and his hostility seems justified when directed toward gamblers and dance hall girls harboring designs on his hard-earned wealth.

Barks had been a staunch believer in the work ethic since childhood. His imagination had been sparked by tales spun by his older brother, Clyde, as they lay in bed at night. The stories concerned a gang of ingenious boys who continually outwitted their contemptuous boss, the "flat butt man." In this idealization of hardworking heroes, office workers who sat on their rears all day were to be despised. Barks had also been inspired by a book, *The Speedwell Boys on Motorcycles*, written by Edward Stratemeyer, a protégé and collaborator of Horatio Alger and ghostwriter of some of his novels. "It gave me the feeling that if I worked hard enough and worked well at anything, that I might get a reward out of it," Barks recalled.[7] With only an eighth-grade education, Barks had lived the ethic of pulling oneself up by his bootstraps and was an autodidact who taught himself English grammar, science and mathematics, history, and archeology to further his cartooning career.

Barks grew up in rural Oregon, so it was natural for him to invoke the frontier myth to valorize Scrooge's fortune. The artist undoubtedly had heard romantic tales of the Klondike gold rush from visitors to the family ranch and the cowboys whom he and his brother idolized. The Klondike gold rush also made sense in terms of Scrooge's age, making him a young man when it began in 1898. The frontier myth's image of America as a virgin land where territory was available for the taking helped bolster the rags-to-riches saga. The notion that a lone individual could dig a fortune out of the ground unaided by others affirmed the individualist ethos on which both the frontier myth and the Horatio Alger ethic rested. Barks explained, "I never thought of Scrooge as I would think of some of the millionaires we have around who have made their money by exploiting other people to a certain extent. I purposely tried to make it look as if Uncle Scrooge made most of his money in the days before the world got so crowded, back in the days when you could go out into the hills and find the gold."[8] Significantly, Scrooge never mentions his parents, although he recalls at one point that his grandfather wore a miner's cap (*US #29* [1960]). He seems to have always been on his own, scratching out a living from childhood. Thus, his reclusiveness, objectionable in a miser, becomes the independence of the self-made man.

It's a nice image—but a myth. The most successful turn-of-the-century entrepreneurs were known as Robber Barons, and with good reason. Their pursuit of wealth had an unsavory side. The Scrooge adventures continually dance around this issue yet never come to terms with it. In a 1979 interview, Barks acknowledged that "Uncle Scrooge himself was based on Gould and Harriman and Rockefeller. All those guys made their fortunes in railroads and mines and so on by being just a little bit unscrupulous with the way they eliminated the competition. . . . Scrooge had to be in that mold, or he couldn't have made it in an era when he was up against all those plutocrats."[9]

However, not only the Robber Barons' ruthless elimination of competitors was an issue: they also exploited and abused workers. A huge gap between rich and poor defined the Gilded Age. When John D. Rockefeller became the country's first billionaire, more than 90 percent of Americans lived in poverty. Despite toiling twelve to sixteen hours a day, 80 percent of workers stayed poor despite the country's great economic growth and high employment. Robber Barons exploited the huge immigrant pool and destroyed unions to keep wages very low.[10] Scrooge pays Donald and the nephews the pittance of thirty cents an hour, making them the "ideal" corporate family. But because his workers are members of his own family who love and support him, this abuse can be ignored.

In effect, Barks's portrait of Scrooge conflates early-nineteenth-century entrepreneurs with the Robber Barons of the later part of that century. Whereas the former were small farmers, mechanics, or proprietors, the Robber Barons were owners of large trusts, cartels, and monopolies and avowed enemies of free enterprise. As John D. Rockefeller famously put it, "The age of combination is here to stay. Individualism is gone, never to return." [11] Although the Robber Barons touted themselves as indi-vidualistic apostles of free enterprise, they created a corporate economy that was the antithesis of the ideals they proclaimed.

As Rex Burns points out, although most Americans equate the idea of success with great wealth, this did not occur until the mid–nineteenth century. Previously, "beginning with the Puritans, and modified by the Enlightenment, success was most often associated with a figure of mid-dling wealth who worked his own fee-simple farm, the yeoman." [12] The term *self-made man* first appeared in 1827 but described not the business tycoon but the yeoman mechanic. [13] This idea of success was based on three major elements: competence, independence, and morality, defined as wealth somewhat beyond one's basic needs, freedom from economic or statutory subservience, and society's respect for fruitful, honest labor. In the philosophy of "enlightened self-interest" of this period, the pursuit of material gain should be balanced by a duty to society. Benjamin Franklin, who epitomized the virtues of the self-made man, argued that although a man had a natural right to the fruits of his labor, surplus profits were the creation and ultimately the property of society. The real value of a sur-plus, Franklin claimed, was its promise to do greater good for humanity. [14] Only with the rise of the Robber Barons did great wealth, competitively won, become equated with success. However, the huge fortunes, corrup-tion, scandals, and lavish lifestyles associated with the Robber Barons represented a perversion of the Protestant ethic's emphasis on thrift, tem-perance, and virtue. Thus, even the archfabulist of the self-made man, Horatio Alger, adhered to this earlier definition of success and railed against wealthy tycoons for perverting it. [15]

Barks masked yet privately acknowledged these contradictions in his depiction of Scrooge. Arguing against the commonly accepted image of Scrooge as an archcapitalist, Barks asserted, "He is the complete enemy of the capitalist system. He would destroy it in one year's time; there would no longer be any competition or free enterprise. He would freeze all the stuff that keeps capitalism going—that is, the spending of money. The faster money is spent, the more prosperity everybody has. Scrooge never spent anything, so everybody would grow progressively poorer as he accumulated more of his or her money, and in time nobody would have any money but him."[16] However, the point is that other people spend money on Scrooge's goods to enrich him. Barks's Uncle Scrooge tales often made the old duck a monopolist, but the author never addressed the issues that this raised and the "universal poverty" that he believed would result from the miser's monopoly power.[17]

Nevertheless, many of Barks's stories foreground the contradictions within capitalist ideology. Scrooge's battle with the Maharajah of Howduyustan (*WDC&S* #138 [1952]), for example, implicitly examined the conflict between the Protestant ethic of thrift and hard work and the ethos of conspicuous consumption emblematized by the ultrawealthy. The story devolves on Scrooge's attempt to prove that he is the world's richest man by battling with the Maharajah over who can build the biggest, most spectacular statue of Duckburg's founder, Cornelius Coot. The story exemplifies a number of escalation stories in which the male's desire to dominate and prove his superiority over a rival becomes progressively more ridiculous.[18] In one splash panel, Barks suggests the absurdity and wastefulness of Scrooge and the Maharajah's competition and its contradiction to an earlier, rural America: several cows look in astonishment at the tycoons' massive statues, which dominate and seem to crush the city.

In the ethos of consumer capitalism, wealth must be displayed rather than simply owned. "A crazy world!" Scrooge complains to Donald. "A man's wealth isn't what he's *got*, it's what he spends!" Consumer capitalism leads to orgies of lavish consumption epitomized by wasteful spectacles of wealth and status put on by the very rich, the story suggests. Although the tycoons begin by disguising their displays of ego behind the facade of civic giving (building statues of Cornelius Coot), their egoism is soon on display as they erect bigger and more opulent replicas of themselves. When the Maharajah is bankrupted by his lavish spending and reduced to wearing a barrel for clothes and begging to survive, Scrooge refuses to give him any money, asking Donald, "Do you think I'm a doggoned spendthrift?" Barks's story points to the ironies of wealthy elites being willing to spend millions on wasteful displays of ego but nothing to help the poor.

This story sparked Barks's editors to send him a letter of complaint from a reader. He responded, "I don't blame that woman for writing a letter afterward saying that she thought it was a gross misuse of money to build these enormous statues all crusted with diamonds when there were so many things that could have been done with the money, like building schools and better jails." Barks wrote back to the office complaining that "the woman missed the point entirely. . . . All that money had created a tremendous amount of work: work for jewelers, and goldsmiths and concrete men and the hydraulics experts. Everybody had a job out of that, so that the money hadn't been wasted any more than it if it had been used in the building of hospitals." [19]

However, the question involves priorities, not just economic expenditures. Barks seems defensive here: spending money on building hospitals would produce not only jobs but also social benefits. The main point is that this story was a satire of self-promotion and waste rather than a defense of it. But the criticism made its mark. Barks admitted that he later softened Scrooge's character because "some fan letters I saw about that time [1951] made me feel that capitalists were not too well loved." [20]

Barks's ambivalence about the success ethic carried over into the first Uncle Scrooge adventure. The artist admitted that he pried "into the old boy's past, into how he founded his fortune . . . all to prove that he deserved to be so rotten rich." [21] However, this story also critiqued the ideology of materialism and affluence that gripped America in the 1950s. Rather than offering comfort, security, and luxury, the American dream had a hollowness at its core. Scrooge's pursuit of wealth has made him a lonely, anxious, insecure old man. The tale foregrounds the way capitalism works as a necrophilic alchemy that abstracts people from their senses and alienates them from their pursuits, from other people, from nature, and even from themselves.

Scrooge's stinginess and denial of sexuality and the senses lead him to displace his erotic desires onto his money. The romance of wealth becomes the major love affair of his life. As German critic Klaus Theweleit has argued, the famous splash page of Scrooge's money dam's eruption and spewing of millions of coins into the air can be interpreted as a break-down in male fantasies of control and mastery.[22] Patriarchal capitalism erects a reductionistic concept of desire, delimiting it to a lust for profit and material objects, and constructs a fear of floods and bodies in which desire flows freely. Water, for example, has been an archetypal symbol of sexuality, and the breaking of the dam can be interpreted as a return of the repressed—the unleashing of Scrooge's libido after decades of privation.

Money traditionally has been viewed as "filthy lucre" and wallowing in it as akin to a child's playing with its own excrement. Barks retained these associations in early stories. When he first introduced Scrooge's money swim, for example, it was as a pollutant. Barks depicts Scrooge as a skinflint who threatens to foreclose on Donald because his payment was a penny short. Even though he has mounds of coins, Scrooge demands, "Hurry up and get that penny! I need it to make my pile deeper!" (WDC&S #104 [1949]). For Scrooge, wealth has become an obsessive quest of accu-mulation for its own sake, divorced from human needs and values. In this context, it's no wonder that Donald (and implicitly Barks) finds Scrooge's money swim "utterly disgusting." As a punishment for his extreme greed, rolling in his money has made Scrooge allergic to it, and he is deprived of the thing that he loves most. He is banished to a sunless cave as bereft of light and companionship as he is of humanity.

However, Barks inverts this value system in "Only a Poor Old Man." The miser's money fetishism is no longer a curse but a means of redemp-tion. Barks transforms Scrooge's love of money into a form of joy and sensual play that his miserliness once precluded. We no longer see his wealth as a form of greed but as bound to sentiments of which he had seemed incapable. Scrooge's fortune had previously seemed a sign of his unscrupulous tactics; now it came to signify his honesty and character. "I made it by being tougher than the toughies, and smarter than the smarties!" he tells the nephews, who are enraptured by his tale, "and I made it *Square!*"

The story's ending more befits a hero than the rogue he once was. He tricks the Beagle Boys into following him in a money swim, and they knock themselves out on the hard coins, allowing him to recoup his fortune. This resolution is a deus ex machina, possible only by attributing magical powers to Scrooge: "I don't explain how he does it because I don't understand it myself," Barks admitted. Throughout the tales, Scrooge has a natural affinity for money. He can do things that are impossible for ordinary mortals. He can smell the presence of precious metals, speak foreign dialects, and has a seemingly infinite amount of knowledge gained from a lifetime of experiences as an entrepreneur.

The radical individualism of the success myth rests on the fantasy that we deserve the rewards we reap because we earn them relatively unaided by others. As Lawrence Chenoweth points out, "[I]f an individual continues to have an exaggerated belief in self-reliance and unrealistic goals, he may resort to the fantasy that he is a god capable of magic powers." [23] But even Horatio Alger's heroes required both pluck and luck—in the form of aid from a wealthy benefactor—to attain success.

The money bin constitutes a central icon in Scrooge's mythology. It is initially located on a hill overlooking Duckburg and later moves to the center of town, a sign of the way Scrooge's wealth and power dominate the city and the world. Barks first named the bin "Money Barn no. 68," implying that Scrooge had other money bins all around the city (*WDC&S* #104 [1949]). Scrooge's money becomes concentrated in one spot, looking like a giant safe, a metaphor for the concentration of fabulous wealth and power in the hands of one individual. Although seemingly impenetrable, the bin's high visibility makes it open to constant attack. Barks develops it at the same time that he developed the Beagle Boys, the robbers who constitute Scrooge's chief nemeses.

The money bin is protected by a moat, radar, booby traps, and other devices. This is an apt metaphor for Fortress America in the 1950s, which embraced a paranoid vision of itself as constantly under attack by communists and other deviants. Popular culture during the 1950s was rife with fears of invasion, often by an unrepressed nature as in *Them!* a film about giant ants. In *Invasion of the Body Snatchers*, pods from outer space take over people's bodies, and in *Forbidden Planet*, "monsters from the id" menace a group of space explorers. The invasion metaphor evokes an us/them mentality and reflects the era's obsession with subversion, typified by McCarthyism. While the Soviet Union loomed as an abstract threat, the real fear was domestic subversion and the notion that America was being whittled away from within.

The money bin is a prosthetic self and can be seen as a metaphor for what Theweleit calls the armored body.[24] In masculinist psychology, body and psyche are united in erecting a psychic armor that defends against "feminine" weakness, emotional vulnerability, and softness, modes of expression that must be controlled by the rational, dominant male. Although made of solid steel, the money bin is perpetually in danger of spilling out its contents, just as the armored male is besieged by fears of the contents of his inner psyche spilling out into the outer world. Scrooge must continually defend the bin from earthquakes, cracks, eruptions, and various forms of penetration. Most often these chinks in the money bin's armor function as a return of the repressed. The bin is associated with the threat of nature, such as earthquakes caused by the Terries and Fermies (*US* #13 [1956]), moths and rats (*US* #386 [1952]), trained animals (*US* #70 [1967]), and supertermites (*US* #386 [1952]). "*My* bin and my *ground* and my *ways* will stay the same forever," he brags to himself as he looks at the citadel (*US* #15 [1956]). But this is only hubris: Scrooge must continually change the bin's location to make way for progress and exchange coins for greenbacks to try to find a place that is invulnerable, fixed, and immutable. But he never can, unmasking the masculinist illusion of a fixed, separate self.

The money bin originated in local California history. Multimillionaire financier William F. Whittier founded the town of Hemet, where Barks lived, and built the Lake Hemet Dam, creating a reservoir to supply water for the city. Barks modeled Scrooge's reservoir in "Only a Poor Old Man" after the dam, whose propensity for flooding the San Jacinto Valley may have inspired the famous money-dam explosion. Whittier's filter plant, located on the crest of Park Hill, inspired the location of Scrooge's money bin.[25] Observing a fleet of armored tanks bearing Scrooge's fortune, Donald exclaims, "They're unloading at that old water tank on Park Hill!" (*US* #493 [1953]). Like Scrooge, Whittier was a hoarder; he monopolized the water supply in Hemet to feed his developments, making it into a one-man town. As a result, Hemet became known as a "moneyed city," in contrast to its poorer neighbor, San Jacinto, a difference immortalized in Barks's "A Christmas for Shacktown" (*DD* FC #367 [1952]).

Barks juxtaposes the money world with the world of life in a number of stories. Scrooge projects his identity into objects that are hard and impervious to change to escape transience, time, and ultimately vulnerability to the natural world and relationships to others. The Midas myth in Greek mythology becomes a central mode of exploring these tensions and illusions. King Midas rules the province of Phrygia, an ancient nation in Asia Minor. In return for a favor, the god Dionysius offers to grant Midas a wish. Midas asks that all he touches be turned to gold. His wish is granted, but when he turns food, drink, and even his daughter to gold, Midas realizes that his wish was actually a curse. He now has gold without limit but at the price of life and of the daughter he loves. Trading life for money is a bad bargain, the tale implies, because life and only life gives meaning and value to money.

Barks's tales unmask the illusion of equating money with wealth, showing that life is what is most truly valuable. He first uses the Midas myth in "The Magic Hourglass" (*DD* #291 [1950]), which shows that diamonds and gold, like money, are intrinsically worthless and that life-giving water is the true wealth. "The Philosopher's Stone" (*US* #10 [1955]), deepens this contrast. Scrooge discovers the ancient alchemist's stone that turns base metals to gold and now has unlimited wealth and power. But possession of the stone threatens capitalism itself. Creating a monopoly of gold threatens to undermine the gold standard, just as excessive greed and power will undermine the market by removing all forms of competition. Possession of the magic stone also endangers Scrooge's life. His eyes become yellow and his joints stiffen as he begins to turn to gold. The miser's denial of the body leads him to turn hard, to harden his heart, and to turn him into a thing like the money and gold he worships.

"The Philosopher's Stone" reflects the unlimited power and wealth of the transnational corporations that experienced their greatest expansion after World War II.[26] Scrooge travels from country to country in search of the stone, ready to pillage each land in pursuit of unlimited profit. Like transnational corporations, which are noted for their unethical and often illegal practices in extracting foreign wealth, Scrooge is dogged by the Law, in the form of a bewhiskered little man who is the inspector of the money council. The nephews admonish their jewel-bedecked uncle, "Put those jewels back, Unca Donald! They belong to the Cretan *govern-ment!* Not *us!*" and remind Scrooge that the Philosopher's Stone belongs by law to the Cretans. Scrooge replies, "I'll file a claim for it first thing in the morning!" "Then I can use it all I like!" "Okay! Okay! that will make it *legal!*" a nephew agrees. But this is a token gesture, assuming remarkably that the government would relinquish an infinite source of wealth to any-one, let alone a foreigner. This is one of the few stories that point out that Scrooge does not have a right to indigenous wealth, a fact that is usually conveniently overlooked.

Barks's contrast of the world of money with that of life grew out of his rural roots. In "The Twenty-four Carat Moon" (*US* #25 [1958]), Muchkale is king of a moon made of solid gold whose monetary wealth Barks con-trasts with the agrarian bounty of the land. As his name implies, Muchkale is an alter ego of Scrooge who once desired to be the richest man on his world. He lives on the gold moon for eight centuries, "eating nothing, drinking nothing!" a metaphor for the deprivation that gold lust entails. He sells the moon to Scrooge for what the miser considers a steal: a lump of dirt. But the dirt is the source of true riches—that is, growing things. It provides the "seeds" out of which the king constructs an entire new world, with an atmosphere, lakes, forests, and his beloved skunk cabbage. "I *live* again!" he yells in joy. "I was quite impoverished before with only gold to work with! But now I have a *world* of my own with *food* and *drink* and *life!*" The new planet also offers a way to end his solitude and to go home to Venus. Sensual enjoyment, an appreciation of nature's bounty, and the joy of human connection are all necessary elements of human happiness, Barks claims. In a rare moment of self-reflection, Scrooge confesses, "Doggone if I don't think he got the *best* of the bargain!" To confirm his judgment, the crown falls off the head of a golden statue he has made of himself, and the miser places a dunce's cap on the figure's head.

Nevertheless, Barks's portrait of Scrooge is always ambivalent. "Back to the Klondike" (*US* FC #456 [1953]) is the first story to present Scrooge as a benevolent character and the only one to reveal a romantic side. Scrooge's egoism is shown to be a mask, which drops briefly to reveal a softer side. McDuck never admits that he has been generous to his old flame, Glittering Goldie. Only through Donald's detective work do we learn how the skinflint rigs his mining race so that Goldie might win his claim and cache of nuggets. In this way, Barks could retain Scrooge's cranky persona while showing that he had a "little bit of humanity."[27] A four-page flashback censored by Barks's editors (and restored in later reprints) works to justify Scrooge's less agreeable side. Only when he flashes the Goose Egg Nugget is his presence acknowledged and his order for coffee taken. His subsequent drugging and the theft of his gold by Goldie and her gang of thieves justifies his retaliation and fifty-year grudge against the dance hall girl.

Depicting a younger Scrooge gave Barks the chance to give the old duck a frontier toughness that he had not previously shown. On close inspection, however, the sequence reveals the tensions subtended by this characterization. The scene in which Scrooge takes on a whole roomful of ruffians gives him the invincibility of a matinee idol. With one blow, he decks an entire row of attackers; another man does double duty by falling against two additional assailants, knocking them out. The hyperbolic quality of this scene parodies the Western stereotype of the barroom brawl, where the hero begins by taking on a few outlaws but ends up in a fight involving the entire bar. The sequence reveals Scrooge as a teller of tall tales in the vein of folk heroes like Davy Crockett and Paul Bunyan. Scrooge's quarrel is with Goldie, and the fight with the other men seems both gratuitous and self-aggrandizing since it is narrated by Scrooge himself. Walking up a pile of bodies to reach Goldie, perched on the balcony, acknowledges the contrived nature of the scene and the way the old duck has exaggerated events to cast a heroic glamour over his past.

In effect, Barks shows Scrooge creating his own myth, which serves to cover up some rather shabby behavior. His insistence on teaching Goldie how hard a miner must work fits the image of the self-made man as a struggling prospector but obscures the fact that he has kidnapped her and turned her into an underpaid laborer. This detail is one of the reasons editor Alice Cobb objected to the flashback. Goldie knows that she is being exploited and protests by flinging her wages back in Scrooge's face. When Donald suggests that Scrooge invoke legal help against the feisty old lady holed up in his cabin, he admits uncomfortably that the claim is no longer legally his because he never paid back taxes on it. To regain his property, he must become a claim-jumper himself. In this way, the strands of Barks's earlier portrayal of Scrooge as an archetypal self-made man began to crumble, revealing the contradictions at its core.

Barks wrote "Back to the Klondike" on the road, sojourning in northwestern motels after having closed a difficult divorce. In Seattle, feeling at loose ends, he took to browsing bookstores. There he came across a copy of Ethel Anderson Becker's *Klondike '98*, a slim volume of vintage photographs and romantic commentary on the Klondike gold rush.[28] "Reading this is how I got off on this wild beat of having Scrooge have the big fight in the saloon, kidnap this gal, and take her out to the hills and make her work out her debt," Barks recalled.[29]

Even more than the rowdy details, Barks was influenced by the stories of instant riches that inflamed a nation's dreams and greed. "It was the last time that common people could have an adventure, other than going to war," the Duck Man observed.[30] Barks would keep returning to the theme of sudden fabulous wealth, but there was a dark side to the success myth. Most sourdoughs failed to strike it rich or lost their fortunes at the gambling table.

Having considered himself a born loser, Barks could not help wondering what had happened to the miners and misfits who never made a killing and had to scrape along in poverty after the boom subsided. Goldie represented these forgotten losers. "Nostalgia about the gold rush country and the old dance hall girls had a lot to do with my thinking on that story. There were still some dance hall girls alive and around, and they'd get a write up in the paper once in a while. I tried to make Goldie a believable person because I thought people were interested in what became of these girls." [31]

Barks's portraits of women are generally unappealing, from harridans like Daisy to ugly spinsters like Angina Arthritis to femmes fatales like Madame Triple-X. But Goldie is a figure of great dignity and sympathy. Though a scrawny old woman, she is tough and resilient, having managed to scratch out a living for fifty years on a played-out claim. If in the beginning she is the head of a gang of swindlers, she evolves into a poor but honest old lady who has given up her claim to the Blackjack Saloon to aid the orphans of deceased miners. Like Grandma Duck, Barks's only other major positive female character, Goldie is a frontier woman who possesses the "masculine" virtues of toughness, hard work, and thrift, which he admired. She represents the dark side of the gold rush and the success myth: the fact that Scrooge is the exception, not the rule, and the fact that rather than reaping rewards for their labor, the majority never realize their dreams of great wealth and status. By having a woman represent these losers, Barks could also retain the notion of the male as a rugged and successful entrepreneur.

Barks based Goldie's appearance on turn-of-the-century chanteuse and actress Lillian Russell. When Scrooge recalls his first meeting with Goldie, he remembers her singing "After the Ball," one of Russell's signature tunes. The lyrics invoke the trope of lost love and suggest Scrooge's melancholy in recalling his one flirtation with romance.

After the ball is over,
After the break of morn
After the dancers' leaving
After the stars are gone
Many a heart is aching,
Many the hopes that have vanished
After the ball.

The gown, pearls, and tiara worn by actress Alice Faye in the 1940 film *Lillian Russell* served as models for Goldie's fashions. Russell was noted for her hourglass figure, a standard for feminine beauty in the Gay Nineties. Like Goldie, who combines "masculine" toughness and self-reliance with "feminine" beauty, Russell transgressed gender binaries, shocking audiences by dressing in men's clothing and smoking cigarettes.

Barks's editors excised five pages showing the young Scrooge's epic encounter with Goldie. Barks unwittingly broke more taboos in this short sequence than in any other story. "It was quite awhile afterwards before I found out why they cut it," Barks recalled. "I got a letter from the office, or was told in my next visit to the office, that I had violated a lot of their taboos and should have had sense enough to know it wouldn't work." Barks's parody of Western brawls violated his publisher's ban against showing excessive violence. "I knew I couldn't put in much in the way of violence and it had to be comical because that didn't seem to hurt anybody." There were also objections about the seedy barroom atmosphere. "I was skeptical of whether I could get away with such a barroom atmosphere but I did it anyway for fun." [32] More objectionable was Scrooge's relationship with Goldie, whom he abducted and forced to live with him and work his claim for a month. "That was kidnapping," Barks admitted. "He picked her up and carried her out to his claim and made her go to work. . . . It didn't look like kidnapping, yet it was." Although Scrooge's actions seemed justified, "He was taking the law into his own hands, and that is not lawful." [33] In his editors' eyes, Barks had thus implicitly justified criminal behavior. Just as serious was the sequence's implication that Scrooge and Goldie might have been sexually involved. The monthlong sojourn at Scrooge's claim raised the question, "What did he do with her at night? I had really overstepped the bounds, and I realized it when the editors cut the sequence out." [34]

Barks's Klondike saga was not just a paean to the self-made man but grew out of his feelings about a bitter divorce. Clara Balken had come with him to Los Angeles when he got a job at the Disney Studio in 1935, and the two had set up housekeeping together in at small apartment near the studio. "It was that way," the artist explained. "I was still married to my first wife. I wasn't going to pay for any darned divorce. Let her pay for it." Pearl Barks eventually got a sugar daddy to pay for the decree, and Carl married Clara in 1938. However, she developed a bad drinking habit and took to abusive behavior. The Duck Man recalled, "That first Uncle Scrooge, *Uncle Scrooge* #1, I drew that in a motel down in Los Angeles, where I had taken refuge. She would have torn up my drawings and probably chopped me up with a meat cleaver or something on one of her big drunks. So I had taken all my drawings and drawing paper and skipped out, in the dark of the night, and went down there, Los Angeles, and got into that motel at the corner of Alvarado and Washington Streets." [35]

Goldie's role as a gold digger who stole Scrooge's fortune symbolized Barks's feelings about Clara: "She divorced me in 1951, took everything I had. And I paid her $250 a month alimony for 13 years." It also galled him that he paid for her entire medical expenses and even invented an artificial limb for her after she had part of her leg amputated when she was diagnosed with a cancerous mole on her foot. Barks ended up "living in a little room that they had made for me in the corner of a warehouse," not far from where he had lived with Clara. "I had two blankets that I had gotten out of the whole deal and my drawing board, of course, and my *Geographics*." [36]

Barks's acrimonious feelings about the divorce inspired not only the shysterism of lawyer Sharkey in "The Golden Helmet" (*DD* FC #408 [1952]) but also Barks's third Scrooge adventure, "The Horse-Radish Story" (*US* FC #495 [1953]). In that story, Scrooge's fortune is threatened because of an ancestor's failure to deliver a bale of horseradish a century earlier. The buyer's last descendant, Chisel McSue, bears a striking resemblance to Sharkey, and both stories deal with legal shenanigans used to try to wrest a fortune from the ducks. Echoing Barks's dispossession by his ex-wife, Scrooge faces the threat of being left with nothing but his clothes and a blanket as a result of McSue's manipulation of legal technicalities.

Barks's transition from the Donald to the Scrooge adventures reflects a change in attitude that mirrors the artist's sobering life experiences. Whereas Donald is consumed with trying (and usually failing) to make a fortune, Scrooge's first few adventures show the miser more interested in preserving than making wealth. The change in ethos marks a note of retrenchment on Barks's part. "Scrooge had his problems, trying to preserve what he had worked hard for, what had come to him by hook or crook—to the preservation of his situation. He's gotten himself a nice comfortable spot where he's wealthy and secure, and he wants to preserve that. Sure, I've come up against those problems, trying to preserve what little feeling of security that I might have accumulated. [Barks's third wife] Garé would say, 'What are you getting so damned tightwad about? Get out and spend your money.'"[37] By invoking Americans' deepest dreams and fears, Barks made Scrooge a unique and highly popular character.

In the process of softening Scrooge, Barks projected the old duck's former negative taints onto other characters. Villains become doubles of Scrooge who assume his former greed and amorality, muting these traits so that he can become a less unsympathetic and unattractive protagonist. In "The Horse-Radish Story," for example, Barks created a new ancestral line for the McDuck family, refiguring the one in "The Old Castle's Secret" that showed that Scrooge had descended from gluttons and money fetishists. He now became the descendant of an honest sea captain, Seafoam McDuck, who had been cheated out of all his possessions because he could not read the fine print on a contract to deliver a bale of horseradish. Scrooge's former capitalist ruthlessness is projected onto villain Chisel McSue, who possesses the duck's Scottish ancestry and like him is "the last of his line." Whereas McDuck had been a hard-hearted moneylender who repossessed a poor laundry woman's washing machine because she owed a nickel (*WDC&S* #124 [1951]), "The Horse-Radish Story" hinges on a financial agreement by a ruthless shylock who tries to appropriate Scrooge's entire fortune because of an ancient contract for an insignificant debt.

Barks intentionally set out to make "Scrooge more likable" in this story. Even though McSue tries to kill the ducks and saving him apparently will cause Scrooge to lose his fortune, the old miser has a pang of conscience at the last minute and rescues him from drowning. "If I had the nephews tie Scrooge down so that they could rescue the crook, you wouldn't have had much sympathy for Scrooge, but the fact that he helped to rescue the guy and got kicked in the face made him sweet."[38] Scrooge's later antagonist, Flintheart Glomgold, is an even more obvious double of Scrooge, down to his look-alike appearance, spats, money bin, and tightwad persona. But in their battle to determine who is the world's richest duck, Glomgold shows a ruthlessness that Scrooge abjures (*US* #15 [1956], #27 [1959]).

Barks continued this process of projection and displacement in his next Scrooge adventure, "Menehune Mystery" (*US* #4 [1954]), in which the Beagle Boys pose as sailors and take over Scrooge's ship. In Hawaii, they make the ducks into virtual slaves who do all the work while the thugs loaf. This narrative inverts the traditional image of capitalist and worker, transforming the capitalist into the one who is exploited and whose labor is appropriated while the Beagles act the part of a leisure class. Scrooge and the ducks receive the imprimatur of nature. They are rescued by the Menehunes, elfin people in native garb who are invisible except when seen in a mirror. Garé Williams, whom Barks married in 1954, suggested the story. She had grown up in Hawaii and was intimately familiar with the legends of native little people.

In the late 1940s, Barks had depicted Scrooge as a ruthless plantation owner in Africa (*DD* FC #238 [1949]) and in the 1950s had made the old man a symbol of western colonialism's destruction of native cultures by introducing a money economy into their society (*US* #6 [1954]). In the next Scrooge adventure, the artist virtually rewrote the history of the West's conquest of indigenous peoples, displacing Scrooge's—and by implication, western imperialism's—role in their demise by displacing it onto the Beagles.

"The Seven Cities of Cibola" (*US* #7 [1955]) was the first Uncle Scrooge treasure hunt. It was inspired by Barks's visit to his friend, Al Koch, manager of the Riverside welfare office in Indio, California. Koch was an authority on local Indian tribes and told Barks about an old Indian trail near Thousand Palms. Barks explored the trail and decided to use it to set the ducks on the road to Cibola. As a form of acknowledgment, the artist drew Koch into the story, kicking the Beagle Boys out of the welfare office.

Musing over the idea the next day, Barks felt that he only had enough material for a ten-page story. Then, in a restaurant, he overheard an old rancher's windy yarn about the Lost Ship of the Desert. Though he knew the tale was bogus, Barks felt that the legend would provide a good vehicle for developing his story. Researching the details, he found that "little accounts had cropped up in the paper every once in a while of people who were delirious from thirst who saw the ship. I found that at one time it was believed to have been a ship lost from a survey party going up the Colorado, and at another time it was believed to be a flat-bottomed barge that got picked up by a tidal wave generated by an earthquake. There was an earthquake in the very early 1800s that might have accounted for that one. . . . I figured I could go to town on that idea because nobody could say I was wrong."[39] Further research revealed that a Spanish galleon had actually disappeared up the Colorado, and Barks only needed to move the earthquake back two hundred years to make the story cohere. To lend his account credibility, he invoked the name of an actual Spanish captain, Francisco de Ulloa, who had explored the area and suffered storm damage to one of his ships.

Even before the discovery of the New World, Europeans had been entranced by dreams of finding El Dorado, of cities harboring vast quantities of riches and streets paved with bricks of gold. In March 1536, a party of Spaniards scouting the Gulf of Mexico encountered a half-naked white man, Álvar Núñez Cabeza de Vaca, who claimed that somewhere in the desert lay a fabulous city in which the inhabitants lived in great houses decorated with jewels and possessed unlimited quantities of gold. In 1539 a Franciscan monk, Fray Marcos de Niza, claimed to have found the fabled cities, and an expedition headed by Francisco de Coronado was mounted in 1540. Coronado did find and conquer Cibola, but the Seven Cities turned out to be small mud pueblos and cliff dwellings in what is now called the Zuni Pueblo. The Spaniards searched in vain throughout the Southwest for the fabled cities of gold but left for Spain broken and disillusioned.

In Barks's tale, Donald dismisses the legend of cities paved with gold: "Aw! that story was a *fake!* The seven cities were found to be poor *mud pueblos!*" But Barks reversed the history of the villages, embracing colonial fantasies rather than the facts. Barks's story works to efface and displace the West's responsibility for colonial depredations, projecting them onto the canine criminals. He presents the Beagles as alter egos of Scrooge who represent the dark side of his money fetishism. Barks establishes the parallelism by cutting back and forth between the two groups. The ducks and the robbers clink their glasses simultaneously in a toast to the expedition and traverse the same route to the cities. The Beagles first show themselves to their adversaries dressed as conquistadors, displacing the narrative away from Scrooge as a representative of western imperialism. And, when the Beagles discover a bin of jewels in the fabled cities, they dive into it, aping Scrooge's fabled money swim. Scrooge's cupidity almost leads him to grab the emerald idol that contains a device that will pulverize the Seven Cities, but the nephews stop him, recognizing the danger. As if to complete Scrooge's action, the greedy Beagles seize the statue and trip the booby trap.

This story is unusually inactive. We never meet the inhabitants of Cibola: they survive only as a ghostly presence knowable through the traces they have left behind. We see them only in the scratchy drawings on the canyon walls. The story shows that they have died of disease. The only action in the story comes in a return of the repressed: when the Beagles trip the booby trap, it releases a huge rock that destroys the entire city, fulfilling the natives' revenge for the criminals' invasion and attempted dispossession of their wealth. The Cibolans function as an absent center, allowing Barks to repress the genocide that has caused their decline. Contrary to Barks's tale, the natives did not die of disease, although many were killed by the invaders. They were enslaved and forced to pay tribute to Spanish settlers and to become Christians. In 1680, a pueblo religious leader named Popé organized a revolt against the Spanish, killing about a quarter of the Spanish population, although the invaders reconquered the region in 1692. The clash of cultures established the beginning of almost five hundred years of Europeans' mistreatment of Indians in the Southwest. Although Barks's story occludes the history of western colonialism, in the end it opposes neocolonial dispossession: neither the ducks nor the Beagles can remember anything about the cities, and both groups fail to be rewarded for their attempted theft of the Cibolans' treasure. The lust for fabulous wealth and imperial conquest is only a fevered dream.

During the twenty-year run of Uncle Scrooge stories, the Beagle Boys are the miser's most frequently used villains and chief bêtes noires. The artist claimed that they were inspired by the Mafia and were "kind of a play on Capone's gang and the different bunch of hoodlums around the country." [40] Like the Mafia, the Beagle Boys are a family comprising an organized criminal gang; indeed, they are the only complete family in the Duck comics and have the biological relations (father and grandfather) denied to Donald and his kin. However, befitting a Disney comic, the Beagles never use guns and never harm Scrooge.

Dorfman and Mattelart interpret the Beagle Boys as proletarians and muted agents of class struggle, writing, "Disney can conceive of no other threat to wealth than theft. His obsessive need to criminalize any person who infringes the laws of private property invites us to look at these villains more closely. The darkness of their skin, their ugliness, the disorder of their dress, their stature, their reduction to numerical categories, their mob-like character . . . all add up to a stereotypical stigmatization of the bosses' real enemy, the one who truly threatens his property." They add, "This caricature of workers, which twists every characteristic capable of lending them dignity and respect, and thereby identity as a social class, turns them into a spectacle of mockery and contempt." [41] They become infantilized as naughty children who are always beaten.

With bulky bodies and unshaven faces, the Beagles appear at first glance to fall into the pop culture stereotype of the dimwitted proletarian who uses brute force in his crimes and always fails in the end. However, they do not represent muscle versus the bourgeoisie's brains, as Dorfman and Mattelart claim, but are instead fairly intelligent, using high-tech weapons and ingenious schemes to rob Scrooge. [42] They even earn doctorates while being imprisoned (US #65 [1966]). Nor is there any evidence of class struggle: they are never shown as exploited or downtrodden but on the contrary want to exploit Scrooge. They want to steal Scrooge's money, not overthrow capitalism. Indeed, in some stories they reveal that they want to protect Scrooge—and by implication capitalism—as a way of making money for them to live on (*US* #70 [1967]). Their aim is not primarily wealth but to live without working. Thus, they represent the antithesis of Barks's affirmation of the work ethic.

The Beagle Boys embody Barks's conservative beliefs and animus against the welfare state. As mentioned previously, in "The Seven Cities of Cibola," they are welfare cheats whom Al Koch kicks out of the welfare office because of their refusal to work. And in "The Doom Diamond" (*US* #70 [1967]), they are loafers, complaining, "Ho Hum! We haven't robbed a bank since labor day!" as their trained blue jays steal coins from Scrooge's money bin while they idly play pool. However, contrary to Barks's conservative ideology, the Beagles are as diligent, innovative, and industrious in trying to steal Scrooge's loot as any apostle of the work ethic.

Conservative ideology castigates liberals for their endorsement of federal regulation, tax-and-spend policies, and championing of big government. The Beagle Boys embody the antithesis of this conservative ideology, representing forces of collectivism that were believed to be undermining the individualism, independence, and work ethic symbolized by entrepreneurs such as Scrooge. They are interchangeable organization men distinguishable only by the different prison numbers on their chests, which change surreally from story to story. Indeed, they are members of a secret, conspiratorial corporation, as evidenced by the "Inc." emblazoned on their sweatshirts. They are emblems of groupthink who function like a single organism and sing, dance, and worry in unison. Even their prison numbers are permutations of each other. Reflecting their innate criminal nature, they always wear their masks and prison togs, even when they are not incarcerated.

Criminal organizations have existed for centuries, but fictional narratives about organized crime are a recent phenomenon. Even the nation's most highly publicized crime fighter, J. Edgar Hoover, denied the existence of a national crime organization until the mid-1950s. Since then, the fantasy of an all-powerful criminal organization has become increasingly popular, looming ominously from the pages of senatorial investigations, popular novels, and films, reaching its apogee in the late 1960s and 1970s in the *Godfather* novels and films. This new crime formula "ambiguously mirrors a world in which the individualistic ethos no longer satisfactorily explains and orders society for most members of the public. The new center of value is the large organization and its collective power." [43] The drama of the criminal gang has become a kind of allegory of the corporation and corporate society. The Beagles represent a corporate mentality onto whom are projected traits denied in Scrooge. In this way, Barks could preserve Scrooge's identity as an individualistic entrepreneur even though he is a corporate monopolist who threatens free enterprise.

The Beagle Boys are also members of a union, what conservatives see as an archcollectivist and anticapitalist organization. Thus, they embody Barks's antiunion biases. One of Barks's pig-faced villains, Porkman de Lardo, hires them from the "Burglars, Thugs, and Pirates Union, Local 6½" to hijack Scrooge's money convoy (*US* #41 [1963]). The pirates' insistence on being paid more for their thievery expresses the conservative shibboleth that unions create inflated wages. "We're union pirates, we demand the union scale!" the Beagles tell de Lardo.

Antiunion humor is a continual theme in Barks's work. When Donald and Scrooge spy on Martians trying to retrofit their flying saucers, Scrooge exclaims, "They don't seem like union members! Never saw a shop steward letting a workman use four wrenches at once!" (*US* #46 [1963]). In conservative ideology, unions create slowdowns and unreasonably limit production so that wages will not be undermined. In "Dangerous Disguise" (*DD* FC #308 [1951]), trainmen abruptly stop and leave their locomotive in the middle of nowhere because the union has called a strike. Ironically, the train stops just before running over Donald's neck while he sleeps after being drugged by Madame Triple-X. The mayor yells at the workers to derail the careening, runaway locomotive, but the switchmen refuse because they are on strike. Barks saw union workers as slackers and strikes as selfish and potentially dangerous.

This sentiment went back at least as far as the 1941 Disney strike. "I wasn't affected by the strike," Barks noted. "The story department wasn't striking. It was the animators and in-betweeners who were striking." Yet his conservative philosophy made him oppose the attempt to unionize the studio: "I was against the strike myself. I felt that they were destroying something there. The Disney Studios were a place where there were no time clocks—you would come to work when you felt like it in the morning, and if you attended to your job and worked well and did plenty, you got paid darn well. If you were one of the shirkers and a complainer and all, why, you would never get a raise. So it was the shirkers and complainers who had organized the strike." [44] However, dismissing the strikers as "shirkers" and "complainers" discounts the important issues of low wages, arbitrary pay scales, lack of credit, and favoritism raised by the strike. [45] Approximately half of the employees at the studio struck, revealing widespread discontent at the fantasy factory. Although a company union existed, it failed to bargain for Disney workers, and thus an industry-wide union was needed.

With the coming of the 1960s, Barks became more reactionary, dismayed at the transformation taking place in American society. During this period the U.S. Supreme Court was led by noted liberal, Earl Warren, and between 1963 and the early 1970s, the Warren Court issued a number of decisions that increased the rights of criminal suspects, causing conservatives to launch an unsuccessful campaign to have him impeached and thrown out of office. "My contempt for the 'Warren Court' is of nauseating proportions," Barks wrote to Mike Barrier in 1967. [46] In his later stories, Barks made the Beagle Boys into an emblem of a permissive America that took on conspiratorial dimensions: "The Beagle Boys represent the over-privileged criminal class that controls most of America's courts and legislatures and schools and entertainment media," he wrote to an Italian interviewer in 1973. [47]

One of Barks's shibboleths, stemming from his cynical view of human nature, had been that it was impossible to reform a bad man, and his later stories lampooned liberal beliefs of rehabilitation and lenience toward criminals. In "The Giant Robot Robbers" (US #58 [1965]), for example, the mayor has built a number of huge robots to "ease man's burdens." Echoing Barks's Republican beliefs and cynicism about progress, Scrooge complains of the taxes used to build such seemingly unnecessary machines. The story centers on a satire of the way liberal permissiveness has undermined law and order. When the Beagles capture the robots and go on a crime spree, the mayor refuses to let the police stop them for fear of damaging the enormously expensive devices. "Alas!" sighs one cop, "This is the darkest day in the history of law and order!"[48]

Barks's ultimate satire of permissiveness toward crime is "House of Haunts" (US #63 [1965]). In the story's opening, the Beagles recline in prison, studying for advanced degrees so that they can use their new abilities to create more ingenious ways to rob Scrooge. Barks's editor, Chase Craig, found the story troubling: "Your story synopsis sounds fine! The only thing that did not sound good to me was your reference to the Beagle Boys learning all kinds of new crime tricks while attending prison school. The idea of teaching crime in prison does not sound very well for our law-enforcing friends. You no doubt have something else in mind here, but the way I read it would put our prisons in a rather bad light. Why not just have the boys going to crook school somewhere and Scrooge gets word that they're about to graduate, etc.?"[49] In Barks's published version, the Beagles attend the "Studious Hours" prison school and instead of being educated by other crooks learn honest, high-tech trades from the warden, applying them to stealing Scrooge's money.

Since his *Calgary Eye-Opener* days, Barks had found judges and courts a fertile ground for humor. After the Beagles are apprehended for their crimes in this story, the judge asks, "How many times have I sentenced you ruffians to be released?" to find that they have been set free ten times. "I sentence you to be re-re-rehabilitated again!" he gasps in a fit of exasperation. "Golly!" a Beagle Boy replies, head down in guilt, "They sure take a lot of trouble with us naughty boys!" In Barks's universe, the rehabilitation of criminals is an oxymoron.

However, Barks's stories are polyvocal and can be read in different ways by different people. Befitting a Disney comic, the Beagles are not murderous felons but "naughty boys," charming rogues whose crimes are games with a well-matched adversary. As Disney comics became more sedate under the increased censorship of the 1950s, the Beagle Boys took on the rebellious impulses that were now disallowed in the nephews, tormenting Scrooge much as the nephews had once plagued Donald. The Beagles became rebels against capital and paternal authority, inventing increasingly ingenious schemes to rob Scrooge of his wealth and depose him from his patriarchal power.

The Beagles' appeal was not lost on readers. In 1953, when the Scrooge adventures were just getting under way, an enthusiastic twelve-year-old fan named Richard Greenberg wrote to the studio requesting permission to form a national Beagle Boys fan club. The idea had occurred to him from reading the scene from the backup story in the third Scrooge adventure in which the Beagles almost get away with stealing the old miser's money vault, now a steel drum, by rolling it down a hill. The thought of a Disney fan club for criminals, inspired by the depiction of an almost successful robbery, was anathema to Disney officials. Frank Reilly, then head of the studio's comic strip department, wrote Greenberg a discouraging reply:

> We are happy to learn of your high opinion of the Walt Disney comic maga-
> zines, especially the one featuring the antics of Donald, his nephews and Uncle
> Scrooge McDuck. . . . About your suggestion for forming a Beagle Boys fan
> club, however, we are not so happy. We will be frank to say that we do not think
> it is a very good idea. . . . While only comic characters, the Beagle Boys are
> designed to cause trouble for Donald and the others. In practically all books,
> movies, plays, comics, etc., the story is built around the conflict between right
> and wrong, between the heroes and the villains. In Scrooge McDuck stories the
> Beagle Boys represent the wrong; they are the villains. They are the lawless ones
> who have no regard for the possessions of other people. We believe it would be
> wrong for you and your friends to identify yourselves with wrongdoers, even
> though they are merely comic creations. A Beagle Boys fan club could possibly
> lead to some mischievous and irresponsible actions by lads too young to realize
> that they are emulating lawlessness.[50]

Though he acknowledged that the Beagle Boys were only fictional cre-
ations, Reilly followed comic censors' simplistic argument that portrayals of crime in comics caused juvenile delinquency. He also ignored the fact that Barks was careful to show that the Beagles' crimes always led to their downfall and often to their arrest and imprisonment. Barks's editors were not blind to these facts and were sympathetic to fans who wanted to enjoy the Beagles' escapades as harmless fun. In this spirit, Carl Buettner sent Barks copies of both letters and commented, "I am considering writing Master Greenberg myself, applying for membership."[51]

The treasure hunt motif undergoes a marked change in the late 1950s. For the most part Barks avoided overt representations of politics in his comics, omitting anything his editors might consider controversial. However, the artist was not operating in a vacuum and was affected by shifts in modern American social and cultural currents. His stories of the late 1950s, for example, register the changes in international relations that were transforming the face of geopolitics. In the late 1950s and early 1960s, the struggle between capitalism and communism shifted to the site of what came to be called the Third World. The postwar era was marked by the rise of anticolonial and nationalist revolutions that began in China and Southeast Asia and spread to Africa and Latin America. The communist victory in China in 1949 signaled that Third World nations could follow another model of economic development besides capitalism, and many began flirting with or embracing socialism. As a result, the United States became involved in an internecine struggle with the Soviets to win the hearts and minds of the peoples of developing nations.

Part of the reason for this shift was a change in Russian leadership. In 1953, Soviet dictator Joseph Stalin died. In the mid-1950s, new Russian leader Nikita Khrushchev became a famous figure on the world stage. In "Dangerous Disguise," Ironland had been Barks's name for the Soviet Union. When Donald's double is unmasked as a spy, he commits suicide rather than being sent to the salt mines by Brutus, a thinly veiled reference to Stalin. "Brutopia" became Barks's satire of the Soviet Union under Khrushchev.

At this time the worst of the anticommunist hysteria in America had abated, and the Cold War had devolved into a stalemate maintained through the threat of mutual destruction if either side unleashed its nuclear arsenal. In 1954, following the United States by several years, the Soviets tested their first hydrogen bomb, escalating the danger of nuclear holocaust while simultaneously keeping the arms race in murderous balance.

"A Cold Bargain" (US #17 [1957]) negotiates the anxieties surrounding this situation. The contentious competition for the world's supply of Bombastium at an auction lures Scrooge into the bidding against a corpulent Eastern European arms merchant. Barks claimed that he only intended to portray a generic arms dealer: "Was the Brutopian ambassador anybody in particular? Nope. He was a composite of power-hungry arms buyers from many nations. I should have probably given him the face of one of my sneering pig villains that appeared a lot in later years, but I wanted to make him look compositely international." [52]

Barks's desire to portray the arms merchant as a generic foreigner may have resulted from an attempt to avoid the taboo on precise political identification. However, the character's bulky build, bald dome, thick eyebrows, and high cheekbones mark him as Russian—more particularly, as Khrushchev himself. [53] The Soviet leader became famous for his temper and boorishness, such as pounding the table with his fists and interrupting speakers at the UN. In 1956, he told western diplomats, "We will bury you," giving him a belligerent persona. [54] Barks recycled this negative image. When Scrooge wins the bid, the Brutopian calls him a "rich pig of a duck," indexing the Soviet's anticapitalist ethos. The Brutopian's bid of one trillion dollars plus "all the kitchen sinks of its happy people" references Barks's satire of the Soviet Union as a despotic dystopia.

Bombastium represents a play on words (bomb and bombastic) that negotiates Cold War hysteria surrounding the arms race and the threat of Armageddon provoked by the development of the H-bomb. [55] Barks's tale is also grounded in fears about radioactive fallout. Although the dangers of nuclear fallout had been known for years, in 1954 the U.S. test of a hydrogen bomb in the archipelago of Bikini made fallout a significant public concern for the first time in America. American officials attempted to reassure the populace that those outside the test area were safe, but radioactive strontium 90 had been found in the food supply, and Japanese crewmen on an ironically named fishing boat, the *Lucky Dragon*, had been charred by the blast. [56]

Like radioactive material, which is stored in cooling pools to keep it from overheating, Bombastium has to be kept frozen, lest it "melt down." Scrooge's mad dash after the ball when it escapes into the city reflects Americans' fears of radioactive fallout gone out of control. When Scrooge takes the ball to the North Pole to prevent it from melting, the

Brutopian appears with a military submarine and steals the Bombastium. "What Brutopia wants, Brutopia *takes!*" he declares. Barks's portrayal of the Brutopians as bent on world conquest reflects Cold War ideology. The Brutopian wants the rare element to further his country's desire for world domination, and he disgustedly abandons the ball when he learns that it is good only for making multiflavored ice cream. Indeed, throughout the story the ball looks suspiciously like sherbet. "In Brutopia the happy people *do not eat ice cream!*" he growls. Scrooge triumphs in the end, selling the Bombastium for double the trillion he paid for it to the Leaky Ice Cream Company. As in the film *Ninotchka* (1939), socialism is shown to be a dour and puritanical ideology, inferior to the hedonism of American consumer culture.

The mother, whose existence is repressed in Disney comics, is the vehicle for saving the day. Scrooge's victory represents a triumph of nature and the nuclear family. When Scrooge loses the ball in the snow, it is recovered by a bereaved mother penguin who thinks it is her lost egg: "My trillion dollars is back in the family again!" Scrooge crows. In the end, Scrooge manifests a sentimental streak that demonstrates his harmony with nature. Standing apart from a group who wouldn't consider bidding on a "worthless" egg, Scrooge performs his annual ritual of buying hen fruit as a gift for the penguin, demonstrating that friendship, even with an animal, is more important than making money. However, given that he had been driven by profit throughout the story, this is a tokenistic gesture.

In "Ancient Persia" (*DD* FC #275 [1950]), Barks had presented a stark and terrifying image of radiation fallout. But in this story he turns the danger into cathartic comedy. The increased atmosphere of censorship in the mid-1950s undoubtedly made the topic of radiation too hot to handle. Moreover, Barks's portrait of the Soviet Union as bent on world conquest reiterates Cold War stereotypes that occlude the ambiguities of Khrushchev's regime. In reality, Khrushchev was responsible for liberalizing the Soviet Union and shocked Soviet leaders by denouncing and condemning Stalin for fostering a "cult of personality" and the mass murder of thousands of suspected dissidents. Perhaps because of the Soviet Union's position of economic and military inferiority, Khrushchev advocated "peaceful coexistence" with the West and participated in arms reduction talks with U.S. Presidents Dwight D. Eisenhower and John F. Kennedy.

The Scrooge adventures of the late 1950s often conclude with Scrooge undergoing a change of heart, usually provoked by the nephews, admitting his humanity, and generously giving up part of his riches to the needy. In "Pipeline to Danger" (US #30 [1960]), for example, Scrooge invades the pygmy Arabs of Casbah Crater with his giant tractors and sandcats to build a reservoir to store his oil. A self-proclaimed "big operator," he disdains "little operators" like the nephews and unknowingly threatens to inundate the Arab village. To protect their homes, the Arabs sabotage his machines. Taken to their village, he learns of their plight and is shamed into realizing that his moral blindness has made him a "little operator." When the nephews rescue him, he comes to the Arabs' aid and turns their desert wasteland into a lush garden. "I suppose I was making a comparison between happy hidden civilizations and unhappy uncivilization," Barks commented. "Those idyllic civilizations of euphoric imagination were idyllic only because they were simple in political structure, and peopled by citizens whose minds all followed the same set of simple principles. To introduce them to Duckburg's greeds and hates and pushiness was like infecting them with cancer." [57]

This story utilizes the pastoral imagery of earlier little people tales but has some notable differences. Unlike those stories, the Arabs' home is not a paradisiacal valley but a wasteland that Scrooge must turn into a garden. This moral shift is signaled by a physical change in the foreigners' stature. In earlier tales, preindustrial little folk had been closer to the ducks in size and could easily overpower them. By making the little people tiny in this story, Barks emphasized their vulnerability, and a paternalistic, even imperialistic tone crept into his tales. Although earlier native communities had been self-sufficient, in this adventure they would have remained impoverished without Scrooge's aid.

These changes register the transformation of U.S. foreign policy in the postcolonial era. The Eisenhower and Kennedy administrations abandoned traditional policies and military strategies in the Third World. U.S. leaders decided that America must fight covert wars to stem the tide of nationalist resistance movements and put increased amounts of aid into the hands of indigenous elites to secure their countries' loyalties.

The prospect of modern capitalism flooding traditional cultures had already been the subject of two Scrooge adventures (*US* #6 [1954], #26 [1959]). A year after Barks wrote "Pipeline to Danger," he planned to use a similar idea for an Egyptian Scrooge adventure: "I'm kind of mulling over the idea of having him take a contract to move the ancient Egyptian palaces and statues that are threatened with flooding by the Aswan Dam. Naturally he finds a hidden shaft leading down into the bowels of history, and therein finds uncountable sparklers. The rains come early to the Ethiopian highlands, mighty floods rush down the Nile toward the newly completed dam. The shaft and all the toiling ducks in the awesome treasure pits will be submerged as the roiling torrent slams against the unyielding barrier of the towering new dam."[58] This concise summary is all that survives of Barks's idea: "I changed my mind about the Aswan Dam plot," he wrote to a fan. "It would have followed too soon after the Sahara locale featured in the 'Pipeline to Danger' story."[59] Many years later, however, he gave a different explanation for shelving the story: "I never finished the script. . . . [T]he project had become so messy with politics that I was afraid to risk it."[60]

Other political currents proved more hospitable to Disney storytelling. In 1957, the Soviet Union launched Sputnik I and II, becoming the first nation to put satellites into orbit around the Earth. The Soviet lead in the space race caused a mood of U.S. national malaise and self-questioning as shocked Americans learned that a country they regarded as primitive and totalitarian could take the lead in science and technology. For Barks, however, the launches became grist for several new Uncle Scrooge adventures. In "The Twenty-four Carat Moon" (*US* #24 [1958]), he portrayed Scrooge, the Beagles, and an Indian maharajah in a race for space riches. "Island in the Sky" (*US* #29 [1960]), another little people story, features a futuristic Duckburg with flying buses, jumping autos, and pneumatic tubes that zap carpools of commuters to the suburbs in minutes. Scrooge is involved in this race to colonize space, seeking to find and claim a deserted planetoid where he can hide his money from "snoopers."

It had been common to conflate America's colonization of outer space with its conquest of the frontier. Thus, the film *Zardoz* was a remake of the Gary Cooper Western *High Noon*, while *Star Trek* invoked space as the "final frontier." The same metaphor also played a central role in President Kennedy's political platform, which he dubbed the New Frontier. Barks draws on this imagery in "Island in the Sky." "What a beautiful sight!" Scrooge exclaims as he spots the space wheel where he wants to refuel, "like Fort Laramie must have looked to the pioneer wagon trains!"

The ducks land on a large, uninhabited planetoid that is teeming with trees, birds, fish, and fruit—a "plush paradise." Barks again uses the archetypal image of the garden to describe a tribal culture, but this time with a surprising twist. Across the chasm of space is a small, barren asteroid, the perfect place for the tycoon to hide his hoard. However, it is inhabited by pygmy Indians who worship the ducks and bow down to them "like the American savages kneeled to Columbus." In drawing on this analogy, Barks re-creates the history of western colonization of America with aliens representing Native Americans. Indeed, they sport grass skirts, feather headdresses, and Mohawk haircuts, and the ducks call them "Apaches" and "Siwashes." In a fit of bravado, Donald tries to scare the natives off by firing his gun in the air. Instead, however, he frightens away a population of birds whose eggs are the asteroid Apaches' only food supply, much as frontier Americans killed off the buffalo, destroying the Plains Indians' means of subsistence.

By inaugurating covert wars and attempting to win the hearts and minds of Third Worlders to wean them away from the attractions of socialism, Americans had to confront the evils of colonialism and imperialism that the West had perpetrated and continued to perpetrate. Thus, it is appropriate that the narrative in this story trades on Scrooge assuaging feelings of guilt over his miscreant acts, and he decides that he must make amends to the natives by creating a tightrope so that they can navigate from one planet to the other. In the process, he uses so much fuel that he has to fill up at the space station, paying their exorbitant rates.

Barks's intent in this story was to portray the plight of the impoverished: "It gave me the chance to have Uncle Scrooge finally relent and do something to repay the damage he and his nephews had done." The author elaborated, "It was a situation that is very much duplicated in real life, where the people who have nothing are always in sight of plenty but unable to reach it. That is one of the things that causes so many of our social problems. The people that have nothing have such a difficult time getting anything. It can be passing by in big Cadillacs in front of them, but they can't have any of it because of some barrier between them and it." [61] However, Barks's solution is anodyne. He makes the barrier between classes physical rather than social, and Scrooge can cross it merely by providing the Apaches a lifeline to the adjacent planet. Consequently, no transformation of the economic structure is necessary: the only solution possible is individual philanthropy.

This solution is a metaphor for offering reparations to dispossessed and slaughtered Native Americans. [62] The story negotiates guilt about the colonization of the Third World and the nations whose traditional cultures Barks so admired. Barks's portrait of Indians reiterates the imperialist tone discussed previously. They are "savages," in the ducks' words, with virtually no language or culture (they make only primitive sounds like "nik, nik"), and would die without the ducks' intervention. Nevertheless, in recasting the genocide of Native Americans as lying at the heart of frontier development and by analogizing it to the colonization of Third World "natives," Barks's story invokes a potentially progressive critique of western modernity.

Barks's imperialist tone in these stories may have arisen from his increasing disillusionment about preserving traditional cultures. From the late 1950s onward, the Scrooge adventures express skepticism about the hope of finding a self-contained Eden isolated from civilization. "Prize of Pizarro" (US #26 [1959]) expresses this motif. Scrooge donates a Spanish galleon to Duckburg to commemorate the Spanish conquest of the New World. History has become a spectacle of consumption, the story shows, with the mayor, city council, the town's children, and other citizens agog over being able to board the ancient vessel but showing no interest in its past.

The ducks set off to the Andes on a search for a hidden Inca gold mine, in effect reenacting the journey of the conquistadors. In previous stories, Barks led the reader to gape at the spectacle of a pastoral valley protected from the corrupting effects of civilization. In this story, however, the hidden oasis is dominated by booby traps. The natives have been corrupted by a desire to join the modern world. "Let's *quit* this boring body guard job and go down to Cuzco and live like *other people!*" a young guard exclaims. Another brags, flexing his muscles, "Yeah, man! Let's join the army and show the emperor what *brave* soldiers we are!" In earlier adventures, the ducks encountered and were transformed by denizens of the past; this time, the Indians can hear and see the ducks, but the ducks cannot see or hear them. Past and present have been irreparably severed, and communication between them is no longer possible; modernity is irrevocably cut off from tradition, and tribal culture no longer offers an alternative vision to modern life.

Neither side can live up to its former glamour. The ducks don the armor of the conquistadores but evince none of their presumed bravery. The ducks evade the Indians' booby traps only because they are too short to be destroyed by them. As Lonnie McAllister notes, the ducks look like walking teakettles, mocking the heroic stature of the colonial hero.[63] "Give us *men* that are worthy of our booby traps!" the guardsman groans. The natives, too, lack valor. For all their bragging, they dive behind the rocks when they hear the ducks coming and run like frightened children when Donald fires a shot in celebration of finding the lost Inca mine. The Indians spring their last booby trap, hoping to rid themselves of the invaders, but only manage to wash their enemies and the gold out of the tunnel. Although the paradisiacal valley remains unharmed, the guardsmen can think only in capitalist terms: "Pan 400 years of back *wages* out of this sand, guardsmen and take to the hills! I've got a strong hunch we're *out of a job!*" The gold floods the city, proving worthless as usual in Barks's cosmology, flooding the town's electric plant and leaving the people with no heat or light. "Down to ten cents a ton," says a citizen. Unlike earlier tales, Scrooge cannot return the people to the land he has despoiled. Fearing that he will be sued for ruining the city, Scrooge muses, "When will I ever learn to leave other people's *mail* alone?"

In later Scrooge adventures, Barks comes to depict McDuck's stinginess and love of money as an eccentricity rather than a character fault, thereby further occluding the miser's greed. In "City beneath the Sea" (*US* #46 [1963]), for example, Scrooge blithely declares his intention to "buy Mt. Everest, the Taj Mahal, and Hong Kong, and move them to my amusement park in Duckburg!" This would entail ecological catastrophe and the rape of both natural resources and national treasures for the sake of creating more trivialized entertainment for Americans. But it is only a toss-off joke, and its calamitous consequences are never shown. Rather, the plot is displaced onto the effects of the Martians' exhaustion of their environment, a surrogate for global capitalism's depletion of earth's natural resources through its quest for profits.

In Barks's last little people story, "Micro-Ducks from Outer Space" (US #65 [1966]), the once avaricious miser has suddenly become an exemplar of the honest businessman. He meticulously gives exact change to the micro-ducks, proving himself the exception to their belief that earthlings are all "*Robbers and monsters.*" But Barks decontextualizes the little people in this story. Unlike earlier pastoral tales rooted in history and local culture, the micro-ducks are aliens from outer space, allowing Barks to elide the colonial past and war-torn present of Third World nations.

Yet like Barks's other little people tales, this story expresses utopian longings and a populist message: The micro-ducks are surrogates for Earth's "little people," who possess no great wealth but deserve the honor and respect of the rich and powerful. Scrooge comes to value the small deal of selling each micro-duck three kernels of grain and corn rather than the megamillions that usually lure him. Scrooge starts out desiring to use the micro-ducks to make a billion dollars by proving to the Skeptics Club that aliens and flying saucers really exist. But he becomes more interested in honesty and fairness than in making a large profit and professes faith in the aliens, in contrast to the skeptics' cynical debunking of beliefs. In the sentimental conclusion, Scrooge has lost a billion dollars because of his inability to make the aliens visible to the Skeptics Club, but he awaits the space people's return, when he can make that "*big deal* eight years from now . . . to buy *twenty kernels of corn!*"

Portraying Scrooge as the exception to amoral capitalism showed how far Barks had departed from his original concept of the miser and how much the Duck Man's critique of capitalism had atrophied in later adventures. Barks emphasizes Scrooge's personal morality while ignoring the structure of capitalist oppression that guides his financial decisions. This makes for a muddled portrait: Scrooge is seemingly out of place in a world dominated by greed and skepticism yet governed by an obsession for accumulating wealth, both the apotheosis and antithesis of corporate capital. In this way, Barks attempted to reconcile the contradictions in American mythology rather than to expose them as he did in earlier tales.

Barks's Donald stories of the 1950s offered a different take on the success myth. By the middle of the decade, he was dealing so frequently with Donald's attempts to master jobs that these tales form a subgenre of their own.[64] Donald is sometimes self-employed, running his own fix-it shop or pet service (*WDC&S* #161 [1954], #200 [1957]), but most of the time he is a laborer doggedly pursuing a trade. These stories gave the duck a new image. The Donald of the 1940s was too arrogant and impulsive to hold a steady job. He pursued get-rich-quick schemes and instant fame and as a result constantly set himself up for a fall. His counterpart in the 1950s is still avid for success but is less obnoxious in his pursuit of it. He seeks now to be accepted as a member of society. In these tales, Donald struggles with the everyday realities faced by ordinary people rather than has exciting adventures, achieving a certain nobility and even heroism in these less-than-successful efforts.

Shame and guilt are keynotes in these stories, motivating Donald from without rather than within. The nephews harp on the fact that their uncle is a nobody—"only a delivery boy for a skunk oil factory!" (*WDC&S* #165 [1954]). When Donald holds a respectable job, he finds that he must guard against errors that could disgrace his employer. In struggling to fend off the poor opinions of others, he becomes a victim of social prejudice and thus a more sympathetic character. These changes are first visible in 1953, when Donald becomes a mailman (*WDC&S* #150). He takes the job seriously, studying hard to pass the mail carrier's exam. His first deliveries are clearly important: a pension check and a soldier's letter to his mother.

One woman calls him "noble," but the only person really aware of his effort is a fellow employee, the postal clerk who reproves Gladstone for expecting a mailman to deliver a valentine through a blizzard.

Because Donald initially rebels and throws away the valentine, he is made to feel guilty, and the hardships he endures in recovering it seem deserved. But the story's conclusion also shifts blame onto Daisy and Gladstone for their uncaring attitude. Instead of recognizing Donald's efforts, Daisy gushes over the admirer who "walked clear down to the post office in this horrible storm." The Junior Woodchucks, too, come in for a measure of criticism. While they play at lifesaving games, their uncle strives to deliver the U.S. mail. For this he receives no reward, but his bowed and snow-covered posture on the last page identifies him with Mike, the noble mailman "who never lost a letter."

Donald's work as a stationmaster is similarly thankless (*WDC&S* #162 [1954]). He hopes at first to succeed by emulating movie heroes, but the story shows that Hollywood romance does not work in real life. The capture of Hairy Harry becomes farce when the fearsome train robber proves to be a buck-toothed oaf. Donald's real act of heroism, it seems, is the sacrifice of his food and blankets to keep alive a cargo of baby turkeys. As a reward, he gets to keep his position at the deserted station at One Whistle, which, ironically, will net him a pension of twenty dollars month if he can keep at it for "another sixty years!"

The hotel story (*WDC&S* #206 [1957]) further satirizes the Horatio Alger ethic, ending with Donald in a lower job than the one from which he had sought to rise. This is a result of the success myth never anticipated but a very real possibility in a society that prevents upward mobility at the same time that it encourages it. Scrooge offers Donald a chance to prove himself as manager of a hotel but really sets him up for a fall by giving him the impossible task of making a going concern of a ghost-town ruin. When Donald miraculously overcomes every obstacle, Scrooge imposes an additional test: he is so concerned with catching his employee in a mistake that he pays no attention to Donald's accomplishments and never considers his own responsibility as an employer in causing Donald's troubles.

This relationship is not the result of Scrooge's miserliness. Barks showed it to be a business norm, no matter for whom Donald works. Bosses in Barks's stories are often conspicuous by their absence, though the worker is constantly made to feel the threat of judgment and reprimand. Because Donald is forced to think for himself, his errors seem to be his own fault: "I should have asked the boss *how* to evict eagles, but thought I knew!" he says in one story. "I guess that was the start of all our trouble!" (*WDC&S* #204 [1957]). Because of his arrogance and impetuosity, Donald is usually to blame for his failures. At the same time, however, Barks implies that the system creates opportunities for these errors. When bosses are on hand, they offer no help or guidance but simply bellow orders. In such a situation, the old-fashioned virtues of "being tougher than the toughies and smarter than the smarties" (*US* #386 [1952]) no longer apply. Resilience and intelligence have been supplanted by callousness and aggression, typified by Mr. Brasshorn of the Break and Bruise insurance company. "To be a *salesman*," he tells Donald, "you have to climb right up on peoples' chests and scream your sales talk in their faces! And when they collapse from shock, you shove a pen in their limp fingers and scrawl their names on the contract!" (*WDC&S* #180 [1955]). To be somebody, the employee must become as obnoxious as his boss. Not only is success in modern Duckburg hard to achieve, it is no longer even admirable. Thus, it is actually to Donald's credit that he is out of place in a city where everyone else strides pugilistically down the street, determined to let nothing get in his way.

Though most of Barks's tales present Donald as a misfit, he emerges in several stories with a curious valor. As a rule, Duckburg awards fame and fortune only to the powerful, talented, and glamorous, but these stories give the loser a measure of dignity. The tale of the city's Olympic tryouts (*WDC&S* #188 [1956]) both portrays the public attitude toward athletes and reveals what Barks believed should be valued in a sportsman. Prominently on display at the stadium is a billboard with the motto, "It is not to win, but to *try* that is important." But judges, athletes, and spectators fail to take this creed into account. The crowd is so used to glamorous images of success that it derides Donald's humble efforts. Even the announcer picks up the insulting tone, speaking of "the not so fabulous Donald Duck."

But Barks showed the star athletes to be just as human as Donald, disqualifying them through the weaknesses that usually plague his hero: nagging women, greed, stupidity, and a bad back. One scene in particular is suggestive: The javelin thrower Fulldrip Pulpbugle is a caricature of the artist, having the bulbous nose Barks always drew on caricatures of himself and the allergies that caused the artist to leave the Disney Studio. When Pulpbugle is disqualified "for the dandelion season" and Donald takes over the javelin, he too, succumbs to hay fever, completing the identification.

The end of the story returns us to Barks's moral, as the nephews award Donald a tin trophy inscribed with the billboard motto. They had earlier wanted to boo him but have gradually come to recognize his effort. Their shift in attitude signals a change in Barks's stories in general. Earlier tales of Donald's failures only hinted that we should sympathize. Now the quality of perseverance that led him into continual failure is shown as a virtue.

The meritorious seldom get their reward, Barks's stories imply, while the undeserving may succeed through no merit of their own. In contrast to the success myth, many of these tales suggest that work must be an end in itself, without thought of achieving great wealth or acclaim. "I believe we should preserve many old ideals and methods of working," Barks explained, "honor, honesty, allowing other people to believe in their own ideas, not trying to force everyone into one form. The thing I have against the present political system is that it tries to make everybody exactly alike." [65] One can easily see Donald as Barks's alter ego in these stories. Laboring for decades in anonymity in the lowest rung of the Disney merchandizing hierarchy, in a medium thought to be expendable, receiving little pay and no public recognition for his entire career, he nevertheless invested his work with honesty, individuality, and integrity.

7

THE POSTMODERN CRACK-UP

uring the 1960s, Barks was in regular contact with fans. Although still praising his work, they noted a marked change in his stories. "What I miss in your strips is not action, but the distinctive personalities your characters used to have," Mike Barrier complained in 1966. "Uncle Scrooge isn't the wonderfully greedy, egotistic bastard he used to be; he's younger, certainly, and more the stock adventure hero."[1] Fans expressed similar opinions about Donald being "less vital." Barks explained, "I can only point to the fact that taboo after taboo has been imposed upon us scripters' freedom of material." Barks also blamed himself for the decline. His letters to fans are filled with melancholy musings on age and fatigue: "I can't blame the editorial office for the slowdown in Donald, however. The truth is that I am just getting old and tired. Will be 60 next March. I don't visualize action with the verve and feeling that I used to. . . . I don't see humor in many things that at one time would have inspired me to write half the night." But, as always, Barks felt a deep sense of obligation to his fans and to his work. "The letters I have received from fans like you have made me realize that I've got to push my chin off the floor and get back on the ball."[2] As a result, many of Barks's later stories show a renewed vitality, and some are among his most significant tales.

From the mid-1950s to the early 1960s, Barks recycled a number of old plots because of his increased workload and "a desperate effort to get ahead of deadlines."[3] "The Terrible Tourist" (*WDC&S* #248 [1961]), for example, is a rewriting of an unpublished, banned Christmas story from 1945; the Donald Duck story in *Walt Disney's Comics and Stories* #186 (1956) is a new version of "Rival Boatmen" (*WDC&S* #45 [1944]); and "Froggy Farmer" (*WDC&S* #236 [1960]) was inspired by a 1947 story (*WDC&S* #77). Thinking that he was writing for a younger generation of readers who would be unfamiliar with his earlier tales, the artist was unaware of those readers who still had or were familiar with earlier stories. Barks's editors also encouraged this rewriting because they thought that his ideas were too good to be used only once and then buried. But the practice made Barks feel that his creativity was ebbing. "The mind is not a bottomless well of ideas," he complained to a fan in 1960, "and mine is about pumped dry."[4]

However, Barks had little control over some changes in the quality of his work. "I suppose you've noticed the heinous butchery that took place" in the April 1961 issue of *Walt Disney's Comics and Stories*, he groused to a fan.[5] "That ad Dell is rerunning in the middle of the book caused the editors to take one page from my story of Gyro's fish hatchery for Donald, the best gag page, of course. I think the shortened story falls flat on its face." Barks tried to outmaneuver his editors in later issues. "Scrooge 35 will have no unplanned cuts," he announced. "I found out about the ad stunt in time to write material to fit."[6] This strategy seemed to work for several issues, but then Western resumed its old habits. To make room for a Cheerios ad, the publisher cut a page from "Rug Riders in the Sky" (*US* #50 [1964]), and "How Green Was My Lettuce" (*US* #51 [1964]) was shaved by two pages.

The greatest atrocity was the loss of two pages and much of the climax from "Mythic Mystery" (*US* #34 [1960]) so that Western could utilize a centerfold for a merchandising campaign. Wrote Barks to a fan, "My chin hit my knees when I saw . . . the big half-page stupender I did of Thor and Vulcan and a nephew riding above the busiest street corner in Duckburg in the gold chariot missing. Thor's horse terrified, thousands (at least) of people gaping upward in disbelief; autos bumper to bumper, smoking, clanking. In short, I gave Vulcan something to be scared about. All wasted effort."[7]

Barks became so discouraged by the butchery that he began inserting a page or two of "plain old padding" into his stories so there would be something for Western to remove without destroying his story line.[8] The artist also virtually stopped drawing splash panels, one of the hallmarks of his adventure stories. "The climatic fight in the next Paul Bunyan [tale] could have been improved with a half-page spread of Scrooge's and the Beagle Boys' giant robot hacking each other to pieces," Barks complained to a fan, "but I was afraid the editors would delete such a scene as being too violent."[9] Western's desires to make cuts diminished the epic quality of the Scrooge adventures by shortening them, forcing Barks to break them into a feature, a short, and maybe a gag page or two.

In the 1940s and early 1950s, Barks had worked relatively free of editorial control. He had not received a list of specific taboos, but seven years of training at the Disney Studio and a habit of being "tooth chatteringly careful" about what he wrote gave him an idea of the limits within which he could work.[10] However, more censorship occurred during the 1950s than in any other period: three of Barks's complete stories were banned, and others were significantly altered. The new mood of restrictiveness surfaced with a vengeance when "The Golden Apples," a ten-page Donald Duck story that was to appear in the September 1952 issue of *Walt Disney's Comics and Stories* (#144), was scrapped. Although the art for the story has vanished, Barks remembered it being a modern version of the myth of Atalanta and the golden apples. Barks explained, "I can only recall that I had Daisy quite angry with Donald because he was trying to win the hand, I guess, of this queen of the apples festival. . . . Daisy was so jealous that she was throwing things at Donald and was not acting lady-like. . . . [T]hat was the only excuse they ever gave me for cutting it."[11] Since Barks cast her as a volatile termagant, Daisy had often before acted unladylike, throwing things at Donald in fits of rage, but the ideology of domesticity imposed on women in the 1950s demanded a more sedate image.

Anything with a hint of sexuality, however arcane, was taboo. In "The Golden Fleecing" (*US* #12 [1956]), Scrooge searches for the legendary golden fleece but is kidnapped by two Arab-looking traders who turn out to be Harpies in disguise. "I almost had to eat those 32 pages of drawings," Barks complained. "It seems that Harpy or Harpie is an obscure nickname for a streetwalker. I managed to save the story by renaming the old girls LARKIES."[12] The editor also found fault with a panel in which Barks drew Agnes and her sisters wheeling madly through the sky, thinking that such behavior connoted insanity, something beyond the pale for a Disney comic. Barks salvaged the situation by redrawing the panels and muting the Larkies' behavior.

The more timorous atmosphere of the 1950s made a return to earlier motifs difficult. When he attempted to recapture some of the Gothic aura of earlier stories in "Trick or Treat" (*DD* #26 [1952]), Barks again experienced censorship problems. Likewise, Barks's return to stories featuring clashes between Donald and the nephews that had been de rigueur in the 1940s now were considered impermissible. In the February 1955 issue of *Walt Disney's Comics and Stories* he recycled a plot from the preceding decade involving rivalry between Donald and his nephews. When he wrote a conflict plot for the third time in the July 1956 issue, Barks's editor, Alice Cobb, sent him a letter from a mother "which we feel is a fair criticism." In addition, "we usually use 'quiet!' instead of 'shut up!'" Cobb cautioned. Barks sent back a vitriolic reply:

> Very well, I will avoid any more stories using conflict or rivalry between Don & the kids. Also no more "shut ups!"
>
> I have bought a number of *Tom & Jerrys*, *Porky Pigs*, *Chester Chipmunks*, etc., and will confine my plots and gag situations to "switches" on the material I find in those *safe* family journals.
>
> Seriously, I think that the woman who wrote this letter and sent the marked pages of the comics is a *neurotic* and so is her sniffling son. <If you wish to alienate the interest of 99% of your readers in order to pander to the narrow tastes of the 1% lunatic frige, I'm with you 100%. It will be so much easier to.>
>
> <You might be alienating the interest of *many* of your normal readers if you insist on pleasing the narrow tastes of the 1/10 of one percent who compose the lunatic fringe. But that is none of my business. I only work here.>
>
> <Down with child psychologists!>
>
> In the past few years I have <referred> returned from time to time to the early duck <stories> plots that I <did> used in the years when Disney

comics was <mushrooming in sales> growing up, thinking that the <growth record> increased sales of the magazine in those times proved that these story-types were sure-fire. And, as I didn't want to stray too far from the beaten track, I switched the plots on a few of them. The objectionable Ice Boat Taxi plot is a switch on a story in June 1944 Disney Comics called "Rival Boatmen" [*WDC&S* #45]. The Swimming Race theme coming up in next month's (July) Disney Comics [*WDC&S* #190] is a switch of the skating race plot from March 1945 [*WDC&S* #54].

<In the "early" years> when I worked in the Disney <Studio's> story department in the Duck unit the basic theme in a great number of the Donald Duck shorts was *rivalry* between the kids & Donald. Certainly the main body of the public didn't object to this theme, for during those years Donald and his nephews overtook and passed Mickey Mouse and *his* nephews in box office popularity.

After starting to work for Whitman I kept to the proven story lines as much as possible. The 10-page Donalds through the first several years were liberally sprinkled with rivalry plots and with no *crime* stories among the offerings. It's possible that the contests between Donald & the kids satisfied the reader's desire for triumphs of good over bad, the boastful over the meek, etc! At any rate, the magazine didn't seem to go broke.

Now comes a neurotic female with a cramped, fault-finding mind and a crybaby son, and proves that all those millions (well, dozens at least) of boys and girls who have bought and read Disney Comics over the years were and are sadists, masochists, murderers, lechers, and *worse*! I agree with her.

From now on you will see *changed* stories coming from this former breeding place of vice. You will see stories that will cause Ruth Downing to write another letter to say that she just *loves* the Donald Ducks. For every time she reads one to her little nose-picking crybaby, he goes to sleep in the middle of the second page.

Forward to better child psychology!

P.S. All of this letter except the first paragraph is so much jousting with windmills.[13]

Barks's run-in with his editor did not dissuade him from reusing other old plots. But when he tried to use a story harking back to the violent fights between Donald and his neighbor, Jones, Western banned the tale "because Donald was too mean to the villain."[14]

Barks's troubles in the 1950s stemmed partly from his relative lack of experience with censorship. He was sometimes unclear about where to draw the line because Western had never issued any explicit policy prohibiting certain subjects until the company's censorship of the Glittering Goldie sequence from "Back to the Klondike" (*US* FC #456 [1953]). "Western didn't give me much direction," the Duck Man recalled. "It was years after I had made a few mistakes that I found out that they had a list of taboos. Alice Cobb got me the sheet one time and showed it to me. You couldn't use the word 'kill' or use a gun in a dangerous way; you couldn't have poison or sickness or crippled people."[15]

Called "Hints on Writing for Dell Comics," this list was Western's first explicit statement concerning tabooed subjects and was written at the height of a national controversy over the effects of comic books on children. It tells writers to "avoid sophisticated and adult themes" and not to show "anything dealing with minority races, politics, religion, labor, suicides, death, afflictions (such as blindness), torture, kidnapping, blackmail, snakes, sex, love, female villains, crooked lawmen or heavies of any race other than the white race." It also admonishes writers to "try to avoid atom bombs, Communists and international intrigue generally" and not to "make fun of the law or portray law officials as stupid, dull-witted or cruel." During his career, Barks had dealt with most of these topics, and some of the taboos may have been partly inspired by his transgressions of them.[16]

The new mood of restrictiveness has to be viewed in the context of the period—a time of McCarthyite witch hunts, blacklists, and anticommunist hysteria. In April 1954, a month before Dell's "Hints" to writers were issued, two events brought the comics controversy to a head. Child psychiatrist Fredric Wertham published an impassioned attack on comic books, *Seduction of the Innocent*, in which he linked them to an alleged increase in juvenile delinquency and argued that they led children to commit crimes of lust, violence, and anarchy. Around the same time, a U.S. Senate subcommittee investigating the causes of juvenile delinquency began exploring the evils of comic books. Although no firm evidence pointed to an upsurge in juvenile delinquency during the postwar era, a Gallup poll showed that 70 percent of Americans believed that "crime-type" comics and crime and mystery television and radio shows were at least partly responsible for an alleged upsurge in juvenile crime.[17]

Wertham's opinion of funny-animal comics was ambivalent. On the one hand, he wrote, "Among the 'good' comic books whose quantity counts at all are usually reckoned the animal comics, the Disney comics and their imitators, classical books in comic-book form, comic books that are reprints of newspaper comic strips, some teen age girl comics and some boys' sport comics. The mainstay of the 'good' comic books are the animal comics and a few of the relatively innocuous related comics."[18] On the other hand, Wertham thought that funny-animal comics could also mimic the evils of crime comics: "The same theme of race ridicule is played up in the good animal comic book *Bugs Bunny*. Colored people are described as 'superstitious natives' and you see them running away. The injury-to-the-eye-motif is added, Bugs Bunny being shown throwing little diamonds into the eyes of the colored people. They are 'big enough to blind a feller!' says Bunny. 'Awk! I can't see!' says one victim. Is that not the same crime-comic-book ingredient adapted to the youngest set?"[19]

Fearing adverse legislation, the comics industry banded together in self-defense and formed the Comics Code Authority in 1954. All comics were to be submitted to the Code, and only those approved were permitted to bear its seal. Wholesalers could then identify and refuse to distribute titles deemed objectionable. Only two companies refused to join: Dell and Classic Comics, the publisher of adaptations of literary works. At this time, Dell published no crime and horror comics, which authorities had deemed the chief offenders; the company declared its line "clean" and "wholesome." In response to pressure to join the Comics Code, in 1955 Dell began publishing a "Pledge to Parents" with the slogan, "Dell comics are Good comics." Dell's censorship of content was even stricter than the Code: "The Dell code eliminates entirely, rather than regulates, objectionable material," it pledged.

With the coming of the Comics Code, crime and horror titles began to disappear, and entire companies went out of business. Total sales of comic books showed a dramatic decrease from a peak of 59.8 million in 1952 to 34.6 million in 1956 to just 20 million in 1989.[20] However, the industry might have recovered if not for the rapid spread of another medium, television. In 1946, only eight thousand Americans owned television sets;

by 1960, the number had increased to 57 million. By the 1960s, 99 percent of the public owned televisions.[21] Studies showed a decline in movie attendance, library patronage, and literacy rates.[22]

The funny-animal comic was particularly hard hit because television sapped its young audience. This threat was not lost on Barks. "The comics with these funny animal movie characters are definitely on the downgrade," he concluded in a 1962 interview. "There's too much of it on television. You know, the kids can sit for hours and watch these cartoons—*Popeye* and *Yogi Bear* and even old Disney characters. They're seeing so much of them that there's no point in going to the newsstand and paying 12¢ to see more of it. The day of the animal characters, I believe, is past. The human characters are the coming thing."[23]

Dell had been the world's largest publisher of comics during the 1950s, accounting for about a third of all comic book sales, and *Walt Disney's Comics and Stories* had been America's best-selling comic book, with each issue purchased by more than 3 million readers. By 1960, however, the title's sales had declined by almost a third from its 1953 high point.[24] In 1961, Dell raised the price of its comic books from ten to fifteen cents, although the industry standard remained at ten cents for several more months before rising to twelve cents at the beginning of 1962. The price change caused an even greater decline in sales. By 1962, *Walt Disney's Comics and Stories* had lost half its circulation.[25] Even a drop in price to twelve cents did not help, and by 1968 circulation had declined to over a tenth of its peak.[26]

Part of the decline resulted from a glut of Disney comic book titles in these years. But such a dramatic drop in circulation can only be attributed to a general loss of interest in the magazine. At this time, Marvel Comics, with young antiheroes such as Spider-Man, had captured a large share of the comic book market. Comic books appealing to a new, hipper audience had displaced older, more sedate fare. The funny-animal comic in particular and comics generally produced for a younger audience, which had been Dell's specialty, were moribund, never again to reach their former heights.

The funny-animal comic was undermined by a tectonic shift in American culture during the 1960s. Most accounts of the period frame it as a decade during which rebellious youth became pitted against conservative adults. However, the truth is more complex. The 1960s saw the rise of what Peter Braunstein has called a "rejuvenation culture" that encompassed both youth and adults alike.[27] LSD historian Jay Stevens has observed that in the 1960s, "it was as though the country as a whole was undergoing a late adolescence."[28] By the middle of the decade, the media had endowed youth with heroic qualities that would have seemed shocking in the 1950s. Until 1964, journalists still regarded youth as a "quiet generation": University of California President Clark Kerr made the retrospectively embarrassing assertion that "employers are going to love this generation" because it would be "easy to handle," and pop charts were filled with songs about teenage angst such as "Teen Angel" and "Leader of the Pack." By the mid-1960s, however, radicals were voicing their disillusionment with mainstream America in terms of a critique of errant adulthood. The valorization of the young led to a more inclusive sense of youth. No longer just a demographic group to which ads could be pitched, youth had become a dissident state of mind, a consuming identity to which all could aspire.

The role of youth as a cultural vanguard led advertising and business elites to a new fascination with targeting this demographic group, "under 24 and over 90,000,000 strong in the United States alone," exclaimed *Vogue* magazine in 1965.[29] These imposing demographics foretold of a new zeitgeist—"youthquake." Forty-two and thirty-one years old, respectively, in 1960, the new president, John F. Kennedy, and his wife, Jacqueline, brought a new sense of style as well as the "excitement of danger" and the "heroism of sacrifice" to the White House.[30] Across the Atlantic, the Mod revolution among England's youth was setting new trends in music, clothes, and fashion. By 1964, the miniskirt, long hair, and idiosyncratic new dance crazes began sweeping the United States as it embraced the ethos of Beatlemania and the British Invasion. The new youth ethos and the tumultuous events of the 1960s undermined the notion of childhood and the funny-animal comic book as a timeless, apolitical realm free of topical references. Indeed, as Neil Postman observes, the notion of childhood as a realm separate from that of adults was breaking down.[31]

Barks was well aware of these changes. In the 1960s, he attempted to keep up with teenage music and slang to make his stories more contemporary. His comics show both fascination and anxiety about the spread of youth culture. "The Great Wig Mystery" (*US* #52 [1964]), for example, is the first *Uncle Scrooge* adventure to utilize hip language. "The kookies of Duckburg have gone for wigs in a big way!" announces a narration box above a scene of bewigged teens entranced by their new look. "I dig those wigs! They send me!" quips Uncle Scrooge—"To Europe that is," he adds. Barks's story articulates the relationship between teen fads, mass conformity, and corporate profits. Scrooge is on his way to buy "planeloads" of wigs to sell to "Duckburg's wig-stricken girls."

Barks shows that teen music had created a kind of universal language that subverted traditional culture by imposing a homogenizing American culture. In "The City of Golden Roofs" (*US* #20 [1957]), Donald and a native of the East Asian city of Tangkor Wat (Angkor Wat in Cambodia) exchange the universal greeting of all fans of Shoeless Pashley, a spoof of Elvis Presley. They talk hip talk and call each other "calypso cat." Foregrounding the workings of American cultural imperialism, the story reveals that the locals' addiction to Shoeless Pashley music enables Donald to make a killing by selling midget hi-fis. But the music has a deracinating effect on native culture. "Hold those waxen poses, girls," says the king's factotum to the monarch's dancing girls, "You must look like statues to please the king." They start gyrating to the pulsing music, destabilizing traditional definitions of femininity. "Girls, girls! It's not graceful to dance like that!" says the king's majordomo.

But Barks's story undermines this critique by obscuring Scrooge's amoral tactics. When the raucous sounds of rock music played by his subjects drive the king batty, Scrooge manipulates him into buying one of his giant stoves to drive them from the palace. The miser then cons the king into giving him a barrel of gold when he cannot pay his debt. The ending justifies the corporate practice of dumping excess products unsalable in the United States into the Third World for big profits: Donald appropriates a fortune in gold from the natives for his cheaply produced hi-fis and Scrooge for his giant heater, useless in Asia's hot climate.

Barks's animus toward hippies is evident in several stories. As usual, his references are anachronistic. The hippies of 1960s youth culture metamorphose into 1950s-style beatniks. In "The Not–So-Ancient Mariner" (*WDC&S* #312 [1966]), the Duck Man transformed the errant loafer Gladstone into a beatnik artist. "The Hall of the Mermaid Queen" (*US* #68 [1967]) continues this conceit. The ducks encounter a race of mermen who have long hair and beards, and Donald calls one a "submarine beatnik." In "Queen of the Wild Dog Pack" (*US* #62 [1966]), an enraged Scrooge voices Barks's animus about the trivializing effects of rock music: "Beat singers are making all the money," he fumes, "and my Shakespearean drama house is going broke!" A fierce wild woman with tusks for teeth succumbs to the sounds of the English rock singer Tweedy Teentwerp, a name that connotes Barks's feeling about the British Invasion's diminution of the culture. Even wild nature, in Barks's eyes, has succumbed to the sentimental sop of teen music. The last panel shows her after having been "civilized," combing her hair blissfully while looking in the mirror in narcissistic self-absorption and listening to teen drivel.

In the mid-1960s, artists such as Andy Warhol and Roy Lichtenstein both critiqued and valorized mass-produced art by using rows of Campbell's soup cans, movie icons such as Marilyn Monroe, and comics figures such as Popcyc and Dick Tracy as the subjects of paintings. Camp and Pop Art became all the rage, embodied in a spate of new television shows including the *Man from U.N.C.L.E.*, the *Avengers*, and *Batman*. Camp operated according to a dual address. It could be read by hip and straight audiences in different ways: *Batman* was both a straight adventure show to younger audiences and a satire of authority grown silly and no longer prepossessing to older viewers. Camp emphasized artifice and a denaturalization of cultural conventions. "The essence of camp," writes Susan Sontag, "is its love of the unnatural, of artifice and exaggeration."[32] Through its emphasis on excess, irony, and stylization, camp deconstructed cultural codes, revealing them to be artificial and arbitrary. Thus, it expressed a legitimization crisis in the genres and the identities they subtended as authority, institutions, and cultural norms were becoming challenged by an antinomian counterculture.

Barks's stories of the 1960s embody this camp aesthetic. "The Cattle King" (*US* #69 [1967]), for example, deconstructs the genre of the

Western. In such earlier parodies as "The Sheriff of Bullet Valley" (*DD FC* #199 [1948]), Barks maintains a sense of realism and sympathy for its hero by invoking a love of the Old West while simultaneously parodying the Western. However, "The Cattle King" wholly embraces silliness and lack of depth, operating only on the surface. Dialog is composed of sight gags and one-liners more befitting a sitcom than a horse opera. Gone is any semblance of Scrooge's entrepreneurial ethic and the frontier ethos of the Klondike days. "I'm leaving you lads to learn the cattle business by experience," Scrooge tells the nephews. "I learned that way! That's why I became a banker!"

The Old West has been shorn of its romance. Donald and the kids are totally uninterested in the West and resist Scrooge's attempt to teach them the cattle business. Camp displaces realism or suspense: a horse faints when the bullets start flying, and all of Scrooge's wranglers are totally corrupt. The story also engages in wild anachronisms: Scrooge fights the rustler Snake McViper in a duel between whirlybirds rather than six-guns. Contemporary references continually intrude, and different genres commingle, making the story into a pastiche that can barely hold together the shards of its narrative. The tycoon's helicopter has giant tentacles, making it seem like a monster from a 1960s horror film: indeed, Scrooge has designed the vehicle "to scare teenagers out of my drive-in movies!"

Media genres function to secure and stabilize social identities by resolving social and cultural contradictions. Thus, genres help to maintain coherent subjectivities within ideological discourses in the face of contradictions. However, when such discourses are undermined by overwhelming discrepancies from popular experience, the assumptions on which a genre is based can be called into question, and it may lose credibility. These cultural assumptions thus can come to seem unnatural and unrealistic.

Befitting the turn to youth culture, the nephews suddenly metamorphose from precocious children into teenagers. "Yoo hoo, I'm a cheatin' teen from Abilene!" a nephew announces to the love-starved rustlers. Dressing in drag epitomizes the gender bending of long-haired youth in the

1960s and its subversion of the macho masculinity embodied in Western myth. "Feminine" wiles supplant the Western's usual emphasis on toughness and strength. The boys lure the rustlers to their chuck wagon and defeat them through the very unmanly device of giving them stomachaches from eating concrete biscuits.

Both to forestall controversy and as a means of ensuring their international appeal, Disney comics (and films) were noted for eliding topical references, creating an apparently timeless universe innocent of contemporary events. But during the 1960s, contemporary references intrude. In "The Cattle King," Barks references teen dances such as the Watusi and President Lyndon Johnson. The author also alludes to the generation gap as Donald identifies himself and the kids as "students" in Scrooge's "cattle college" and at the adventure's end proclaims himself a "drop-out," invoking the youth counterculture. These camp anachronisms reveal the Western's trouble in appearing credible during the turbulence of the Vietnam War. "What's the next bit of violence you've planned for us peace-loving students?" Donald asks Scrooge.

Nine years after penning the story of Glittering Goldie, Barks returned Scrooge to the Klondike to prospect for gold in "The Golden Nugget Boat" (*US* #35 [1962]). For the first time, we get to see the old sourdough in action, not just lecturing Goldie beside the sluice box. But the Duck Man's portrayal of prospecting, with its demonstration that Scrooge needs luck to succeed, undermines the work ethic on which the success myth was based. With the rise of a postmodern consumer culture, the entrepreneurial myth and the values of work, thrift, and asceticism on which it rested were losing their credibility.

Even more than the barroom flashback, with its strong streak of frontier boasting, "The Golden Nugget Boat" suggests that Scrooge's vision of the Klondike is a myth. His reminiscences on a television show have the flavor of a tall tale, and facial expressions clearly indicate that neither Donald nor the announcer believes a word of Scrooge's story. Neither, it seems, does Barks, since the rest of the story shows Scrooge trying desperately to live up to his own romance—and failing. In the end he does find gold, but only by the same freak of fortune that located a nugget for Gladstone. Scrooge tosses the same pebble over his shoulder that Gladstone used, finding gold in exactly the same way. When the citizens of Chilblain, dazzled at the size of his strike, ask him to reveal his working methods, Scrooge only smiles and fobs them off with Gladstone's line: "It's a professional secret!" In a disturbing destabilization of the success myth, Barks leaves us no rationale for distinguishing between Scrooge's success and that of his polar opposite, the lucky loafer Gladstone. The artist's drawing of the ducks sailing down the Yukon in a swan-shaped craft of hammered gold, singing as they go, approaches the realm of dreams rather than a credible resolution to the story. It is as if the work ethic, having failed, can only be salvaged by fantasy. At the same time, by starting with a small nugget boat and ending with a large one, Scrooge has demonstrated once more his knack for turning a sizable profit.

"The Looney Lunar Goldrush" (*US* #49 [1964]) relegates its search for nuggets to second place while madness and mercantilism come to the fore. In an echo of "Back to the Klondike," a gold nugget is found, stolen, and used to clobber one character on the head, but there is no focus for these events. When Goldie threw the Goose Egg Nugget at Scrooge, it epitomized the whole running battle between them: Donald's use of the moon nugget to knock out an already groggy Dan McShrew is simply a throwaway gag: "I knew that nugget was good for something!" The story opens with Scrooge lecturing a troop of Junior Woodchucks about the "bitter disappointments" of the gold fields. "For every glory-holer that strikes it rich there are thousands who struggle home without a shirt-tail!" Once again, his reminiscences have more than a touch of the tall tale, and the troop commander has to intervene at one point to protect Scrooge from embarrassing questions. "As an old prospector let me say that *I* would never join another gold rush!" Scrooge insists. Yet when gold is discovered on the moon, he joins the lunar stampede as avidly as the rest of Duckburg.

This time, however, Scrooge travels to the gold fields as a proprietor of a country store, selling soda pop and knickknacks to the real sour-doughs at cutthroat prices. When villainy rears its head, it takes the form of a business hijacking rather than a jumped claim, and the barroom brawl that fueled a page of epic violence in "Back to the Klondike" devolves into a comic-opera parody of Robert W. Service's "The Shooting of Dan McGrew." It is not just that the old romantic formulas no longer work. Scrooge's closing words suggest that he was always more of a merchant than a prospector: "I'm going *home* lads, like I did from all the other rushes—*richer* than *all* the miners!" From behind a thick shield of satire, Barks was finally facing the reality of who made a killing in the gold fields.

Barks's creation of Magica de Spell as Scrooge's archnemesis in the 1960s tells us much about the destabilization of the times. In 1952, when *Uncle Scrooge* debuted, Barks resurrected beliefs that were already becoming anachronistic. Ten years later, American mythology was self-destructing, and Scrooge's treasure hunts had lost much of their romantic glamour. Captains of industry were looked on as robber barons, much as had been the case during the Gilded Age; foreign intervention was seen as American imperialism; and the work ethic had been superseded by a consumer ethos that prized pleasure above virtue. Faced with this subversion of American mythology, Scrooge's adventures underwent a change.[33] Unable to justify Scrooge's hoard to a generation that was losing faith in heroic tycoons, Barks consigned McDuck's success to luck, with fortune as a synonym for a lack of explanation, like magic.

Disney animation had been built on the Gothic thrills that witches provided to an audience of children. Legend has it that the seats in Radio City Music Hall had to be reupholstered after the premiere of *Snow White* because so many frightened children had wet their pants when the witch appeared. But Barks wanted a new take on the notion of the witch as an old hag. "Disney had witches in just about every movie they made," he recalled. "At least it seemed that way to me. So I thought, why not invent a witch? If I made her look kind of glamorous, with long sleek black hair and slanty eyes, instead of one of those fat, hook-nosed old witches, she could be an attractive witch."[34] Barks modeled her on Morticia, "the dark-haired witch from the Charles Addams family cartoons in the *New Yorker*, which I liked very much." Magica was "downright sexy," claimed Barks. "That's why she's Italian and, of course, very popular with readers in

Italy."[35] Magica lived on Mount Vesuvius, where the intense heat enabled her to fuse the dimes of rich men into a powerful "Super-amulet."

Bark created the character of Magica as a psychological double of Scrooge, a dark avaricious twin who shares his lust for wealth and power and desires to displace him as the richest person on earth. However, she ascribes to a philosophy directly antithetical to Scrooge's apotheosis of work, thrift, and self-denial. Believing that wealth inheres in objects, Magica inverts the whole ethic that built Scrooge's fortune. Having no accomplishments of her own, she seeks to assume the power and wealth of others through an alchemical charm fashioned from the first dime that Scrooge earned. Nothing delights her more than garnering profit without work. For instance, in one story, "Raven Mad" (*WDC&S* #265 [1962]), she even invents a way to absorb good fortune through sunlight. "I'll get *extra-rich* every time I get a sunburn!" she crows. "*Laziest* way to make money I ever heard of!" growls Scrooge. She is a kind of vampire who seeks to live off the blood and sweat of others, amassing a fortune while earning nothing for herself through her own labor.

Barks's invention of Magica as Scrooge's archnemesis symbolizes the hegemony of a consumer society based on media spectacle and appearance that assumes dominance in the 1960s. Magica is an archetypal consumer, convinced that possession of the right object will make her happy. In contrast to Scrooge, who never obtains any physical comforts from his wealth, Magica is obsessed with achieving total leisure and luxury: "I'll live in a palace with Jewels and mink, and handmaidens and Butlers!" she declares in one story (*US* #40 [1963]).

Magica is also a shape-shifter. She can assume any person's identity after immobilizing him with her magic wand. This power is imbricated with consumer culture. Consumerism depended on fluid ego boundaries in which the persona could be continually adapted to the latest (continually changing) images, styles, and fashions. The female is often taken as representative of these traits. Writes Barbara Ehrenreich, "What had been understood as masculinity, with its implication of 'hardness' and emotional distance, was at odds with the 'feminine' traits appropriate to a consumption-oriented society, traits such as self-indulgence, emotional lability, and a 'soft' receptivity to whatever is new and exciting."[36] Western modernity perceived women as exemplifying the pitfalls of mass culture, more vulnerable to and having less distance from the intoxications and blandishments of images and mass consumption.[37] Magica's shape-shifting captured the essence of this new form of identity and the threat its polymorphousness posed to rigid forms of masculinity.

Barks valued science over superstition and at first explained Magica's power naturalistically. Her foof bombs are chemical pellets stored up her sleeve, and her stun ray operates by battery. But he later shows us that she can command hurricanes, thunderbolts, and even the planets (US #43 [1963]) and possesses the power of Circe to change the ducks into animals with the wave of her magic wand (US #41 [1963]). Knowing that her terror lies not in her sorcery but in the threat to Scrooge's identity it portends, Barks becomes cavalier about explaining her powers.

Magica combines the sexual threat of the femme fatale with the image of the witch as crone: she is a solitary spinster with no man in her life. "Her looks gave her an extra element of power," Barks explained.[38] But her beauty is never a prelude to Scrooge's seduction: only money could pluck his heartstrings. Rather, the fears she engenders in him are of another order. She differs significantly from Scrooge's other adversaries. The Beagle Boys want only to possess Scrooge's wealth, while Flintheart desires only to displace Scrooge as the world's richest duck. Magica wants to destroy Scrooge's identity as a way of empowering herself. "I'd like you better as a *churchmouse!*" she tells him. "The symbol of *poverty!*" (US #40 [1963]). She symbolizes male fears of female domination, anxieties that became more acute in the 1960s as women began to assert their strength and independence and achieved greater entrée into the workforce and public sphere. The decline of traditional values, which had supported the work ethic, created a legitimation crisis in male identity, which was based on masculine achievement in work.[39]

Under patriarchy, the assertion of female power is viewed as tantamount to emasculation and a loss of male identity. Hence, Magica has an aggressive and domineering persona: "Move over everybody, I'm on my way to get riches!" she declares as she pushes a policeman and another bystander aside ("For Old Dime's Sake," *US* #43 [1963]). In "The Ten-Cent Valentine" (*WDC&S* #258 [1962]), Magica, dressed as a young girl duck out jogging, pushes Donald to the ground, yelling, "Move over, you weak-looking flabbyduck! Give a strong, agile musclegirl running room!" In several stories she even assumes Scrooge's identity, taking over his physical appearance and mocking his claim to be himself (*US* #43 [1963], *US* #48 [1964]). She never competes with another woman for power or for the attention of another man, like Daisy; rather, Magica devotes herself to seeking power like the men, thus abandoning the traditional female role. In a male-dominated society, she can be cast only as deviant and threatening, her behavior cruel and unnatural, like the magic she wields. Her desire to become powerful and wealthy seems abnormal, while Scrooge can assume the mantle of heroic entrepreneur. Because she is a villain, Magica can indulge in the "unladylike" behavior that Barks's editors prohibited in Daisy. Magica plays the role of the stereotypical hysterical woman at the end of most stories, having hissy fits and pelting the ducks with rocks after they recapture Scrooge's revered coin.

However, much like the femme fatale, Magica can be read alternatively as a rebel against male authority, offering readers pleasure in the subversion of male power. This was an important aspect of Disney comics' appeal in the 1960s, when a large number of readers were young girls. In *Uncle Scrooge* #36 (1962), Magica takes over the mayor's persona and stuns male bureaucrats with her foof bombs. And in "Isle of Golden Geese" (*US* #45 [1963]) she shanghais the Beagle Boys and makes them into her crew, forcing them to call her "ma'm" and to carry out her orders by chastising them with thunderbolts. Her melodramatic flair with words and possession of superhuman powers makes her a charismatic figure. Her soliloquy in "For Old Dime's Sake" (*US* #43 [1963]) is one of the greatest in Barks's oeuvre. All nature is at her command. "Dance a fandango, you thunderbolts! Do the *twist*, you hurricanes! From outer space I summon the boogermen of the universe! . . . I Magica de Spell, have become so ornery the world will tremble at my slightest scowl!" Intended by Barks as a parody of the preternatural powers of superheroes and witches, her omnipotence borders on camp. Even Mother Nature shudders at

Magica's power: when she hisses at a potted tree in the last panel, it sheds its leaves, trembling in fear.

Magica's obsession with Scrooge's first dime marks it as another one of Barks's fetish objects. Barks's initial depiction of the first money that Scrooge earned appears in "A Christmas for Shacktown" (*DD* FC #367 [1951]), where a framed bill, labeled "My First Dollar," is chained to the wall, an emblem of his stinginess and hoarding, not thrift like the first dime. All the characters in this story—Donald, Daisy, the nephews—unite in a rare demonstration of selflessness to buy gifts for the destitute kids of Shacktown, with the boys contributing the money intended for their own Christmas presents as well as Donald's. Even the amoral Gladstone aids the cause. Only Scrooge abstains. After being badgered by Donald, he agrees to give twenty-five dollars for turkeys but he refuses to spend an equal amount on what he considers a "useless" toy train, even though his money bin is so full that he can barely keep it from overflowing.

Barks's story was highly innovative for its time, showing that Duckburg was divided into separate areas for the well-off and the poor and contained a ghetto of impoverished and unhappy children. The artist was courageous in writing about poverty in the postwar period, a time of presumed national affluence when poverty was invisible. Its existence was not officially acknowledged until the 1960s, by the Kennedy administration and President Johnson's War on Poverty. Thus, "Shacktown" had a huge impact on many baby boomers.[40]

This story foregrounds the power of a dime, and prefigures Scrooge's lucky coin—but with a crucial difference. When Donald gives Scrooge a dime as a joke, the miser deposits it in his cache. But the coin serves as a punishment for the skinflint's selfishness; it causes his bin to cave in and Scrooge loses his entire fortune.[41] Only the toy train, the gift that he failed to offer, can save his loot, but it will take almost 273 years for the locomotive to retrieve it. Scrooge is forced to live his life in solitude in a cave, an emblem of the alienation from humanity wrought by his parsimony and, by poetic justice, destitute, like those for whom he had no compassion.

Rather than the symbol of Scrooge's thrift it would become, the dime is an emblem of his mean-spiritedness and a vehicle of punishment for his lack of empathy—bad luck rather than good luck. This is an index of how much Barks would transform the skinflint's mythos in the later Uncle Scrooge adventures. But Barks created a utopian message as well: Scrooge promises to give the boys the toy train's next carload of money. When it brings out a thousand dollars, the miser must give the Shacktown children the best Christmas of their lives. "My opinions about poor people are very biased," Barks told an Italian interviewer in 1973. "I have always been one of them."[42] However, Barks's recommendation of individual philanthropy as a solution to poverty fails to challenge the distribution of wealth from which such inequality derives.

The first story to call the first dime by name is "The Midas Touch" (*US* #36 [1961]), which marks Magica's debut.[43] When Donald tells Scrooge that his first dime is a good luck charm and is the secret of his wealth, Scrooge dismisses the idea: "Bah! Mere superstition! *Thriftiness* is the secret of my wealth!" But Barks's stories seem to confirm Magica's belief in the magical power of Scrooge's revered coin. When she hurls a molten meteor at Scrooge's money bin, it simply deposits gold and jewels on his land, making him even richer. As a result, Scrooge stops talking about the hard work and thrift that built his empire and accepts the myth that wealth can be produced by a good luck charm. When she steals his dime and turns his nephews into pigs in "The Oddball Odyssey" (*US* #40 [1963]), he wails, "That is the end of the line for my *fortune*!" "With my old number one dime gone, I'll no longer care what becomes of my other trillions of dimes! Nor will I care what becomes of *me*! My nephews are lost—*all* that I valued in the world is lost!" However, Barks hedges the issue: Magica never possesses the first dime long enough to prove its power.

"The number one dime should not be treated as a *good luck charm*. It contradicts the way Uncle Scrooge *really* made his fortune," Barks observed. "But woe is me! I blatantly violated that rule in at least one story."[44] "City beneath the Sea" (*US* #46 [1963]), a story in which Magica does not appear, shows the dime to be the sole cause of the profitability of his global empire. When the coin disappears beneath the sea, his businesses start to crumble, and only when he retrieves the dime from a group of Martians does his wealth return. The dime thus comes to assume the property of luck with which Magica invests it. Scrooge falls victim to the same fetishism of the dime that bedeviled Magica, a mystification that he had initially dismissed. At the same time, Barks makes the power of the dime undecidable, reflecting his ambivalence about the myth of the entrepreneur. In "City beneath the Sea," Scrooge is released by the Martians when he finds a large iron deposit that they need to save their depleted planet. But the reader does not know whether Scrooge's regaining his first dime or his expertise in finding precocious metals enables his discovery.

A key nodal point in the dime's transformation is "Raven Mad" (*WDC&S* #265 [1962]). After this story, Scrooge comes to believe that the coin is a magical charm. Scrooge exhibits his dime at a bazaar to raise money for Duckburg's rocket shot to the sun, but no one is interested. "Duckburgians have *terrible* taste!" he grouses. The story reveals how the entrepreneur's values, symbolized by the dime, have lost their luster in the 1960s. "They'd rather watch hula dancers than view my dime!" he snarls. However, after Magica tries unsuccessfully to steal the coin, the crowd grows intrigued. "Golly!" says one bystander, "a girl tried to steal that dime!" "It must be worth something!" says another. A third one demands, "I want to see that!" Members of a crowd then begin to poke their bulbous noses over the glass enclosure that houses the revered coin.

Here Barks reveals how commodity fetishism works in a consumer society. A seemingly worthless object becomes invested with glamour and becomes an object of fascination by its association with spectacle and the imaginary desires of others. This form of commodity fetishism differs from Marx's concept, which holds that in attaining a mystical aura, the commodity masks the surplus labor of the producer. Rather, this type of mystification might be called cultural fetishism, in which the connotations transferred to certain objects (through advertising, marketing, and visual spectacle) endow them with a magical, hyperbolic value that gives an aura of status to their owners. Cars become symbols of sexual potency, diamonds become emblems of love, and sunglasses connote the image that one is cool.

Barks was acutely aware of the way in which America was increasingly imbricated in commodity spectacle. In "The Status Seeker" (*US* #41

[1963]), for example, Scrooge enters a glitzy party at the swank Brasstoria Hotel where jewel-encrusted society matrons look disdainfully on him as a party crasher. A snobbish pig-faced maître d' informs him that he does not belong because the party is "only for important people." The entrepreneur and his work ethic have become anachronistic. In a society where status rather than just wealth counts, lavish display rather than work and thrift are most important. Barks reveals the absurdity of this transformation. A woman wears a diamond on her necklace so big that she has to carry it around in a wheelbarrow. The artist also mocks the triviality of fashion culture and its cycles of planned obsolescence: One matron says to another, "Mrs. Snooty's wearing a new Gior gown!" "At yesterday's party it was a new Gassini!" Even a bearded bum in rags who mooches off the buffet is invited to the party because he owns the "Pink Fakaso," Barks's gibe at the phoniness of modern art.

Although he owns the hotel, the guests look down on Scrooge because he possesses no status symbols. "Just another social climber trying to make an impression with *nothing* of importance!" say the pigface and two other status climbers in a huff after Scrooge fails to produce the candy-striped ruby, the world's foremost status symbol, which he claims to own. But Scrooge buys back the ruby from the chief of Rippan Taro, to whom he had traded it. The Third World too has succumbed to commodity spectacle, and the chief is addicted to status. He trades the ruby for a bunch of candy because having a fat tummy is a status symbol in his society. The story ends with Scrooge attaining status at last: he appears at another party of the glitterati, wearing the famed ruby. The snobby guests then bemoan seeing him too often, complaining that "He's stingy, dowdy, and dreadfully *boring*! All he can talk about is money!" But they have to invite him to all the parties because of his ownership of the glamorous jewel.

Contemporary theorists claim that we have recently entered an era of postmodernity. They place the transition from a modern to a postmodern society somewhere in the 1960s and 1970s, although some claim that we remain in the transition phase. They argue that changes in society during the postwar years accumulated to produce a society whose institutional, cultural, and epistemological condition is sufficiently different from that of modernity to warrant the new label. Frederick Jameson has theorized a transition to late capitalism that is global and in which all realms of personal and social life and spheres of knowledge have been turned into commodities. Jean Baudrillard asserts that information technology, mass media, and cybernetics have effected a transition from an era of industrial production to an era of simulation in which models, signs, and codes determine social order. The culture of postmodernity is thus often characterized by "consumerism, commodification, the simulation of knowledge and experience; the blurring if not the disappearance of the distinction between representation and reality, an orientation on the present that erases a sense of both past history, and of a significantly different future."[45] These shifts entail a decline in epistemic and political authority and a fragmentation of experience and personal identity.

The United States was the first country to adopt mass production and mass consumption, which became established in the 1920s after the birth of the assembly line, installment buying, and saturation advertising in mass-circulation magazines and over broadcast media such as radio. Consumerism was diminished by the Great Depression in the 1930s and war in the 1940s but then came to dominate America again. Consumer society reached fruition in the 1960s when the full power of television as a mass medium bombarded America with an exponential growth of advertising, media imagery, and free home-based entertainment that saturated the entire culture.

When asked in 1961 if he ever watched television, Barks quipped, "I don't have a TV and don't intend to."[46] Even after he had owned a set for several years, Barks's animus toward television had not abated: "In this country, the set is never off, and what is offered is 99 percent junk," he told an interviewer in 1980. "One can't stress the influence of American television on its population enough—it breaks people down and poisons them."[47] Barks's earliest stories about the medium express a concern about television's power to distort reality. In one ten-pager (*WDC&S* #195 [1956]), Donald is a boob tube junkie who watches his favorite shows with slavering devotion. Barks contrasts Donald's addiction to the fantasies of the tube with the nephews. He becomes obsessed with a fictional train wreck on television, missing the news flash that enables the nephews to prevent a real accident through their engineering skills.

In this story, television has positive uses, but by the 1960s Barks perceives the culture as so inundated by TV messages that people's sense of reality has come under threat. "The Lost Frontier" (*WDC&S* #246 [1961]) is Barks's penultimate satire on the effects of television. The nephews are no longer scientific pragmatists but TV addicts, enthralled with Captain Gadabout's battle with an abominable snowman. In this story, TV images become more real than reality, creating what Baudrillard calls the "hyperreal."[48] Conflating fiction and reality, the nephews think that the battle is real and that Gadabout is the intrepid hero he claims to be. Donald fumes at such credulity, but his melodramatic diction betrays the fact that he too will succumb to television's simulations: "That Captain Gadabout is a two-bit fraud! A pernicious prevaricator! A prince of hokum, and high hipster of hogwash!"

The next week, the adventure hero is going to the Grand Canyon to investigate rumors that prehistoric creatures are living in isolated mesas. Donald takes the kids to the canyon to prove once and for all that the captain is a "faker." However, when the ducks fly down to the mesa, they discover a family of cave people. Barks believed that many television shows were "offensive to civilization" and were "putting people back into savagery."[49] Hence, he appropriately satirized typical TV addicts as cavemen. They embrace the ducks' addiction to television, wear the ducks' clothes, and act out the fictions they see on the screen: the father apes a body slam he sees on a wrestling show and throws the hapless Donald to the ground. Entranced by an instructional program on television, the simian creatures think that they can fly a plane with no prior experience, a mordant satire on television advertising's inculcation of prepackaged, instant knowledge. Captain Gadabout then arrives with a fleet of helicopters. Thinking the ducks are cave people, he films them for his next TV show. However, when the ducks protest that they are really civilized people, an odd bargain is arranged. Gadabout agrees to rescue them on the condition that they keep their true identities secret. By consummate irony, Donald not only cannot expose Captain Gadabout for the faker that he is but also has to sit and watch himself be portrayed as a caveman on the screen before an audience of millions. Television not only creates a society based on mass delusion but also reduces its audience to a state of lobotomized passivity.

Barks explores the relationship between image and spectator most fully in "Big-Top Bedlam" (*DD* FC #300 [1950]). Out of money, Donald goes to hock Daisy's valuable heirloom brooch to buy tickets to the circus for himself and the kids. He loses the pin just before Daisy unexpectedly arrives, and to cover his deceit, he tells her it has been stolen. He must save face when Daisy orders him to get the pin back from the "circus ruffians" she mistakenly believes have stolen it. Daisy's attempt to maintain these dissimulations sets up his entrapment in the funhouse hall of mirrors that is the circus.

The brooch represents what psychoanalytic theorists have called a "lost object of desire." Jacques Lacan, for example, posits a stage in early childhood, called the mirror stage, when the child is still uncoordinated and not yet fully formed, and comes to identify with an illusory image of itself in the mirror that provides the unified and coherent self that it lacks. Lacan calls this imaginary alter ego the ideal ego. After the subject enters the stage of the Symbolic, or the accession to language and culture, this imaginary unity is broken, and it becomes impossible to return to the earlier fusion of self and image, although its ghost haunts the subject. This experience of misrecognition (*méconnaisance*) is characteristic of the ego and persists throughout the Symbolic and into the subject's adult life. The ego directs the subject into a futile search for an illusory unity that forms the basis of its entrapment by imaginary images, fantasies, and ideologies.[50]

The lure of this fictive self leads the subject to search for a "fullness of being" that can never fully be possessed, forever alienating the subject from his or her self-identity. Lacan draws a distinction between the penis and the phallus, between the actual biological male and the idealized image of masculinity in Western culture. The male forever tries but can never fully live up to this idealized masculinity, thus creating a perpetual gap between lack and its object that fuels desire forward.[51] Daisy's brooch is such a signifier of masculinity: Donald will go to any length, suffering humiliation after humiliation, in order to cover up his inadequacies as a male and to protect himself from Daisy's castrating anger.

Barks uses the circus as a metaphor to satirize the way the media enable such misrecognitions and brutalizes and debases the subject.[52] Instead of becoming a spectator, Donald becomes an object of the audience's sadistic pleasure and emasculating gaze. His relationship to the audience reflects changes in postwar America when the media began to challenge and supplant the family as an agent of children's socialization. Critics of the period saw America being transformed from a society of publics into a nation of consumers. Americans were increasingly becoming part of a mass society of isolated individuals and groups who participated together collectively more and more through the mediation of the media.

A mass audience is characterized by the viewing of media events in "collective isolation" and is composed of individuals and groups, cut off from communication with each other. They form a collectivity only by virtue of simultaneously watching the same media event. Because of the mass circulation of these images, viewers become more and more induced into believing in media simulations. An image on television or film replaces our direct experience of people and events which, if uncritically imbibed, creates a self-perpetuating form of mass delusion.

"Big-Top Bedlam" references these changes. Each set of characters in the story perceives others *only* through false impressions, unable to distinguish appearance from reality or to correct their errors. Zippo, the circus's quick-change artist, thinks Donald looks like a bill collector and is unaware that he is only seeking the brooch, which Zippo has found. As a result, he tries to scare Donald off by subjecting him to humiliating tricks and dangerous stunts. The audience also is misguided, believing Donald's daredevil stunts and abuse by the other clowns to be part of the act. "That clown on the high wire is *wonderful!*" exclaims a woman, unaware that Donald is fighting for his life. The nephews mistake Donald's motives and believe that he has gotten a "*plushy* job in the circus" and has forgotten them. Thinking that he is becoming "too *popular*," they hit him with a slingshot, furthering his abusive treatment, although he is ignorant of their involvement. Donald also misrecognizes events: Zippo's mastery of disguise makes the duck think that his brooch-flipping tormentors are different people rather than one person wearing different costumes. Like movie fans who idolize stars for their heroism or bravery, he confuses the actor with the role, unable to distinguish the two.

"Big-Top Bedlam" is one of Barks's most graphically innovative stories. He drew irregularly shaped panel designs to evoke the nightmarish world of the circus. The panels are fairly regular until the appearance of the circus, the first shot of which is a large-sized panel that weighs oppressively on a diminutive panel of Donald below. The effect suggests the oppressive force of the circus and the weight of the lie that he has told Daisy. The most irregular panels occur in the aerial sequence, in which Zippo forces Donald to traverse a high wire on a spring-propelled bicycle. The jagged panels point to Donald on the wire, threatening to pierce him and cut him in two, while another sharp-tipped panel points to the great distance below, evoking Donald's peril. When Donald almost falls, a jagged panel points to Zippo, his persecutor, and the applauding audience in the panel above. These graphics encode anxieties about the fragmentation and dissolution of identity under the mass gaze of the audience.

The circus is a mad, hellish world in which all individuals and groups operate separately but form an interlocking mass that mocks Donald's intentions. Indeed, Zippo disguises himself first as the devil, then as a skeleton. Barks drew irregular panels to show how the world of the circus created a fragmented male ego, forever split off and alienated from itself. In one corner, Donald races up the high wire after Zippo releases Donald's bike, with the audience howling with laughter. But he is aimed directly at an image of himself being held prisoner by Zippo, as if Donald will collide into an image of himself. This suggests the self-destructiveness of his act and the divided, alienated self that results.

In the finale of his act, Zippo announces that he will change identities so fast that "*nobody* will know who I am!" suggesting the way the media's production of a plethora of illusory identities was destabilizing the public's grasp on reality. When he dresses in drag, he seems to do the impossible—to change into two identical women. This doubling foregrounds for the reader the difference between self and image, the fact that paradoxically, for the image to represent the self it cannot be the self, image and referent being two different things. The fact that one of these women wears the brooch seems to point to the real Zippo, allowing audience and reader a temporary grounding in reality and a respite from the kaleidoscope of different identities. When Donald finally obtains the brooch from Zippo and explains why he had been chasing him, it seems as if the duck finally has access to the Real and has escaped from the circus's simulations.

However, Donald never gives up the search for an ideal ego. He struts home, believing that Daisy will welcome him as a "hero" for recovering her brooch. But the nephews think that he is gloating at his new celebrity, and one shoots him with the slingshot, causing Donald to lose the pin. The circus's simulations inflect the nephews' perceptions even after they have ceased being audience members. Barks aligns the reader's gaze with the weapon and augments the identification by drawing the panel in the Y-shape of the slingshot, bringing the reader into complicity with the artist's subversion of Donald's desire to be a hero.

In a twist of fate, the loss works in Donald's favor, excusing him from attending a museum banquet with Daisy. After hearing of his travails, she decides to reward him, even though he has been a miscreant. Donald looks at himself in the mirror, evoking the subject's illusory identification with his reflection in the mirror stage, and gloats, "Who says that *crime doesn't pay*?" Such hubris sets him up for a fall. When the nephews unexpectedly turn up with the brooch, he has to go to the banquet after all. Donald has finally obtained the object he so desperately sought but now no longer wants, for its possession signals his domination by Daisy. She forces him to attend a boring lecture, and he again is imprisoned by an audience, surrounded by fat dowagers and shriveled old men, emblems of women's dominance over their mates. To pursue the phallus, this tale suggests, is to perpetuate a cycle of abuse from which one cannot escape and to ensure a vacuum at the heart of male identity.

According to Baudrillard, the media-saturated society creates a world of total simulation. This is apparent in a 1966 story, "The Heedless Horseman" (*US* #65), one of the last Scrooge adventures. The story deals with Derby Day in Duckburg: "The old village goes a little kookie when race time draws near!" reads a narration box (*kookie* being Barks's favorite word for what he believed to be the lunatic fringe in the 1960s). Although Scrooge initially dismisses this as just another fad, the miser gets caught up in the game. He buys Fireball, one of the fastest thoroughbreds on the track, for $10 million, thinking that he can gain Duckburg's adulation by winning the derby. But the horse turns out to be only a robot, "a horsehide covered *computer*," as Donald puts it. The conclusion indicates Barks's growing cynicism in an era in which everything is a simulation and the real cannot be distinguished from the imaginary. Fireball's victory in the race seems justified because all the other horses are also machines: "This makes it fair for all the faked-up fillies," Scrooge consoles himself, subverting any notion of truth and fair competition, key ideals of the capitalist entrepreneur. "It'd be uplifting to look at real honest horses once more!" say the nephews. But the story has no resolution. Image and legerdemain remain the only real currency.

Barks perceived the rise of a media culture based on simulation and images of celebrity glamour as undermining not only the work ethic but the work process itself. This is apparent in the transformation of the so-called mastery stories, which he began writing in 1953.[53] In these stories, Donald is no longer a failure but a master craftsman who awes Duckburg with his feats of skill and imagination. These tales parody modernity's hubris in assuming that humans can fully dominate nature.

The later mastery tales, most of which appeared in the 1960s, reflect an era governed by media culture. The shift in tone that marks these stories can be traced to attitudes propagated by a nation of television viewers. Gone is the glamour enjoyed by the skillful individual; gone also is his sudden fall from grace. The hero, admired for his prowess, is displaced by the celebrity, whose fame rests on being famous. In a nation of consumers, people build identities not on what they do but how they look. The opening page of "Spare That Hair" (*WDC&S* #272 [1963]) suggests that this preoccupation with appearances distinguishes modern from primitive humans. "Where would mankind be without *barbers*?" the narrator asks. "Still back in the *bushes*—that's where!" Donald's first customer is a bush-headed professor who looks like a wild man despite his suit and tie. Donald manages to trim the man down to a civilized state, but the process of the haircut makes an ironic comment on the modern uses of technology.

The nephews' statement that their uncle "has made a science of mowing hair and chopping whiskers" reveals the basic illusion behind Donald's barbering: he has taken advanced knowledge of the "epicranial aponeurosis" and put it to the trivial use of cutting hair. This perversion of technology carries it not forward but backward, as suggested by Donald's use of shears, scythe, and electric hedge clippers. These tools for basic, productive agricultural work once helped people lead better lives. Now they are put in the service of a haircut.

In a society that reads images rather than personalities, people will go to absurd lengths to distinguish themselves through nuances of appearance. "Always I wanted a haircut like nobody else's haircut!" cries the shaggy professor. His belief that he can make himself unique through a change in image is an illusion of the sort that most commercials would push on us. But, drinking a special beer or using a special lipstick will only group one with other people who succumb to the lure of that product. Thus, the man who hopes to acquire a singular identity actually becomes a conformist, adopting a personality that others provide. "My friends call me a square! Many people call me a Square! I'm right in the groove!"

Every gag in the story makes a point about stereotyping. Eight athletes who already look identical receive assembly-line crew cuts; standardized images lead to mass-produced personalities. What happens to the gorilla becomes a metaphor for what happens to humans in a society obsessed with images. Barks's latent misogyny merges here with his critique of mass society. Horrendo the gorilla represents humanity's animal nature. The haircut that Donald gives him perverts his ferocious spirit so that the ape becomes a sissy, an apt metaphor for the domestication and feminization of the (male) consumer in mass culture. Donald's clients lose their selfhood in similar ways, sporting bizarre and grotesque hairdos. But while the customers are pleased with their reflections in the mirror, Horrendo runs in terror.

The circus people are also horrified, but for a different reason. A gorilla that looks like a "cookie pusher" is not marketable. To be entertaining, the circus too must maintain an image—that mastering animals is a dangerous business. But by a final irony, the crowd in the last panel is so caught up in the spectacle—perversely a symbol of its own taming—that it does not notice the shaven ape.

"The Beauty Business" (*WDC&S* #308 [1966]) carries the themes of "Spare That Hair" to their logical extreme. Even the tale's history assumes significance, for it reveals Barks's reaction to having marketing controls on his art and having to conform to an editorial image of what the public wanted. "In the recent contest-survey which was conducted we discovered this magazine [*Walt Disney's Comics and Stories*] has a great girl-reader interest," Chase Craig wrote to Barks in November 1965. "In fact, we got more letters from girls than from boys. Many of them were quite insistent that Daisy be featured and many were indignant that we didn't up-date her dress, makeup, etc. Anyway, we do feel that if we add Daisy as a regular in the Donald Duck we will make a lot of readers happy, so we would like to try it. You might also like to use Daisy's nieces."[54]

Barks chafed at the thought of elevating a character he loathed to a lead in the Donald stories, and he reminded Craig of his impending retirement, adding that writing comics for the past twenty-three years had given him a "pain in the neck."[55] However, Craig persuaded the Duck Man to write two Daisy and Donald stories. The first tale, "The Beauty Business," which appeared in March 1966, clearly expressed Barks's thoughts about having to include Daisy in his stories and of building a plot around points of dress and makeup.

"The Beauty Business" is packed with every variety of female grotesque. Everyone in the story—especially Donald—is obsessed with glamour. In Daisy's case, this preoccupation is a matter of peer pressure: "Oh dear! My girlfriends' boyfriends went to trade school, and all became actors and astronauts and such glamorous things! Donald better be something I can be proud of or I'll just go up in a puff of smoke!"

Seventeen years earlier, Donald had felt humiliated at having to crochet doilies (*WDC&S* #101 [1949]). But in an age when a sausage shop can be remodeled into a "Salon de Charm" and Barks was forced to emphasize female fashions and hairdos in his stories, it is appropriate that Donald has become a "pin-and-curl-mechanic."

The transformation of the hideous Mrs. J. Crowfoot Dryskin shows the artificiality of the glamour business. Donald has to cover her with putty and paint to disguise her whole face. "At last I look like myself!" she exclaims oxymoronically. Barks, however, revealed the incongruity of such manufactured beauty by drawing a beautiful new head tottering away on the spindly body of an old woman. Donald, who until this tale has believed implicitly in his own artistry, knows that he is dealing in shams—very fragile ones. "Don't sing too vigorously, Ma-dom!" he thinks as Mrs. Dryskin waltzes away. "Your whole face could fall off!"

Daisy, who resists being beautified, is nevertheless a conformist. In a town where every woman has been glamorized, she feels "like an asparagus in a field of orchids." However, the panel in which she walks down the street shows her to be the only normal-looking woman in Duckburg. The sophisticated "beauties" around her are all grotesques, with beehive hairdos, bangs covering their eyes, swiveled posteriors, and—in one case—a dress that apes a clown's costume. When Daisy allows herself to be dragged into the beauty parlor, her nieces, April, May, and June, sabotage her with "hag putty" and "ugly duckling de-uglifier." Symbolically, however, Daisy's hideous transformation draws attention to the tenuous line between manufactured beauty and monstrousness. The story closes with Donald reigning as the undisputed "glamour king of Duckburg."

In earlier stories, Donald had worked in such occupations as mail-man, stationmaster, and hotel manager, all of which took place in a private realm where he was answerable to his conscience or at worst a close relative. He gradually moves into a public sphere where failure puts him at odds with all society. By the 1960s, Duckburg has become a character in its own right, filled with spectacles, political speeches, and trivial fads: the melting down of a Civil War canon, a world's fair, a Halloween procession of jack-o'-lanterns, a pet parade, and even a Dutch festival. Barks portrayed it as a mass society, polluted by advertising hype, civic boosterism, and conformist consumption.

"Hero of the Dike" (*WDC&S* #246 [1964]) reinterprets Mary Mapes Dodge's famed story of the "Hero of Haarlem," questioning the possibility of heroism in the postmodern era.[56] The story takes place during Duckburg's annual sea festival, during which all the citizens dress in Dutch costumes. The highlight of the festival is the Wooden Shoe Ball. Donald and Gladstone are on their way to the dance to prevail on Daisy to be their partner when Donald spots a leak in the dike. As usual, Gladstone is a con artist who convinces Donald that he will be the hero of Duckburg if he stays and plugs the hole while Gladstone goes for help. But he goes to the ball and forgets all about Donald. Crosscutting between the ball and Donald, Barks shows the would-be hero's plight. While the whole city and his archrival enjoy the dance, Donald is beset by a finger growing numb and is attacked by ants and a swarm of mosquitoes. Nobody pays any attention to his calls for help. Gladstone finally tells the mayor to get to the dike at once, but the official goes off to make a speech instead. Even the usually conscientious nephews are preoccupied—so enraptured by the warbling of Cutie Teenie and playing their music so loud that they cannot hear Donald calling for help. The mayor too is entranced by rock music and at the Dutch festival dance contest yells, "Swing it, you cats, and may the best couple win the prize!" When Donald asks a hobo for aid, he instead picks the duck's pocket. When the dike finally crashes, Donald is blamed and a mob tries to hunt him down. He escapes in a gondola with Daisy, grateful for a romantic respite in the midst of the witch hunt. "Hero of the Dike" is one of Barks's most cynical stories, embodying the artist's increasing disillusionment with humanity and postmodern consumer culture.

The later Scrooge adventures also express Barks's disillusionment and are strikingly unromantic. Half of them are set in Duckburg or other parts of America, and even the foreign tales have lost much of their exotic allure. Locales are generic rather than evoking specific places and often have just enough scenery to support the narrative. In addition to the loss of local color, Barks's art also undergoes a transformation. Gone are the textures and shading that gave earlier adventures a touch of realism. In their streamlining and simplification of detail, these tales manifest a new graphic economy. Part of the reason for this new style was Barks's disenchantment with the cutting of his stories and his decision to put less effort into his art—such as abandoning splash panels. Barks had also begun simplifying his style and drawing the ducks taller and more angular as a result of a new crop of paper from the office. "In the old days," he wrote to a fan in 1960, "I was furnished with the best grade of Strathmore, and my style was more detailed and the characters more expressive. Nowadays ... the paper furnished us artists has been a clay-coated import from Germany. The result has been a tightening of the lines, less bounce to the characters."[57] Barks claimed that he had always been inclined to draw the ducks too tall and that with the new paper he could not erase them as easily as before, making them look elongated and ungainly. By 1960, after Barks received a new type of paper, the ducks had become short and bouncy again but were simplified and more stylized.

There was another reason for the change in Barks's style. To put away a nest egg for retirement, he took on the drawing (but rarely the writing) of a host of other Disney titles, including *Gyro Gearloose*, *Daisy Duck's Diary*, and *Grandma Duck's Farm Friends*. His page count, including covers, increased from 277 in 1949 to 373 in 1960.[58] Thus, Barks simply could not put the same effort into his later art as he had into his earlier work, admitting, "I think my work was sort of dropping down in quality a bit because of the quantity."[59]

The shift in graphics also occurred because the sense of wonder with which Barks approached foreign lands had diminished. As corporate America increased its global reach, it was no longer possible to find pockets of uncontaminated ancient cultures ripe for exploration. "An ominous drumbeat of doom was rumbling out of Indochina, where ancient kingdoms and cultures of a beautiful people were about to be steamrolled by modernizers," Barks wrote about Tangkor Wat (Angkor Wat), his fictionalized portrait of Cambodia, in "City of Golden Roofs" (*US* #20 [1957]).[60] The contamination spread to the pages of the *National*

Geographic. "Yes, I still get the *Geographic*," he stated in 1985. "The 'Journey up the Nile' article in the May issue was interesting but lacked the historical wallop that made 'Felucca down the Nile' so outstanding years ago. Egypt today is so cluttered with people the *Geographic* can no longer recreate the grandeur of the past; it can only show people and more people, and the ditches they dig to irrigate crops for more people."[61] Rather than providing an escape into a culture that offered relief from our neuroses and strife, foreign locales simply became more and more mirrors of modern America. When asked in 1984 if it was still possible to find an untouched utopia like Tralla La, Barks quipped, "No. The Democrats have already looted it."[62] America's increasing military intervention abroad and political upheaval in many other nations also impacted the adventure story. "I'm running out of nations which aren't fighting or rioting or committing aggression!" Barks complained to a fan in 1962.[63]

Barks could no longer ignore contemporary events, and near the end of his career he wrote three stories dealing with the war in Southeast Asia. "Monkey Business" (*WDC&S* #297 [1965]) was written at a time of increased U.S. involvement in the war in Vietnam and a sudden increase in American "advisers" in that country (nearly twenty-three thousand by the end of 1964).[64] Scrooge's mechanical monkeys fail to sell in America, so he decides to sell them overseas, a reference to the corporate practice of dumping unsalable or dangerous products in foreign countries. Scrooge's monkeys destroy the ecological balance in Siambodia (Cambodia) and Upper Malaria (South Vietnam) and cause conflicts between the two countries, showing how American intervention brings confusion, chaos, and war.

In 1964, when this story was written, Prince Norodom Sihanouk, the Cambodian leader who had overseen his country's independence from the French in 1953, was desperately striving to remain neutral as war escalated in neighboring South Vietnam, which Barks aptly names Upper Malaria, analogizing the war-torn country to a contagious disease. The story's Prince Jambouk combines qualities of both Sihanouk and South Vietnamese rulers. By 1965, after the United States ignored his entreaties for neutrality and American armies were attacking Viet Cong and North

Vietnamese regulars within Cambodian borders, Sihanouk began allowing the North Vietnamese to attack the South from Cambodia. Thus began a cycle of violence that created enmity between both countries.

Scrooge uses the clanging sound of the monkeys to drive the rice birds (symbols of the guerrilla forces) that are destroying the rice paddies to Upper Malaria. This act incites Malaria to invade Siambodia, but Scrooge tells Donald to retune the monkeys to drive the invaders out of the country. In effect, the tycoon has turned the monkeys into military devices to repel an enemy. However, American intervention has unforeseen consequences: by taking sides, Americans have made themselves vulnerable to blame for any failures by their allies. When Scrooge suggests a celebration feast, the ringing of the dinner gong ironically calls the rice birds back from Upper Malaria. King Jambouk orders his men to hunt the ducks down, determined to make Scrooge pay for the mistake, and they must flee the country. Scrooge and the ducks escape with part of the jewels paid for Scrooge's "aid." But in a tokenistic gesture, the nephews force him to donate a quarter of the jewels to the Junior Woodchucks of Siambodia as compensation. Thus, the story seems to have a happy ending. However, the ecological destruction and enmity between the countries indicates that American intervention has proved disastrous. In the real world, Sihanouk's decision to allow North Vietnamese and Viet Cong troops to use Cambodian territory led to massive U.S. bombing, his overthrow, and the rise of the genocidal regime of Pol Pot.

In 1965, President Johnson escalated the Vietnam War, marking the end of the counterinsurgency phase of American involvement and the first use of U.S. ground troops in South Vietnam as well as the first systematic bombing of North Vietnam. "The Treasure of Marco Polo" (*US* #65 [1965]) encodes the devolution into open warfare. It is Barks's most militarily explicit and politically topical story and is fraught with xenophobia, confusion, and panic. The tale opens with a long panel that contrasts the foreign treasure in Scrooge's money bin with a multiarmed statue of Gimme, the God of Alms Takers. His outstretched hands, Medusa-like arms, and patched pants warn that America's search for foreign wealth could end up embroiling it in a costly quagmire. Scrooge has bought a huge jade elephant for a million dollars from Unsteadystan, an allusion to South Vietnam. However, the elephant has been hijacked, leaving only its tail and a bullet-riddled crate. Many years earlier, pirates had stolen the elephant from Marco Polo in a raid in Cochin China (Indochina). Now history repeats itself: the elephant has been stolen again by communist pirates trying to take over Unsteadystan. Soy Bheen, a young stowaway, offers to take Scrooge to Unsteadystan in return for protection from Wahn Beeg Rhat, who is trying to become the country's dictator. "I'm not *about* to go wildly off to a war zone in the silly hope that some peasant kid can help me find my stolen elephant!" Scrooge fumes. But when an ancient map written by Marco Polo shows that the country harbors a fabulous treasure, Scrooge becomes intoxicated by the thought of discovering foreign loot. As he looks over the note, we see a map resembling the contours of the United States behind him with locations marked "here" and "there." As he reads the letter, the map changes shape, and we see locations labeled "nowhere" and "nowhere also." The change suggests the folly of searching for wealth and power in foreign locales so insignificant that they are "nowhere" on the map.

When Scrooge's plane tries to land, it is riddled with gunfire. Perceiving himself a neutral party, Scrooge protests that he is a "Duckburgian citizen," but his shouts are met with a hail of bullets through the airplane's window. American power is no guarantee of immunity against harm on foreign shores but instead marks one as a victim. Nor are good intentions a guarantee of good treatment in an unfamiliar foreign nation: when Scrooge waves a flag of truce, it is shot full of holes. "White flags mean *come out fighting* in Unsteadystan!" Soy tells him. The violence causes Scrooge to lose interest in elephants and hidden treasure, and he tries to hop a ship, but it is torpedoed by Rhat's brats. The ship's name, the SS *Traumatic*, connotes American shock at being bogged down in a confusing, senseless war. Scrooge runs toward the Duckburg embassy for protection, but it is blown up by a guerrilla who shouts, "Wahn Beeg Rhat, yes! Duckburg, no!"

The mask of innocence drops in this story: it is no longer credible to euphemize insurgents as thieves or raiders. They are shown to be guerrillas, and the context is thoroughly military, with tanks, grenades, antiaircraft batteries, and images of battle in defiance of Western's censorship code.[65] However, although the United States had escalated the war in Vietnam and both propped up and instigated coups against South Vietnamese governments, Barks never examines the nature or justice of American involvement. Indeed, the story completely elides images of U.S. military intervention in the war. It evokes mainstream American opinion at this time that the United States was an innocent victim in the war, trapped in a quagmire that it had not created.

Barks utilizes a number of antisocialist stereotypes in this story. Wahn Beeg Rhat's name is a play on Spanish dialect, and he is styled after Latin American dictators. Likewise, the guerrilla's anti-Duckburg chant is a parody of Latin American propaganda slogans, and a soldier takes a siesta in the middle of the war, invoking stereotypes of Latins as lazy and slothful. Barks also alludes to Russian stereotypes when the guerrilla remarks, "Shows that you can't trust these watches from the worker's paradise!" This conflation of Asian, Latin American, and Soviet communists reveals Barks's confusion about the differences among socialist movements as well as his adherence to the shibboleth of a monolithic communist bloc engaged in a conspiracy to rule the world. This simplistic model of communism was embodied in the domino theory, the chief ideological justification for going to war in Vietnam: if one Asian nation fell, all of Southeast Asia would "go communist."

But, Barks's tale does not valorize U.S. involvement in the war and embraces an isolationist position: both sides are called rebel gangs, and the conflict is presented as a civil war in which we should not be involved. Unsteadystan has had "sixty rulers in six months" (South Vietnam had nine changes of rulers from 1963 to 1965), and the name connotes the country's political instability. U.S. intervention is misguided and unwelcome. The usually levelheaded nephews are bunglers who almost get their uncles executed. "Now if you eager meddlers would let *me* run the show *my* way you may be able to save your uncles!" Soy tells them. Soy turns out to be Prince Char Ming in disguise. He steals into the jade elephant and turns a key that makes the elephant's trunk rise, a sign that a "true ruler" has ascended to the throne. He appears in royal garb through the elephant's howdah as both armies bow down before him. "Don't let him spoil my *revolution!*" Rhat yells as he tries to shoot the young prince. Char Ming is saved not by the soldiers, who are passive and rarely shown in the story (not unlike the South Vietnamese army, which was noted for its corruption, low morale, and unwillingness to fight the enemy) but by a well-coordinated football tackle by the unarmed nephews. American sporting prowess, as David Kunzle tells us, has triumphed over military aggression and superior weaponry.[66] However, their heroism is compromised and arrives late in the tale: until they save Soy, they are unable to understand the nature of the conflict and what to do about it. Thus, Soy, not the nephews, is the major hero.

When Rhat orders the erasure squad to fire on Soy, they refuse: "And keep these silly revolutions going forever! No! We suddenly think it'd be nice for Unsteadystan to have a *king* again like in the *good old days!*" says a guerrilla. However, Barks's solution trivializes revolution and the issues at stake in the war: land reform and an end to the political persecution of dissidents by the South Vietnamese regime. The solution is also a fantasy, belied by the name of his hero, Prince Char Ming. He is the only one who can "unite the country and bring peace." But, in reality, the only policy that would have united the country and expressed popular will would have been a negotiated settlement with North Vietnam, an arrangement that would inevitably have ended in the unification of the country under communist leadership.[67] To forestall this result, the U.S. resorted to undemocratic strategies that contradicted its democratic ideology. Under the Geneva Accords of 1954, which ended France's colonial war in Indochina and divided Vietnam into two armistice zones, unification under a single government was to be the subject of an election in 1956. To prevent the country from going communist, the U.S. aided South Vietnamese leader Ngo Dinh Diem in his efforts to abort the election and to establish South Vietnam as an independent nation. However, his regime became tyrannical and repressive, and the Kennedy administration orchestrated a coup that toppled him from power. As the U.S. tried to bolster one failed regime after another it was forced to escalate the war, and the conflict became increasingly an American commitment—and an American liability.

Barks's solution of returning Unsteadystan to kingship was guided by his conservatism and privileging of native tradition and reflects his confusion about the war:

> In the 1960s there was so much of that Vietnam bank burning going on around the country. I realized what people were objecting to in that war, and I just felt that someplace we have got to stop the communists or they're going to take over everything. It was something I couldn't do anything about. . . . In "The Treasure of Marco Polo" I tried to turn the country back, to make people think of the better times the people had before they got so darn mad that they were fighting all the time. Those stories were written at a time I had run out of ideas and would have to do a lot of fabrications in a plot that I didn't know too much about. They weren't my best stories.[68]

Given the conflagration in Southeast Asia, imperialist treasure hunts were no longer morally justifiable. Scrooge cannot be shown to be profiting from nations with whom the United States was at war. Thus, when Char Ming offers Scrooge the jade elephant and twenty urns of Marco Polo's treasure, the miser says he has lost his taste for treasure and gives it and the elephant back to Unsteadystan, even promising to return the tail after he gets home. "The tired and hungry people of Unsteadystan can *use* that wealth!" affirms a nephew. America should send Vietnam money, not bombs, the conclusion implies.

"The Doom Diamond" (*US* #70 [1967]) was the last adventure story Barks both wrote and drew and expresses the problematic nature of the imperialist treasure tale in the contemporary era. It can be read as an allegory about the Vietnam War. Scrooge buys the Zero Diamond, the largest diamond in the world, from South Miserystan (South Vietnam) and delivers the price in gold to their capital. However, the jewel turns out to be a jinx to whomever owns it, and both Scrooge and the Beagle Boys, who steal it, are beset by disaster after disaster. *Zero* means "doom" in the natives' language, and Barks's tale implies that American involvement in Southeast Asia has brought only implacable ill fortune to our nation and thus is a no-win situation. "Goodbye and hurry home!" the natives yell, diving for cover as the Americans leave, suggesting that the American presence had become equally displeasing to the Vietnamese.

The story begins with both Scrooge and the Beagle Boys in a rut. The robbers use trained birds to filch quarters and half dollars and idly dream of making a big heist, while Scrooge futilely chases the animals as his money flies out the window. "We've gotten . . . like people on a dole!" says one Beagle Boy. Only when Scrooge and the Beagles step out of this situation do they court disaster. When Scrooge neglects his money bin to pursue foreign booty, he faces the loss of his fortune. Believing him lost at sea, Duckburg threatens to seize his money and send it to Fort Knox (i.e., the federal government). Such loss also threatens the Beagles and their coin-pinching scheme: they rescue the old duck from a watery grave after throwing him and the jinxed diamond he has accidentally swallowed into the ocean. The story ends as it began, with the Beagles idly watching their trained fowl pilfer coins and Scrooge again impotently chasing them. While this situation is frustrating, it offers security to both sides and suggests a chastened Republicanism on Barks's part. American involvement in Vietnam has robbed citizens through onerous taxation, the tale implies, but it is better to stick with the status quo, even if doing so supports welfare cheats like the Beagles. As Barks put it in 1975, "My own political philosophy is that we've got a pretty good thing the way we've got it now, and we should just leave it damn well alone. We can have Watergates and all kinds of things, but nobody gets hurt, nobody goes to prison; we just have a lot of fun as we go along. Everybody's robbin' everyone else, but it's something you expect."[69]

Barks's doubts about America bringing freedom, technology, and economic progress to undeveloped nations is the subject of a 1962 satire of the Peace Corps, "Buffaloed by Buffaloes" (GG #1267 [1961]). With great fanfare and political speeches, Duckburg sends the first member of its Brain Corps to "uplift citizens of less advantaged lands—it hopes!" Gyro Gearloose arrives in Farbakistan and surveys the needs of the people. To the inventor, the country seems ruled by hard labor, waste, and inefficiency. He observes a herd of buffalo lounging in the water eating lotus blossoms and people spending hours pumping water and weeding rice paddies. When he asks why farmers do not use electric pumps, he discovers that the country has no means of generating electricity. "Your problems are solved," he declares in a moment of hubris, promising to "have you *all on easy street!*" Seeing so much power going to waste, he orders dozens of electric pumps and miles of wire to carry it from the new power plant he plans to build. He invents a "reverse roller coaster" to run the buffalo-powered generator, "freeing" men from the task of pedaling the water pumps. The result is a disaster: more men are needed to push the buffalos than to pump water, and there are no longer people enough left to weed the paddies. When the natives ask him what his next plan is, Gyro says anxiously, "I think I'd better get out of the country before I have another *idea!*" and beats a hasty retreat. "And so, Farbakistan stays un-uplifted—its people toiling like beasts of burden, and its beasts of burden still untoiling!" reads a narration box.

Barks's later Scrooge tales reveal a preoccupation with age and memory. Despite his increased cynicism, he remained a romantic at heart. "North of the Yukon" (*US* #59 [1966]) again evokes nostalgia for Scrooge's days as a frontier hero in the Klondike gold rush. Barks had a sentimental attachment to this story and kept the original art for years. It was based on the story of Balto, the sled dog who saved Nome by carrying medicine to save the city during an epidemic.[70] The artist named his dog Barko, a tip-off that reveals his attachment to the canine. Barko is an old champion, now arthritic and forgotten. Scrooge's antagonist is a pig-faced villain, Soapy Slick, a reference to Soapy Smith, the real-life Dawson con artist whom Barks had added to a crowd scene in "Back to the Klondike" (*US* FC #456 [1953]). As usual, the past haunts the present: Soapy tries to steal McDuck's fortune by claiming he never paid for a grubstake in 1898. Barko and Scrooge prove that the old sourdoughs still have the right stuff: each shows determination, loyalty, and self-sacrifice in the struggle to win back the receipt.

These heroic frontier traits coexist with Barks's cynicism about the media. The newspapermen are pushy and invasive and bear responsibility for informing Soapy about Scrooge, thereby imperiling his fortune. However, Barks's view of the journalists is ambivalent. They also save

Scrooge's wealth by photographing Soapy trying to tear up the receipt after stealing it from Scrooge. The news media thus both threaten individual privacy and guarantee some degree of bean-spilling even in a mass society. But the old heroes and the old values ultimately triumph.

"King Scrooge the First" (*US* #71 [1967]) was the last adventure story Barks wrote. He did not draw it because "I was about to retire and I didn't want the long grind of drawing 'King Scrooge' to run me into overtime."[71] The story is a moving retrospective plea by the sixty-five-year-old author as he faced retirement to be released from the ducks after laboring on them for over thirty years as both storyman and cartoonist. A story within a story, it interweaves past and present. A four-thousand-year-old fortuneteller, Khan Khan, believes that Scrooge is the reincarnation and descendant of King Scrooge the First of ancient Sagbad, capital of Fatcatstan. The swami activates Scrooge's "memory genes" and takes him back to the ancient city in hopes of having him reenact his burying of a secret treasure.

Khan Khan functions as Barks's alter ego: He writes the plot and has the ducks enact it in what functions as Barks's final summing up of all the Uncle Scrooge adventures. The Duck Man reveals the depredations behind Scrooge's fortune and his tales of adventure. Sagbad is attacked by Khan Khan, in his earlier incarnation as king of the Mongolducks, in revenge for sacking Samarkand. Khan Khan visits the revenge of history for all the pillage and violations Scrooge has wreaked on this and other civilizations. The nephews, who are usually Scrooge's helpers and rescue him from dangers, function here as a Greek chorus, condemning him: "There are enemies on every hand," they sing in a camp musical number, "who'd like revenge on Fatcatstan" and want to get back the loot he took from their capital. "Now what capital can that be!" sing the nephews, "And what loot do they mean? King Scrooge-Shah has looted half the world that's yet been seen!" "Oh, he pillaged Parthegenea, Galatia, and Armenia! He made a mush of Hindu-Kush and robbed the Medians blind! He took the bucks of the poor Seljucks and left not a cent behind!" "Always, always it's this way! The younger generation makes fun of their elder's accomplishments!" groans Scrooge-Shah. Barks invokes the generation gap here, portraying youth as truth tellers, not media-addicted adolescents as in his earlier tales, while simultaneously parodying them as a camp chorus.

King Scrooge leads Khan Khan to the treasure, but he wants not gold but the antidote to the powder he took centuries before that had made him immortal. "Riches you wouldn't understand, short-lived one!" he tells Scrooge. The swami shrivels and begins to fade as he shuffles off into the desert to die. He is "tired, and old and lonely! I've had it, as they say young princes!" The last panel shows Scrooge wallowing in jewels and booty, calling Khan Khan a "nut." But a nephew winks at his brother (and the audience), aware of Scrooge's delusion that great wealth can lead to inner peace. "Great words from the voice of *wisdom!*" the nephew says ironically.

"King Scrooge the First" is Barks's epitaph to the ducks, expressing his desire, via his alter ego, Khan Khan, to free himself from the bondage, anonymity, and low pay of writing Disney comics. As a parting shot, the Duck Man broke two of Western's major taboos in his last Scrooge story: the prohibitions on portraying sex and death. In a scene in Sagbad's slave quarters, Donald lusts after several well-endowed slave girls until Scrooge-Shah restrains him, and the usually misogynist nephews drag girl duck slaves around by the chains on their necks. And, in the story's denouement, Khan Khan disintegrates before our eyes, leaving no doubt that he is dying.

On June 30, 1966, Barks retired from Western Publishing. He had turned sixty-five at the end of March and departed from the company as soon as he could. The impending loss was not lost on his editors. Barks had been the mainstay of Disney comics and produced the best-selling comic title of all time. "I had not forgotten about your retirement plans," Chase Craig wrote in November 1965, "but I did not remember the actual date. . . . In fact, I would like very much to forget such a date as it will be a catastrophe for the comic book industry. I'm sorry that 23 years of comic booking gives you such a pain in the neck, but look on the bright side. . . . [T]hink of how many people you've made happy with Uncle Scrooge."[72]

The letter tried to coax Barks into doing more assignments for the company: "Just tell us what you would like to do in the way of work, and we will then make our plans around your decision." Barks agreed to continue providing "some comic work" on a freelance basis to supplement his pension. "Pawns of the Loup Garou" (*DD* #117 [1969]), was the first result of the new arrangement. The idea for the script had come from Barks bibliographer Mike Barrier; however, neither man was happy with the final product. "The thing you noticed about my 'Loup Garou' story is the sort of business I like to forget," Barks wrote to Barrier. The artist had to skirt the issue of whether his menace was actually a werewolf because of Western's prohibitions against horror stories. "Always there were decisions to make. Could a Loup Garou be a real werewolf? Could a witch be a real witch? How far can I stretch the ridiculous without getting in trouble with the office? How far can I push pure fantasy ... ? I leaned toward logical explanations of phenomena in everyday terms and mechanics—just to be safe. I hate to go back into those old stories and revive the struggles I had trying to make explanations interesting and funny and not a dull let-down."[73]

Two more Donald Duck stories followed ("Officer of the Day," *DD* #126 [1969], and "A Day in a Duck's Life," *DD* #138 [1971], both script only). But Barks's most extensive postretirement scripting was for a Junior Woodchucks series. Thanks largely to the persistence of Craig, Barks wrote two dozen Woodchucks stories from 1969 to 1973. His method was the same as in all later scripts: to submit rough drawings in comic panel format plus a brief written synopsis. The stories bristle with the tumultuous events of the 1960s and 1970s (protest marches, political graft, and public apathy), but their most prevalent concern was ecological disaster. In this emphasis, the artist may have been influenced by his reading material. Ecological issues had been heavily foregrounded in American news in the 1970s, and *National Geographic* featured numerous articles on environmental concerns.

Scrooge is the villain in these tales, leading an army of bulldozers to mow down Duckburg's Black Forest to build his model city, polluting Lake Erie with runoff from his vitamin factory, and trying to kill endangered species like whales for their blubber. In these tales, Barks returned Scrooge to his roots as an egoistic capitalist. Until the 1960s, the artist had been unaware of fans' likes and dislikes, but feedback from readers sparked a change in Scrooge's character: "Analyzing all the things you fans have written and said, I've concluded that you all liked him best when he was the menace in the duck stories," he wrote to a fan in 1970. "When he became the hero, with his own book, I had to be careful how bad I made him."[74]

This later Scrooge often regresses to the dirty tricks of his earlier incarnations. In "Eagle Savers" (*JW* #11 [1971]), for example, the nephews tell Scrooge that they will have to report him to Senator Birdfriend if he does not stop driving the bald eagles from their nest and threatening their extinction by drilling a hole in their mountaintop home. "Who cares?" he replies. "With my money I can put Senator Birdfriend in my pocket anytime!" The nephews sometimes take on the characteristics of the counterculture, fighting corporate capital. In "Duckmade Disaster" (*JW* #14 [1972]), they lead a protest march when Scrooge tries to erect his money bin over the site of the cabin of Cornelius Coot, the founder of Duckburg. And, in "Let Sleeping Bones Lie" (*JW* #8 [1971]), they get Scrooge high on "vision weed," an allusion to marijuana, to prevent him from destroying a dinosaur skeleton to build a superhighway.

Ecological catastrophes only hinted at in earlier stories are starkly portrayed and are remarkable for their appearance in a Disney comic. Indeed, nowhere else in comics was environmentalism so openly and consistently embraced. However, with their young heroes, the Woodchucks stories were geared toward a younger audience, and Barks did not address older readers as he had in previous stories. The tales thus suffer from being formulaic and simplistic and from having contrived happy endings. When the Duck Man tried to depart from these limits, he was immediately shot down. Craig asked Barks to change the ending of "Be Leery of Lake Eerie" (*JW* #17 [1972]), for example. In Barks's script, the lake remained polluted, while in the printed comic it has been entirely cleaned up. "The office butchered the ending," the artist commented, "and it all comes out as sweet as rain drops on rose petals."[75]

After drawing ducks for more than thirty-five years, Barks's heart was no longer in writing comics. "Yes, I'm still doing a few scripts for

Gold Key, doggone it!!" he complained to a fan in 1972. "The editor seems so desperate for scripts that I crank up my tired brain and do one now and then."[76] Chase Craig had been so nice to Barks over the years and so important to his career that he did not want to let the editor down. Barks shared his feelings with Western writer Mark Evanier, who passed them along to Craig. "Do you really think Carl wants to stop doing them?" Craig asked. "Because for 20 years, he wanted to quit doing the ducks every two months. He keeps saying he didn't have any more stories in him, and I always keep urging him to try one more . . . and of course, he always came up with something wonderful." So after Evanier assured him that Barks was serious this time, Craig called the Duck Man and told him, "You're free!" Evanier could hear Barks's "Whoopee!" echo through the phone's earpiece.[77]

By this time, the Duck Man had become fascinated with another medium: painting. In 1955, Barks took up watercolors as a diversion but soon found it so interesting that it was taking time away from his duck work and had to quit. After he retired in 1966, he again took up the easel, this time specializing in oils. His third wife, Garé, was an accomplished wildlife painter, and she and Carl went to local art shows to display their work and cultivate sales. Barks specialized in oil paintings of young girls, rural landscapes, and scenes of Southern California Indian tribes before the arrival of the white man. Yet few sold.

However, events soon would radically alter Barks's life. After his name circulated among comics aficionados during the late 1960s and early 1970s, an organized and highly vocal fandom began to grow up around his work. In 1971 a young fan named Glenn Bray asked Barks to paint an oil of a Donald Duck comic book cover, and the former Disney artist's stalled painting career began to take off. Barks's Duck paintings originally sold to fans for the modest price of $150, but when they began being auctioned off, prices rose steadily, with one selling for $6,400 in 1976. Today they can command more than $200,000, putting them in the price range of works by the great masters. When he temporarily lost his license to paint Disney subjects, Barks took up watercolors and created a new series of non-Disney duck paintings depicting "Famous Figures of History as They Might Have

Looked Had Their Genes Gotten Mixed with Waterfowl!" These ribald paintings were reminiscent of Barks's work on the *Eye-Opener*. From 1982 through 1993, Another Rainbow issued a series of fine art lithographs of his Disney paintings. Although Barks's reputation was built on his comic book stories, he spent more years as a painter than as a Disney comic book artist and writer.

In the 1980s, Barks's recognition grew when complete reprintings of his work appeared in collected editions. Michael Barrier's *Carl Barks and the Art of the Comic Book* provided the first detailed bibliography of Barks's stories. Two other books followed: a collection of Barks's Duck paintings, *The Fine Art of Walt Disney's Donald Duck*, published by Another Rainbow, and a limited edition, *Walt Disney's Uncle Scrooge McDuck: His Life and Times*, published by Celestial Arts, with an introduction by George Lucas. Reviews of these books in such national publications as *Time* and *Newsweek* further cemented Barks's stature as a nationally recognized artist. In 1991 he received the Disney Legends Award, the only comic book artist ever granted such an honor.[78]

Garé Barks passed away in 1993, leaving Carl to be cared for by a team of loyal housekeepers. The artist continued to produce drawings of the ducks for Disney conventions until his health began to fail. In 1999, he was diagnosed with leukemia, and he died in his sleep on August 25, 2000, six months short of his hundredth birthday. An atheist, Barks dismissed any thoughts of a hereafter: "I have no apprehension, no fear of death," he told Donald Ault in 1999. "I do not believe in an afterlife."[79] But he did seek one particular form of immortality. In the mid-1990s, Barks was asked what he thought his legacy would be. "Wouldn't it be great if a thousand years from now my stories were like Aesop's fables?" Barks mused. "Just keep right on going [and] never, never die. That would be an ideal situation. I want to check up on that."[80]

Barks's wish is well on its way to being granted. Except for a brief hiatus, his stories have been continuously reprinted since the early 1980s, and new European collections of his complete works are in production. Barks's ongoing popularity testifies to his stories' continuing relevance. Beneath the facade of being innocent children's fare, Barks's tales are inextricably linked to the politics of his time and offer one of the most trenchant critiques of patriarchal capitalism in any popular media. They trace the history of our culture's will to power that goes back five thousand years to the origins of civilization through the era of European colonization and the hegemony of the West to the postmodern society of the present. They call into question the tentacle-like homogenization of both the Third World and the United States by consumerism and global capitalism.

The depth of this critique has led some authors to claim that Barks's vision is primarily nihilistic, a "disenchanted utopia" that offers no solution to the negativity his stories inscribe.[81] This judgment is too simplistic. Although Barks dissuades us from believing in either a bucolic Golden Age or a modern technological utopia, his narratives have an important utopian subtext. They are characterized by what I have called an ethic of balance. As a curb on the quest for unlimited material accumulation, growth, and progress promoted by the culture of western modernity, they offer one of the few visions of communal and ecologically sustainable societies in the popular media as well as an ethic of nonviolence that satirizes the deleterious consequences of masculine aggression, competition, and war. Having grown up in the rural hinterlands before the full onslaught of urbanization, technological proliferation, and monopoly capitalism, Barks invested his stories with a morality of humility, moderation, tolerance, and compassion as an antidote to the domination of humanity and nature of the present paradigm.

Barks's tales thus tales contribute to what we might call a form of reflexive modernity, an awareness of the costs and dangers as well as the advantages of our modern/postmodern world. Barks was a very modernist antimodernist, well aware of the power that his narratives could exert on his readers. Like Alfred Hitchcock and French New Wave cinema, he created a self-reflexive discourse in his works that operated within popular narratives yet promoted a critical spectatorship by his audience. His "open" texts, with their multiple, contradictory worldviews and self-reflexive parodies of popular narratives, empower readers to resist the passive consumption of his work, offering important countertexts to the commodification of media culture. They open up the mind to the clash of divergent worldviews and discourses and undermine notions of male mastery, a unitary self, and totalizing ideology. Just as Donald and Scrooge represent the deluded humans of the present, the nephews are harbingers of a new planetary consciousness, embodying the possibility of the emergence of a new form of humanity. Yet it is important to remember that these child/adults are not charismatic heroes but only representations of ourselves and the potentialities that we all possess in the struggle for self-empowerment and a meaningful life.

A CARL BARKS FILMOGRAPHY

The following is a list of produced Disney cartoons on which Carl Barks worked as a storyman. Unless otherwise noted, all films were Donald Duck cartoons directed by Jack King. An asterisk indicates that Barks drew many or most of the storyboards for that film. Initials SD and SC indicate whether Barks was a story director or a member of the story crew on a film. Although this title was sometimes nominal, the director was generally the most experienced storyman in a unit, the person who explained a storyboard to Walt Disney and to the other gag men in story conferences. According to Barks,

> In most Disney story units, the story director was a sort of corporal with some small amount of authority over the gagmen and sketchmen. He was also the guy who choreographed the story in presenting it before Walt. His ability to grunt, squeal, emote, and howl with laughter at his storyboard gags determined his standing in the studio's hierarchy. In the Duck unit, none of us—except possibly Harry Reeves—wanted any authority, and none of us wanted the job of explaining the crudely drawn storyboards to Walt. His attention was always twenty drawings ahead of the narrator, anyway. I got stuck with the job after Harry was moved up to roving straw boss of the whole shorts division.[1]

Modern Inventions. May 29, 1937.*
Donald's Ostrich. December 10, 1937.
Self Control. February 11, 1938. SD.
Donald's Better Self. March 11, 1938. SD.
Donald's Nephews. April 15, 1938. SC.
Good Scouts. July 8, 1938. SD.*

Donald's Golf Game. November 4, 1938. SD.
Donald's Lucky Day. January 13, 1939.*
The Hockey Champ. April 28, 1939. SD.*
Donald's Cousin Gus. May 19, 1939. SD.*
Sea Scouts. June 30, 1939. SD. Directed by Dick Lundy.*
Donald's Penguin. August 11, 1939. SD.
The Autograph Hound. September 1, 1939. SC.
Mr. Duck Steps Out. June 7, 1940. SD.
Put-Put Troubles. June 19, 1940. Directed by Riley Thompson.
Bone Trouble (Pluto). June 28, 1940. Directed by Jack Kinney.
Donald's Vacation. August 9, 1940.
Window Cleaners. September 20, 1940. SC.*
Fire Chief. December 13, 1940.*
Timber. January 10, 1941. SD.*
The Golden Eggs. March 7, 1941. SC. Directed by Wilfred Jackson.
Early to Bed. July 11, 1941. SC.*
Truant Officer Donald. August 1, 1941. SC.*
Old McDonald Duck. September 12, 1941. SD.*
Chef Donald. December 5, 1941. SD.*
The Village Smithy. January 16, 1942. Directed by Dick Lundy.
Donald's Snow Fight. April 10, 1942. SD.*
Donald Gets Drafted. May 1, 1942. SD.
The Army Mascot (Pluto). May 22, 1942. Directed by Clyde Geronimi.
The Vanishing Private. September 25, 1942. SD.*
Sky Trooper. November 6, 1942.
Bellboy Donald. December 18, 1942.*
The Old Army Game. November 5, 1943. SC.*
Home Defense. November 26, 1943.*
Trombone Trouble. February 18, 1944. SD.*
The Plastics Inventor. September 1944.

Barks also worked on other cartoons that were never produced, including the following:

The Love Nest. February 1936.
Timid Elmer. c. 1936.
Northwest Mounted. 1936.*
Nightwatchman Donald. August 1937.*
Interior Decorators. October 1937.*
Yukon Mickey (*Yukon Donald*). February 1938.*
Lost Prospectors. March 1938.*
Donald Munchausen. April 1938.

Tanglefoot. May 1938.
Donald's Shooting Gallery. June 1938.
The Rubber Hunter. c. 1938.*
Donald's Balloon. August 1938.
The Beaver Hunters. May 1939.*
Traveling Salesman Donald. c. 1940.*
Sculptor Donald. c. 1941.
Madame XX. 1942.*
Donald's Tank. 1942.*

For a description of these cartoons, see Thomas Andrae, "A Carl Barks Filmography, " *Carl Barks Library of Walt Disney Comics and Stories in Color* (Prescott, Ariz.: Another Rainbow, 1996), 51: 13–15.

NOTES

CHAPTER 1

1. Barks, interview by Donald Ault and Thomas Andrae, August 4, 1975. For a collection of Barks interviews, see Donald Ault, ed., *Carl Barks Conversations* (Jackson: University Press of Mississippi, 2003).
2. Barks to R. O. Burnett, December 13, 1960.
3. Malcolm Willets, "An Interview with George Sherman," *Duckburg Times* 12 (July 1981): 12 (reprinted from *Vanguard* 2 [1968]).
4. Leonard Maltin, "The Carl Barks Story: The Creator of Uncle Scrooge Moves into the Limelight," *Disney News* 19, no. 1 (Winter 1983–84).
5. Barks, interview by Paul Ciotti, September 28, 1972.
6. James Freeman, "Donald Duck: How Children (Mainly Boys) Viewed Their Parents (Mainly Fathers), 1943–1960," *Children's Literature* 5, no. 6 (1977): 151.
7. Paul Lyness, "The Place of the Mass Media in the Lives of Boys and Girls," *Journalism Quarterly* 29, no. 1 (1952): 43.
8. Barks, interview by Donald Ault, May 5, 1973.
9. Norbert Muhlen, "Comic Books and Other Horrors," *Commentary*, January 1, 1949, 81.
10. Ibid.
11. Bradford Wright, *Comic Book Nation: The Transformation of Youth Culture in America* (Baltimore: Johns Hopkins University Press, 2001), xvii.
12. Martin Barker, *Comics: Ideology, Power, and the Critics* (Manchester, U.K.: Manchester University Press, 1989), 292.
13. Ariel Dorfman and Armand Mattelart, *How to Read Donald Duck: Imperialist Ideology in the Disney Comic* (New York: International General, 1975), 36.
14. Ibid., 46.

15. Ibid., 64.

16. Ibid., 16.

17. Ibid., 64.

18. Ibid., 73.

19. Michael Barrier, *Carl Barks and the Art of the Comic Book* (New York: Lilien, 1981), 82.

20. Barks to Dick Blackburn, March 8, 1968.

21. Barks to Michael Barrier, August 13, 1978.

22. Dorfman and Mattelart, *How to Read Donald Duck*, 16.

23. David Kunzle, "The Parts That Got Left Out of the Donald Duck Book; or, How Karl Marx Prevailed over Carl Barks."

24. Raymond Williams, *Marxism and Culture* (London: Fontana, 1981).

25. Dorfman and Mattelart, *How to Read Donald Duck*, 67.

26. C. Wright Mills, *White Collar: The American Middle Class* (New York: Oxford University Press, 1953), 263.

27. Dorfman and Mattelart, *How to Read Donald Duck*, 97.

28. Ibid.

29. Ibid., 98.

30. Ariel Dorfman, *Looking South, Facing North: A Bilingual Journey* (New York: Farrar, Strauss, and Giroux, 1998), 252.

31. Tony Bennett, "The Politics of the Popular," in *Popular Culture and Social Relations* (London: Open University Press, 1966), 19.

32. Douglas Kellner, *Media Culture: Cultural Studies, Identity, and Politics between the Modern and the Postmodern* (New York: Routledge, 1995), 98–101.

33. Stephen Kline, *Out of the Garden: Toys and Children's Culture in the Age of TV Marketing* (New York: Verso, 1993), 104.

34. Barks to Elvio Paolini, April 16, 1973.

35. John Tomlinson, *Cultural Imperialism* (Baltimore: Johns Hopkins University Press, 1991), 27.

36. Ibid., 164.

37. Ibid., 27.

38. Although Barks's stories ultimately derive from traditional beast fables, his works differ in offering a complex, ambivalent morality rather than a didactic system of epigrammatic "truths" and in presenting ambiguous characters rather than uniform "human" types.

39. E. B. Boatner, "From Burbank to Calisota," in *The Comic Book Price Guide*, ed. Robert Overstreet, no. 7 (1977–78), A–39.

40. Carl Barks, *Walt Disney's Uncle Scrooge McDuck: His Life and Times* (Millbrae, Calif.: Celestial Arts, 1981), 346.

41. Boatner, "From Burbank to Calisota," A–39.

42. Ibid.

43. Barks, interview by Michael Naiman, August 27, 1993, *Overstreet's Golden Age Quarterly* 2 (October–December 1993): 77.

44. Barrier, *Carl Barks*, 6–7.
45. Barks, interview by Ault and Andrae, August 4, 1975.
46. "A Tribute to Carl Barks," *Lost River Star*, special ed., July 1995, 10.
47. Barks, interview by Michael Barrier, November 22, 1973.
48. Barks to Bill Craig, May 6, 1966.
49. Barks, interview by Barrier, November 22, 1973.
50. Barks to Bill Craig, May 6, 1966.
51. Barrier, *Carl Barks*, 7.
52. Barks, interview by Ault and Andrae, August 4, 1975.
53. Barks, interview by Bruce Hamilton (questions by Thomas Andrae and Geoffrey Blum), June 24, 1984.
54. Barks, interview by Naiman, August 27, 1993.
55. Ibid.
56. Barks, interview by Barrier, November 22, 1973.
57. Barks, interview by Ault and Andrae, August 4, 1975.
58. Barks, interview by Barrier, November 22, 1973.
59. Ibid.
60. Ibid.
61. Ibid.
62. Ibid.
63. Shelley Armitage, *John Held Jr.: Illustrating the Jazz Age* (Syracuse, N.Y.: Syracuse University Press, 1987), 63.
64. *The Unexpurgated Carl Barks* (Prescott, Ariz.: Hamilton Comics, 1997), 43.
65. Barks, interview by Barrier, November 22, 1973.
66. Ibid.
67. Barks, interview by Thomas Andrae, Geoffrey Blum, and Bruce Hamilton, September 24, 1983.
68. Ibid.
69. Boatner, "From Burbank to Calisota," A–41.

CHAPTER 2

1. Barks to Thomas Andrae, April 30, 1987.
2. Barks also animated "a short bit of a shed-like building being blown apart" in the *Three Little Wolves* (Barks to Thomas Andrae, April 30, 1987). "Schnitzelbank" is "a German drinking song that was popular in the beer halls after the repeal of prohibition" (Barks to Thomas Andrae, November 13, 1987).
3. Barrier, *Carl Barks*, 27.
4. Barks, interview by Barrier, November 22, 1973.
5. Barks to Thomas Andrae, November 13, 1987.
6. Barks, interview by Ault and Andrae, August 4, 1975.

7. Barks to Thomas Andrae, April 30, 1987. In 1936, according to Barks, Disney was still "one of the boys": he would drop by the office to talk with storymen and make informal suggestions about their work. After *Modern Inventions*, Barks saw Disney only in formal conferences, after the storyboards for a cartoon were already prepared. Burdened with work on the feature films and with the expanded production of shorts, Disney no longer had time for casual chats.

8. Barks, interview by Ault, May 28, 1973.

9. Ibid.

10. Barks, interview by Ault and Andrae, August 4, 1975.

11. Barrier, *Carl Barks*, 27.

12. Barks, interview by Hamilton, April 29, 1987.

13. Barks to Thomas Andrae, November 13, 1987.

14. Barks, interview by Ault and Andrae, August 4, 1975.

15. Barks to Thomas Andrae, November 13, 1987.

16. Barks, interview by Ault, May 29, 1973.

17. *Mickey's Parrot* (1938), *Mickey's Elephant* (1936), *Mickey's Kangaroo* (1935).

18. Max Horkheimer, "Authoritarianism and the Family," in *The Family: Its Function and Destiny*, ed. Ruth Anshen (New York: Harper, 1949), 381–98.

19. See Michael Kimmel, *Manhood in America: A Cultural History* (New York: Free Press, 1996).

20. Ibid., 205.

21. Anthony Ludovici, "Women's Encroachment on Men's Domain," *Current History*, October 27, 1927, 23.

22. J. B. Watson, *Psychological Care of Infant and Child* (New York: Norton, 1928), 86.

23. Joseph M. Hawes and N. Ray Hiner, eds., *American Childhood: A Research Guide* (Westport, Conn.: Greenwood, 1985), 510.

24. Barks, interview by Ault, May 29, 1973.

25. Cited in David Kunzle, "Dispossession by Ducks" (English manuscript), 11, published as *Carl Barks, Dagobert, und Donald Duck: Welteroberung aus Entenperspektive* [Carl Barks, Uncle Scrooge, and Donald Duck: World Conquest in Ducks' Eye View] (Frankfurt am Main: Fischer Taschenbuchverlag, 1990).

26. *Happy Hooligan* had utilized the uncle–nephew symbolism for parent–child relationships but not the theme of father–son rivalry. Taliaferro's creation of the nephews may have also been influenced by his 1936 adaptation of *The Practical Pig*, in which the Big Bad Wolf had three ravenous sons.

27. David R. Smith, "The Man Who Drew the Mouse: An Interview with Floyd Gottfredson," in *Mickey Mouse in Color* (New York: Pantheon, 1988), 109.

28. Barks, interview by Ault, May 29, 1973. The reference to Dr. Spock is an anachronism, for his theories did not become popular until the 1940s.

29. Hawes and Hiner, *American Childhood*, 503.

30. Ibid.

31. Barks to Thomas Andrae, April 29, 1987.

32. Barks to Thomas Andrae, November 13, 1987.

33. Some of these drawings are reproduced in "*The Hockey Champ*," in *Carl Barks Library* (Scottsdale, Ariz.: Another Rainbow, 1984), set 7, 507–11.

34. Based on my examination of existing storyboards drawn for the Donald Duck shorts located at the Walt Disney Archives.

35. Preliminary outline #23, *Interior Decorators*, October 16, 1937.

36. *Laurel and Hardy: The Boys* [television documentary] (1992).

37. Barks to Thomas Andrae, April 29, 1987.

38. Andrew Bergman, *We're in the Money: Depression America and Its Films* (New York: Harper and Row, 1971).

39. Carl Barks, "Donald's Grandma Duck," *Vacation Parade* #1 (July 1950): 100–109.

40. Notes for *Carl Barks Library*, November 13, 1987.

41. Ibid. Barks designed a sequence in which Donald and Daisy jitterbug so intensely that they dance up a wall, along the ceiling, and down the other side. Banes worked as a storyman from 1938 to 1941.

42. Barks to Thomas Andrae, April 29, 1987.

43. Elizabeth Bell, "Somatexts at the Disney Shop: Constructing the Pentimentos of Women's Animated Bodies," in *From Mouse to Mermaid: The Politics of Film, Gender, and Culture*, ed. Elizabeth Bell, Lynda Haas, and Laura Sells (Bloomington: Indiana University Press, 1995), 107.

44. Barks to Thomas Andrae, April 29, 1987.

45. Jim Korkis, "The Other Duck Man: An Interview with Jack Hannah," in *Carl Barks Library* (Scottsdale, Ariz.: Another Rainbow, 1984), set 1, vol. 1, 149.

46. Barks, interview by Sebastian Durand and Didier Ghez, July 7, 1994.

47. Barks, interview by Barrier, November 22, 1973.

48. Barks to Thomas Andrae, April 27, 1987.

49. Barrier, *Carl Barks*, 4.

50. Barks developed this theme more fully in a series of stories in which Donald is a master craftsman whose attempts to master nature backfire; see Thomas Andrae and Geoffrey Blum, "A Working Class Hero," in *Carl Barks Library* (Prescott, Ariz.: Another Rainbow, 1985), set 9, vol. 1, 9–16, 49–50, 83–84.

51. Richard Pells, *Radical Visions and American Dreams: Culture and Social Thought in the Depression Years* (Middletown, Conn.: Wesleyan University Press, 1973), 25–33.

52. Ibid., 27.

53. Siegfried Gideon, *Mechanization Takes Command: A Contribution to an Anonymous History* (New York: Norton, 1969), 42.

54. Pells, *Radical Visions*, 26.

55. Max Horkheimer and Theodor W. Adorno, *Dialectic of Enlightenment* (New York: Herder and Herder, 1969), 138.

56. Walter Benjamin, "The Work of Art in the Age of Mechanical Reproduction," in *Illuminations*, ed. Hannah Arendt (New York: Schocken, 1969), 217–52.

57. Quoted in Roland Marchand, *Advertising the American Dream: Making Way for Modernity, 1920–1940* (Berkeley: University of California Press, 1985), 3.

58. William Leiss, *The Domination of Nature* (Boston: Beacon, 1972), 161–64.

59. In *Der Führer's Face* (1943), the pressure of laboring on an assembly line drives Donald mad, but this experience is doubly displaced because he is working in a Nazi war plant, not an American assembly line, and because it turns out to be a nightmare. *Donald's Gold Mine* (1942) also features a nightmarish assembly line sequence that is displaced by being located in a mine, not an industrial plant. Barks worked on neither film.

60. See Pierre Macherey, *A Theory of Literary Production* (London: Routledge and Kegan Paul, 1978).

61. Korkis, "Other Duck Man," 149.

62. When Barks reworked this plot for the comics (*WDC&S* #100 [June 1949]), Donald became the one to triumph, opening the schoolhouse and making the boys write "Crime Does Not Pay" on the blackboard. In books that children could read and reread, open rebellion was not as permissible as in a film that flashed by quickly on the screen.

63. See *Sea Scouts* (1939) and *The Vanishing Private* (1942).

64. Barks's action scenes often culminate in a tableau gag, a held picture showing Donald in a ridiculous pose. In *The Hockey Champ*, he receives horns and a pitchfork of ice that make him look satanic; in *Snow Fight* he gets frozen atop a plume of ice, looking like a monkey on a palm tree.

65. Barks, interview by Barrier, October 5, 1974.

66. Ibid.

67. Barks, interview by Jack Hannah, in *An Officer and a Duck* (Walt Disney Home Video, 1985).

68. Barrier, *Carl Barks*, 28.

69. Ibid., 27.

70. Barks to Thomas Andrae, April 29, 1987.

71. Barks, interview by Geoffrey Blum, December 10, 1991.

72. Ibid.

73. Barks, interview by Malcolm Willets, 1962.

74. Thomas Doherty, *Projections of War: Hollywood, American Culture, and World War II* (New York: Columbia University Press, 1993), 68.

75. Barrier, *Carl Barks*, 28.

76. Notes for *Carl Barks Library*, April 29, 1987.

CHAPTER 3

1. Gregory Catsos, "The World's Foremost Wise Quacker, Clarence 'Ducky' Nash," *Filmfax* 26 (April–May 1991): 38.

2. Ibid.

3. Barks, interview by Blum, December 10–11, 1991.

4. Edward Summer, "Of Ducks and Men: Carl Barks Interviewed," *Panels* 2 (Spring 1981): 4.

5. Barks, interview by Barrier, October 5, 1974.

6. Barks, interview by Ault and Andrae, August 4, 1975.

7. Catsos, "World's Foremost Wise Quacker," 38.

8. Barks, interview by Barrier, November 22, 1973.

9. Summer, "Of Ducks," 4.

10. *Donald Duck Best Comics* (New York: Abbeville, 1978), 13.

11. Barks, interview by Ault and Andrae, August 4, 1975.

12. Ibid.

13. Barks, interview by Klaus Strzyz, October 31, 1980.

14. Boatner, "From Burbank to Calisota," A–54.

15. R. W. Connell, "Iron Man: The Body and Some Contradictions of Hegemonic Masculinity," in *Sport, Men, and the Gender Order: Critical Feminist Perspectives*, ed. Michael A. Messner and Donald F. Sabo (Champaign, Ill.: Human Kinetics, 1990), 94.

16. Kimmel, *Manhood in America*, 7.

17. Jeffrey Hantover, "Sex Role, Sexuality, and Social Status: The Early Years of the Boy Scouts" (Ph.D. diss., University of Chicago, 1976), 288.

18. Al Taliaferrro had created the dog in the Donald Duck newspaper strip and had named him Bolivar. Barks had to change the name to Bornworthy because Western Publishing thought that Latin Americans might be offended because the name defamed their national hero, Simon Bolivar.

19. Barks, interview by Ault and Andrae, August 4, 1975.

20. Mills, *White Collar*, 263.

21. See Barbara Creed, *The Monstrous-Feminine: Film, Feminism, Psychoanalysis* (New York: Routledge, 1993).

22. See Isaac D. Balbus, *Marxism and Domination: A Neo-Hegelian, Feminist, Psychoanalytic Theory of Sexual, Political, and Technological Domination* (Princeton: Princeton University Press, 1982), 303–52.

23. Deconstruction is "a mode of reading texts which subverts the implicit claim of a text to possess adequate grounds, in the system of language it deploys, to establish its own structure, unity and determinate meanings" (M. H. Abrams, *A Glossary of Literary Terms*, 4th ed. [New York: Holt, Rinehart, and Winston, 1981], 38).

24. Bugs Bunny was the first funny-animal superhero in comic books. "Super-Dooper Rabbit" appeared in *Looney Tunes* #5 (March 1942). Dana Coty, who gave Barks the idea for a superhero parody, was probably inspired by this story. The name "Super Snooper" came from *Funnyman* #6 (1948), a comic book starring a comedian superhero created by Superman creators Jerry Siegel and Joe Shuster.

25. On Barks's reading of Mulford's Hopalong Cassidy novels, see Barks, interview by Barrier, November 22, 1973. The film concerned the villain's stealing of cattle by

changing their brands, hiding the animals in a secret canyon, and throwing the blame on someone else.

26. Walt Disney, *Donald Duck and His Nephews* (New York: Abbeville, 1983), 9.
27. Barks, interview by Ault and Andrae, August 4, 1975. Dickens was not the only inspiration for Scrooge. According to Barks, "It was Andy Gump's uncle I was thinking of when I first created Scrooge, but I couldn't remember enough about him, so I sort of combined him with Dickens's Scrooge" (Barks, interview by Bruce Hamilton, *Duckburg Times* 17–18 [1983]: 38). Uncle Bim appeared in Sidney Smith's comic strip, *The Gumps*. "Uncle Bim was disappointing to me because I never got to see his wealth," Barks explained, "his bales of currency and stacks of coins. It was partly because of Uncle Bim that I made a fetish in most of Uncle Scrooge stories of showing the old duck's multiple trillions in cash" ("Uncle Scrooge and Money," in *The Best of Uncle Scrooge* [New York: Abbeville, 1979], 15).
28. Barks, interview by Ault and Andrae, August 4, 1975.
29. Ibid.
30. Ibid.
31. Barks, interview by Ault, May 29, 1973.
32. Barks to David Kunzle, January 16, 1975.
33. Barks, interview by Erik Svane, July 7, 1994.
34. Thich Nhat Hahn, *The Heart of the Buddha's Teaching: Transforming Suffering into Peace, Joy, and Liberation* (New York: Broadway, 1999), 7–8.
35. Barks, interview by Ault and Andrae, August 4, 1975.
36. Ibid.
37. Barrier, *Carl Barks*, 55.
38. John Cawelti, *Apostles of the Self-Made Man: Changing Concepts of Success in America* (Chicago: University of Chicago Press, 1965), 112.
39. Barks, interview by Ault and Andrae, August 4, 1975.
40. Al Taliaferro introduced Donald's red coupe into the newspaper strip, but the vehicle originally derived from the 1936 Disney cartoon *Don Donald*.
41. Lawrence Chenoweth, *The American Dream of Success: The Search for the Self in the Twentieth Century* (North Scituate, Mass.: Duxbury, 1974), 94.
42. Ibid., 109.
43. Barks, interview by Ault and Andrae, August 4, 1975.
44. Barks, interview by Ault, May 29, 1973.
45. Lucien Goldmann, *Towards a Sociology of the Novel* (London: Tavistock, 1975), 136.
46. See William Leuchtenberg, *Franklin Roosevelt and the New Deal, 1932–1940* (New York: Harper and Row, 1963), 26.
47. Barks, interview by Ault, June 3, 1999.
48. Barks to David Kunzle, October 27, 1974.
49. Barrier, *Carl Barks*, 86.
50. Barks to Ron Goulart, March 22, 1961.
51. Information from Peter Kylling based on Garé Barks to Dorothy Barks Gibson, date unknown.

52. Barks to Geoffrey Blum, November 17, 1985.

53. Barks, interview by Ault and Andrae, August 4, 1975.

54. Barks, interview by Hamilton, June 24, 1984.

55. Barks, interview by Ault and Andrae, August 4, 1975.

56. Ibid.

57. "Plastic Bubbles Refloat Capsized Ship," *Popular Science*, April 1965, 118–19.

58. Max Horkheimer, *The Eclipse of Reason* (New York: Seabury, 1974), 3–57.

59. Langdon Winner, *Autonomous Technology: Technics-out-of-Control as a Theme in Political Thought* (Cambridge: MIT Press, 1977).

60. Barks drew but did not write this story; however, he reworked it enough so that it bears all the hallmarks of being his work.

61. Barks to Elvio Paolini, April 16, 1973.

62. Grandma Duck is one of the few positive female characters in Barks's oeuvre, representing the hardiness of the frontier spirit. However, Barks rarely used her, and most stories featuring her were written by other writers. She was created by Al Taliaferro in the Donald Duck comic strip, first appearing in a daguerreotype portrait on Donald's wall (August 11, 1940), and was introduced into the strip on September 27, 1943.

63. "I made the duck a little bit different in every story; I changed him to fit the *role* he was playing"; "I made Duckburg whatever it needed to be for a plot" (Barks, interview by Ault, May 5, 1999).

64. Barks to Don Rosa, May 11, 1991.

65. Umberto Eco, *The Role of the Reader: Explorations in the Semiotics of Texts* (Bloomington: Indiana University Press, 1979). See also John Fiske, *Television Culture* (New York: Methuen, 1987), for a discussion of how different types of readers interpret such texts.

66. In a number of Donald Duck adventures, Donald and the boys end up breaking even with or becoming more successful than Gladstone, despite his great luck: see "Race to the South Seas" (*MOC* #41 [1949]); "Trail of the Unicorn" (*DD* FC 263 [1950]); and "The Gilded Man" (*DD* FC #422 [1952]). In "The Secret of Hondorica" (*DD* #46 [1956]), both Gladstone and the ducks fail on their hunt for valuable papers.

67. The young Scrooge shined shoes for a living and gathered firewood in his native Scotland, selling it to the rich for "monstrous" prices (*US* #44 [1963], #22 [1958]).

68. Barks, interview by Ault, May 29, 1973.

69. Ibid. The name *Duckburg* first appears in *WDC&S* #49 (1944).

70. Barks to R. O. Burnett, December 13, 1960.

71. Barks, interview by Ault and Andrae, August 4, 1975.

72. Barks also drew a model sheet of Uncle Scrooge at this time.

73. Mark Evanier, interview by Thomas Andrae, November 29, 2004.

74. Barks to Don Rosa, March 31, 1991.

75. Ibid.

CHAPTER 4

1. Barks, interview by Bruce Hamilton, Thomas Andrae, and Geoffrey Blum, 1987; Barrier, *Carl Barks*, 226. The story was inspired largely by two Pluto cartoons Barks helped to write, *Bone Trouble* (1940) and *Army Mascot* (1942).
2. This title was part of Dell's Four Color series, in which different titles were printed on a one-shot basis at irregular intervals throughout the year.
3. Barks, interview by Naiman, August 27, 1993.
4. Barks, interview by Ault and Andrae, August 4, 1975. The comic strip adventures of Alex Raymond's *Flash Gordon*, Hal Foster's *Prince Valiant*, and Roy Crane's *Buzz Sawyer* and *Wash Tubbs* and the humorous adventure tales of E. C. Segar's *Popeye* were also very influential. Indeed, the Popeye strip adventure featuring detective Merlock Jones (August 1932) inspired the quick-change artist in Barks's Donald Duck tale *Big Top Bedlam* (*DD* FC #300 [1950]).
5. Barks, interview by Hamilton, September 24, 1983.
6. See Bruce Hamilton, "Glitterings of Pirate Gold," in *Carl Barks Library* (Scottsdale, Ariz.: Another Rainbow, 1984), set 1, vol. 1, 127–31.
7. Barrier, *Carl Barks*, 39.
8. Barks, interview by Hamilton, September 24, 1983.
9. Barks quoted in Disney, *Donald Duck and His Nephews*, 10.
10. Barks to Dick Blackburn, March 8, 1968.
11. Barks, interview by Hamilton, September 24, 1983.
12. Details from the museum and palace sequences are drawn from illustrations in William C. Hayes, "Daily Life in Ancient Egypt," *National Geographic*, October 1941, 419–515. The images of tombs and pyramids were taken from photographs in Willard Price, "By Falluca down the Nile," *National Geographic*, April 1940, 435–76.
13. Barks, interview by Hamilton, September 24, 1983.
14. Donald Ault, "Allegories of Apocalypse," in *Carl Barks Library of Donald Duck Adventures in Color* (Prescott, Ariz.: Another Rainbow, 1994), vol. 5.
15. Trevor Corson, "The Race to Bomb" [review of Sven Lindqvist, *A History of Bombing* (New York: New Press, 2001)], *The Nation*, October 29, 2001, 25–30.
16. Barks, interview by Hamilton, September 24, 1983.
17. Ibid.
18. Barks's design for the sea serpent machine in this comic mirrors that in the unproduced cartoon.
19. Barks, interview by Hamilton, September 24, 1983.
20. David Gerber, "Heroes and Misfits: the Troubled Social Reintegration of Disabled Veterans in *The Best Years of Our Lives*," *American Quarterly* 41 (1994): 547.
21. Ibid., 49.
22. Lucy Fischer, "Mama's Boy: Filial Hysteria in *White Heat*," in *Screening the Male: Exploring Masculinities in Hollywood Cinema*, ed. Steven Cohan and Ina Rae Hark (New York: Routledge, 1993), 78.

23. Barks, interview by Hamilton, September 24, 1983.
24. Willaim H. Chafe, *The Unfinished Journey: America since World War II* (New York: Oxford University Press, 1991), 33–34; Larry May, *The Big Tomorrow: Hollywood and the Politics of the American Way* (Chicago: University of Chicago Press, 2000), 168.
25. Barks, interview by Barrier, November 22, 1973.
26. Kunzle, *Carl Barks*, 2.
27. Margot Henriksen, *Dr. Strangelove's America: Society and Culture in the Atomic Age* (Berkeley: University of California Press, 1997).
28. Bradford Wright, *Comic Book Nation*, 69.
29. "Station Whiz Gets Atomic Power," *Captain Marvel Adventures* #131 (April 1952).
30. See "The 10th at Noon," *Weird Science-Fantasy* #11 (January–February 1952).
31. When Another Rainbow reprinted this story in 1990 in the *Carl Barks Library* (set 6, vol. 1, 142), the Walt Disney Company insisted that the ending be changed so that Donald not be shown profiting from people's misfortunes.
32. Geoffrey Blum, "Barks and the Bomb," in *The Carl Barks Collection* (Copenhagen: Egmont Serieforlaget AS, 2006), 4: 9–12.
33. Marty Jezer, *The Dark Ages: Life in the United States, 1945–1960* (Boston: South End, 1982), 96. The evidence against the Rosenbergs was and remains controversial, and it seems clear that they did not get a fair trial. They were executed in 1953.
34. Barks, interview by Ault and Andrae, August 4, 1975.
35. Ibid.
36. See Elaine Tyler May, *Homeward Bound: American Families in the Cold War* (New York: Basic Books, 1988).
37. Barrier, *Carl Barks*, 110.
38. Barks, interview by Gottfried Helnwein, July 11, 1992.
39. Ibid.
40. Ibid.
41. Godfrey Hodgson, *America in Our Time* (Garden City, N.Y.: Doubleday, 1976), 81.
42. William Appleman Williams, "The Frontier Thesis and American Foreign Policy," *Pacific Historical Review* 24 (November 1955): 379.
43. Richard Van Alstyne, *The Rising American Empire* (New York: Norton, 1974), 1.
44. Donald E. Pease, "New Perspectives on U.S. Culture and Imperialism," in *Cultures of United States Imperialism*, ed. Amy Kaplan and Donald E. Pease (Durham, N.C.: Duke University Press, 1993), 23.
45. William Patrick Day, *In the Circles of Fear and Desire: A Study of Gothic Fantasy* (Chicago: University of Chicago Press, 1985).
46. David Punter, *The Literature of Terror: The Gothic Tradition* (London: Longman, 1996), 1: 111–12.
47. Day, *In the Circles of Fear and Desire*.
48. See David Stannard, *American Holocaust: The Conquest of the New World* (New York: Oxford University Press, 1992).

49. Michael Nerlich, *The Ideology of Adventure: Studies in Modern Consciousness* (Minneapolis: University of Minnesota Press, 1987), vol. 2.
50. Barks, interview by Ault and Andrae, August 4, 1975.
51. Ibid.
52. Ibid.
53. Ibid.
54. Barks to Thomas Andrae, October 2, 1983.
55. Lewis Erenberg, *Swingin' the Dream: Big Band Jazz and the Rebirth of American Culture* (Chicago: University of Chicago Press, 1998), 224–25.
56. "Race to the South Seas," *MOC* #41 (1949); "Adventure Down Under," *DD* FC #156 (1947); *WDC&S* #74 (1946).
57. Inez Wallace, "I Met a Zombie!" *American Weekly*, April 3, 1942, 10–11.
58. Barks, interview by Ault and Andrae, August 4, 1975.
59. Barks to Malcolm Willets, April 7, 1968.
60. See photo in Oliver P. Newman, "Bare Feet and Burros in Haiti," *National Geographic*, July 1944, 323.
61. Barks to Geoffrey Blum, November 17, 1985.
62. Robin Wood, *Hollywood: From Vietnam to Reagan* (New York: Columbia University Press, 1986), 73–77.
63. Barks to Donald Ault, September 15, 1972.
64. See, for example, "Luck of the North," *DD* FC #256 (1949); "The Land of the Totem Poles," *DD* FC #263 (1950).
65. Hans Schmidt, *The United States Occupation of Haiti, 1915–1934* (New Brunswick, N.J.: Rutgers University Press, 1971).
66. On the history of voodoo and its appropriation into Euro-American culture, see Gary Rhodes, *White Zombie: Anatomy of a Horror Film* (Jefferson, N.C.: MacFarland, 2001); Laënnec Hurbon, *Voodoo: Search for the Spirit* (New York: Abrams, 1995). The idea of black violence against whites had a basis in reality: black rebels burned two thousand plantations and killed a thousand whites during the war against French colonialism.
67. Laura Mulvey, *Fetishism and Curiosity* (London: British Film Institute, 1996), 2.
68. Ibid., xiv.
69. Jezer, *Dark Ages*, 67–70.
70. Ibid., 68, 69.
71. Ibid., 67–70.
72. Ibid., 70.
73. Dorfman and Mattelart, *How to Read Donald Duck*; Kunzle, *Carl Barks*.
74. Barks, interview by Ault and Andrae, August 4, 1975.
75. Barks to Donald Ault, September 15, 1972.
76. John Christman, *The Myth of Property: Toward an Egalitarian Theory of Ownership* (New York: Oxford University Press, 1994).
77. William Blackstone, *Commentaries on the Laws of England* (Boston: Beacon, 1962), book 2, p. 2.

78. Jennifer Nedelsky, *Private Property and the Limits of American Constitutionalism: The Madisonian Framework and Its Legacy* (Chicago: University of Chicago Press, 1990); Christman, *Myth of Property*.

79. Barks, interview by Barrier, October 5, 1975.

80. Barks, interview by Hamilton, September 24, 1983.

81. Barks to Michael Barrier, January 25, 1971.

82. Ibid.

CHAPTER 5

1. Jean Delumeau, *The History of Paradise* (New York: Continum, 1995).

2. Stanley Diamond, *In Search of the Primitive: A Critique of Civilization* (New Brunswick, N.J.: Transaction, 1987), 106.

3. Paul Radin, *The World of Primitive Man* (New York: Grove, 1960), 106.

4. Ibid.

5. Barks, interview by Ault and Andrae, August 4, 1975.

6. Jack Zipes, *Breaking the Magic Spell: Radical Theories of Folk and Fairy Tales* (New York: Methuen, 1979), 14.

7. Quoted in ibid., 138.

8. Alison Lurie, *Don't Tell the Grown-Ups: Subversive Children's Literature* (Boston: Little, Brown, 1990), 43.

9. Barks, interview by Ault and Andrae, August 4, 1975.

10. John O'Reilly, "South Florida's Amazing Everglades," *National Geographic*, January 1940, 115.

11. Barks, interview by Hamilton, September 24, 1983.

12. Julianne Burton-Carvajal, " 'Surprise Package': Looking Southward with Disney," in *Disney Discourse: Producing the Magic Kingdom*, ed. Eric Smoodin (New York: Routledge, 1994), 131–47.

13. Neocolonialism can be distinguished from colonialism in terms of its project of using native elites to maintain economic, political, and military control by the West over Third World countries rather than its occupation of foreign lands.

14. Barks based his interpretation of the city on photographs in Henry Albert Phillip, "The Pith of Peru," *National Geographic*, August 1942, 167–88.

15. Clark Gable was Barks's favorite male movie star.

16. Beau Riffenbaugh, *The Myth of the Explorer: The Press, Sensationalism, and Geographical Discovery* (London: Belhaven, 1993), 2.

17. Hugh Thompson, *The White Rock: An Exploration of the Inca Heartland* (New York: Overlook, 2001), 79–80.

18. Barks, interview by Ault and Andrae, August 4, 1975.

19. Barks, interview by Hamilton, September 24, 1983.

20. Thompson, *White Rock*, 77–78.

21. Murray Bookchin, *The Ecology of Freedom* (Palo Alto, Calif.: Cheshire, 1982), 246.

22. Wendy Lesser, *Life below the Ground: A Study of the Subterranean in Literature and History* (Boston: Faber and Faber, 1987).

23. Mason Sutherland, "Carlsbad Caverns in Color," *National Geographic*, October 1953, 499.

24. Barks, *Walt Disney's Uncle Scrooge McDuck*, 215.

25. Herbert Marcuse, *Eros and Civilization* (Boston: Beacon, 1969), 34.

26. The story's attraction for the counterculture is evident in an underground paper's discussion of it with a fake interview with Barks in "Terries and Fermies: Underworld People Cause Quakes," *Bugle American*, February 25, 1971.

27. Notes for *Carl Barks Library*, 1984.

28. David C. Korten, *The Post-Corporate World: Life after Capitalism* (San Francisco: Kuarian and Berrett-Koeler, 1999), 51.

29. Barks to Malcolm Willets, April 19, 1962.

30. Peter Bishop, *The Myth of Shangri-La: Tibet, Travel Writing, and the Western Creation of Sacred Landscape* (Berkeley: University of California Press, 1989).

31. Barks, *Walt Disney's Uncle Scrooge McDuck*, 117.

32. Ibid.

33. Leo Marx, *The Machine in the Garden: Technology and the Pastoral Ideal* (New York: Oxford University Press, 1978).

34. See "Adventure Down Under," *DD* FC #156 (1947); "Race to the South Seas," *MOC* #41 (1949).

35. Barks to Thomas Andrae, April 30, 1987.

36. Jean and Frank Shor, "At World's End in Hunza," *National Geographic*, October 1953, 485–518.

37. Published with his illustrations in Barks, *Walt Disney's Uncle Scrooge McDuck*.

38. Marcel Mauss, *The Gift: The Form and Reason for Exchange in Archaic Societies* (New York: Norton, 1990), 69.

39. Lorna Marshall, "Sharing, Talking, and Giving: Relief of Tensions among Kung Bushmen," *Africa* 31 (1961): 245.

40. See "Christmas for Shacktown," *DD* FC #367 (1952).

41. Henry Nash Smith, *Virgin Land: The American West in Symbol and Myth* (New York: Vintage, 1950), 138.

42. Barks, interview by Ciotti, September 28, 1972.

43. Barks to Geoffey Blum and Thomas Andrae, November 17, 1985.

44. Barks could look outside his window and see the San Jacinto Mountains, which form a backdrop in the story. The Estudillo mansion becomes Don Gaspar's rancho, and the Saboba Indian reservation and even the rock into which the ducks' car crashes are drawn from real life (Barks, interview by Barrier, October 5, 1974).

45. In the book, Felipé marries Ramona, something the film only implies.

46. Dydia Delyser, *Ramona Memories: Tourism and the Shaping of Southern California* (Minneapolis: University of Minnesota Press, 2005), 127.

47. See Leonard Pitt, *The Decline of the Californios: A Social History of the Spanish-Speaking Californians, 1846–1890* (Berkeley: University of California Press, 1966).
48. Richard Henry Dana Jr., *Two Years before the Mast* (New York: Mayflower, 1911), 85.
49. Barks, interview by Hamilton, September 24, 1983.
50. Barks, *Walt Disney's Uncle Scrooge McDuck*, 270.
51. Roy Harvey Pearce, *Savagism and Civilization: A Study of the Indian and the American Mind* (Berkeley: University of California Press, 1988), 193.
52. Jack Weatherford, *Indian Givers: How the Indians of the Americas Transformed the World* (New York: Fawcett Columbine, 1988), 133–50.
53. Ibid.
54. James Tully, *An Approach to Political Philosophy: Locke in Contexts* (Cambridge: Cambridge University Press, 1993), 154.

CHAPTER 6

1. Barks, interview by Willets, 1962.
2. Kimmel, *Manhood in America*, 29.
3. Ibid.
4. Erik Olin Wright, *Class Counts: Comparative Studies in Class Analysis* (Cambridge: Cambridge University Press, 1997), 199–200; Chenoweth, *American Dream*, 13.
5. Jill Kasen, "Wither the Self-Made Man? Comic Culture and the Crisis of Legitimation in the United States," *Social Problems* 28, no. 3 (December 1980): 142.
6. Daniel Bell, *The Cultural Contradictions of Capitalism* (New York: Basic Books, 1978), 71–72.
7. Barks, interview by Donald and Lynda Ault, June 13–14, 1997.
8. Barks, interview by Barrier, October 5, 1974.
9. Barks, *Walt Disney's Uncle Scrooge McDuck*, 61–62.
10. Charles Derber, *People before Profit: The New Globalization in an Age of Terror, Big Money, and Economic Crisis* (New York: Picador, 2003), 48.
11. Alan Trachtenberg, *The Incorporation of America: Culture and Society in the Gilded Age* (New York: Hill and Wang, 1982), 86.
12. Rex Burns, *Success in America: The Yeoman Dream and the Industrial Revolution* (Amherst: University of Massachusetts Press, 1976), 1.
13. Cawelti, *Apostles*, 43.
14. Burns, *Success in America*, 8–9.
15. In "The Seven Cities of Cibola" (*US* #7 [1955]), for example, Scrooge owns all the businesses in Duckburg and admits that he is a "regular old *octopus*."
16. Barks, interview by Ault and Andrae, August 4, 1975.
17. Barks, interview by Ault, May 29, 1973.
18. See, for example, "Tralla La" (*US* #6 [1954]) and Donald's competition with Gladstone to become lead in Daisy's play (*WDC&S* #128 [1951]). However, escalation

stories do not always involve competition—for example, the story of Gyro's worms (*WDC&S* #156 [1953]). See Donald Ault, "In Perilous Paths," in *Carl Barks Library* (Prescott, Ariz.: Another Rainbow, 1983), set 8, 733–34, 737–41.

19. Barks, interview by Ault and Andrae, August 4, 1975.

20. Barks to Michael Barrier, June 9, 1966.

21. Notes for *Carl Barks Library*, 1984.

22. Klaus Theweleit, *Male Fantasies*, vol. 1, *Women, Floods, Bodies, History* (Minneapolis: University of Minnesota Press, 1987), 271. Theweleit reproduces the splash panel of Scrooge's dam busting but does not identify Barks as the author.

23. Chenoweth, *American Dream*, 17.

24. Theweleit, *Male Fantasies*, 1: 312.

25. On Whittier and the history of the Hemet water wars, see Mary E. Whitney, *Valley, River, and Mountain: Revisiting Fortune Favors the Brave: A History of the Lake Hemet Water Company* (Hemet, Calif.: Hemet Area Museum Association, 1999).

26. Between 1945 and 1957, the value of overseas exports doubled. Direct investment in foreign countries rose from $7.2 billion in 1946 to $49.3 billion in 1965, representing 60 percent of the world's total. The largest and most powerful U.S. corporations owned this investment (Jezer, *Dark Ages*, 75).

27. Barks, *Walt Disney's Uncle Scrooge McDuck*, 61.

28. Ethel Anderson Becker, *Klondike '98: Hegg's Album of the 1898 Alaska Gold Rush* (Portland, Or.: Binfords and Mort, 1949).

29. Barks, *Walt Disney's Uncle Scrooge McDuck*, 62.

30. Barks, interview by Hamilton, September 24, 1983.

31. Barks, *Walt Disney's Uncle Scrooge McDuck*, 64.

32. Barrier, *Carl Barks*, 133.

33. Barks, interview by Barrier, November 22, 1973.

34. Barks, interview by Hamilton, June 24, 1984.

35. Barks, interview by Barrier, November 22, 1973.

36. Barks, interview by Ault and Ault, June 14–15, 1997.

37. Barks, interview by Hamilton, June 24, 1984.

38. Barks, *Walt Disney's Uncle Scrooge McDuck*, 96.

39. Ibid., 150.

40. *Mickey Mouse in Color*, 107–8.

41. Dorfman and Mattelart, *How to Read Donald Duck*, 67.

42. See for example "The Paul Bunyan Machine" (*US* #28 [1960]); "The Case of the Sticky Money" (*US* #42 [1963]).

43. John Cawelti, *Adventure, Mystery, and Romance: Formula Stories as Art and Popular Culture* (Chicago: University of Chicago Press, 1976), 77.

44. Barks, interview by Helnwein, July 11, 1992.

45. On the strike, see Steven Watts, *The Magic Kingdom: Walt Disney and the American Way of Life* (Boston: Houghton Mifflin, 1997), 203–27.

46. Barks to Michael Barrier, August 9, 1967.

47. Barks to Elvio Paolini, April 16, 1973.
48. Barks's script for "Officer for a Day" (*DD* #126 [1969]) also lampoons the Warren Court's permissiveness toward criminals.
49. Chase Craig to Barks, July 9, 1965.
50. Frank Reilly to Richard Greenberg, December 11, 1953.
51. Carl Buettner to Barks, December 18, 1953.
52. Notes for *Carl Barks Library*, 1984.
53. A pig-faced Brutopian consul reappears in "The Swamp of No Return" (*US* #57 [1965]), where his consulate bears an explicit parody of the Soviet hammer and sickle, a sledgehammer and shackle.
54. This phrase is ambiguous in Russian and can also be translated less belligerently as "We will outlast you."
55. Hendrick, *Dr. Strangelove's America*, 99.
56. Ibid., 44.
57. Barks to Geoffrey Blum, June 5, 1985.
58. Barks to Malcolm Willets, November 17, 1960.
59. Barks to Malcolm Willets, December 30, 1960.
60. Barks to Geoffrey Blum, June 5, 1985.
61. Barks, *Walt Disney's Uncle Scrooge McDuck*, 291.
62. Kunzle, *Carl Barks*.
63. Lonnie McAllister, "The Shapes of Barks' Fiction," in *Carl Barks Library of Uncle Scrooge Adventures in Color*, no. 26 (n.p., 1997).
64. See Andrae and Blum, "Working Class Hero."
65. Barks, *Walt Disney's Uncle Scrooge McDuck*, 346.

CHAPTER 7

1. Michael Barrier to Barks, March 2, 1966.
2. Barks to R. O. Burnett, December 13, 1960.
3. Barks, interview by Barrier, March 27, 1966.
4. Barks to Ron Goulart, March 22, 1961.
5. Barks to Joe Cowles, March 19, 1961.
6. Barks to Malcolm Willets, March 24, 1961.
7. Barks to Malcolm Willets, May 24, 1961.
8. Barks, interview by Ault and Ault, June 13–14, 1997.
9. Barks to John Spicer, April 25, 1960.
10. Barks to John Thompson, October 18, 1962.
11. Barrier, *Carl Barks*, 199.
12. Barks to R. O. Burnett, December 13, 1960.
13. Barks to Alice Cobb, June 4, 1956. Passages in angle brackets were deleted by Barks.

14. Barks to Michael Barrier, November 22, 1974.

15. Barks, interview by Hamilton, September 24, 1983.

16. *Carl Barks Library* (Prescott, Ariz.: Another Rainbow, 1984), set 3, vol. 2, 522.

17. There was no increase in juvenile crime in the postwar era. Indeed, delinquency declined between 1945 and 1952. See Steven E. Mitchell, "Devious Paths, Part 3," *Comics Buyers' Guide*, February 20, 2004, 31. The Gallup poll is cited in Catherine Yronwode, "Fit to Print," *Comics Buyers' Guide*, September 30, 1984, 22.

18. Frederic Wertham, *Seduction of the Innocent* (New York: Rinehart, 1954), 307.

19. Ibid., 309.

20. Roberta E. Pearson and William Uricchio, eds. *The Many Lives of the Batman: Critical Approaches to a Superhero and His Media* (New York: Routledge, 1991), 68.

21. Roger Sabine, *Adult Comics: An Introduction* (New York: Routledge, 1993), 163.

22. See George A. Comstock, *Television and Human Behavior: The Key Studies* (Santa Monica, Calif.: Rand, 1975).

23. Barks, interview by Willets, 1962.

24. Willets, "Interview with George Sherman," 12.

25. In 1962 Western and Dell separated. Western became Gold Key and kept most of its comics licensees, while Dell created a new line consisting largely of its own characters.

26. Willets, "Interview with George Sherman," 12–13.

27. Peter Braunstein, "Forever Young: Insurgent Youth and the Sixties Culture of Rejuvenation," in *Imagine Nation: The American Counterculture of the 1960s and 1970s*, ed. Peter Braunstein and Michael William Doyle (New York: Routledge, 2002), 243–76.

28. Ibid., 243.

29. Ibid., 248.

30. Chafe, *Unfinished Journey*, 188.

31. Neil Postman, *The Disappearance of Childhood* (New York: Vintage, 1994).

32. Susan Sontag, *Against Interpretation* (New York: Farrar, 1966), 275.

33. Barks, *Walt Disney's Uncle Scrooge McDuck*, 317.

34. Ibid.

35. Barks, interview by Strzyz, October 31, 1980.

36. Barbara Ehrenreich, *The Hearts of Men: American Dreams and the Flight from Commitment* (Garden City, N.Y.: Anchor, 1984), 170–71.

37. Andreas Huyssen, "Mass Culture as Woman: Modernism's Other," in *Studies in Entertainment: Critical Approaches to Mass Culture*, ed. Tania Modleski (Bloomington: Indiana University Press, 1986).

38. Barks, interview by Hamilton, June 5, 1985.

39. Kimmel, *Manhood in America*, 291–328.

40. According to Dr. Peter Demyan, superintendent of Schools for San Jacinto, "Shacktown" was modeled on San Jacinto, while the rich lived in Hemet to the south (Demyan to Thomas Andrae, September 27, 2002). Joseph Cowles has noted the

story's impact on baby boomers: see "Memories of Shacktown," August 12, 2000, available at http://www.thegoodartist.com.

41. The dime is initially lucky for Gladstone, but he warns Donald that it may be bad luck for him.

42. Barks to Elvio Paolini, April 16, 1973.

43. The first dime initially appears in *US* FC #495 (1953) in which its sharp edges allow Scrooge to free himself from the Beagle Boys' bonds. However, it has not yet become a good luck charm.

44. Barks to Don Rosa, April 22, 1991.

45. Phillip Bray, "Theorizing Modernity and Technology," in *Modernity and Technology*, ed. Thomas Misa et al. (Cambridge: MIT Press, 2003), 44.

46. Barks to Ron Goulart, March 22, 1961.

47. Barks, interview by Strzyz, October 31, 1980. However, Barks acquired a television in the mid-1970s and came to like watching certain television programs, especially sporting events (information provided by Donald Ault, July 10, 2003).

48. Jean Baudrillard, *Selected Writings*, ed. Mark Poster (Cambridge: Polity, 1988), 171.

49. Bruce Hamilton and Bill Blackbeard, "The Mouse Man and the Duck Man: An Interview with Floyd Gottfredson and Carl Barks," in *Mickey Mouse in Color: Deluxe Edition* (Prescott, Ariz.: Another Rainbow, 1988), 104.

50. See Kaja Silverman, *Male Subjectivity at the Margins* (New York: Routledge, 1992). Silverman argues that rather than taking place during the ages of six to sixteen months, the mirror stage comes into play retroactively, from a moment well within language and sociality, 20–21.

51. See Anika Lemaire, *Jacques Lacan*, trans. David Macey (London: Routledge and Kegan Paul, 1977).

52. See also Barks's satire of the radio quiz show, in which Donald stuffs his head so full of obscure facts that he loses his mind (*WDC&S* #99 [1948]).

53. See Andrae and Blum, "Working Class Hero."

54. Chase Craig to Barks, November 1, 1965.

55. Chase Craig to Barks, November 4, 1965.

56. The story appeared in a chapter of Dodge's book, *Hans Brinker; or, the Silver Skates* (1865).

57. Barrier, *Carl Barks*, 82.

58. Ibid., 81.

59. Barks to Geoffrey Blum, June 5, 1985.

60. The story was inspired by the musical *The King and I* (1956) starring Yul Brenner. Barks did not see the film or stage play but based his story loosely on reviews (notes for *Carl Barks Library*, 1984).

61. Barks, interview by Hamilton, June 24, 1984. Willard Price's "By Felucca down the Nile" (April 1940) was one of two *National Geographic* articles that provided background detail for "The Mummy's Ring" (*DD* FC #29 [1943]).

62. Barks, interview by Hamilton, September 24, 1984.

63. Barks to Malcolm Willets, January 17, 1962.

64. Barks did not write the story but reworked it enough so that it shows all the hallmarks of being his.

65. In the 1980s and 1990s, Disney reluctantly allowed this story to be reprinted but insisted on deleting all references to dictators, rebels, revolution, and civil war as well as Barks's satire of socialist propaganda ("watches from the workers' paradise"), depoliticizing it.

66. David Kunzle, "Dispossession by Ducks," 165.

67. Richard Slotkin, *Gunfighter Nation: The Myth of the Frontier in Twentieth-Century America* (New York: Atheneum, 1992), 543.

68. Barks, interview by Donald Ault, Bruce Hamilton, John Ronan, and Nicky Wright, April 30, 1999.

69. Barks, interview by Ault and Andrae, August 4, 1975.

70. Balto's heroic efforts supposedly enabled the delivery of antitoxin serum to Nome. However, although the news media lionized Balto, Togo, who traveled the lion's share of the journey, was the true hero, "[M]y memory of the saving of Nome was not perfect," Barks admitted. "My recollection was that one dog team pulled the sled the whole way from Fairbanks" (Barks to Donald and Lynda Ault, February 5, 1995).

71. Barks to Don Thompson, October 18, 1962.

72. Chase Craig to Barks, November 4, 1965.

73. Barks to Michael Barrier, January 23, 1968.

74. Barks to Michael Barrier, December 11, 1969.

75. Barks to Michael Barrier, August 16, 1972.

76. Barks to Larry Herndon, September 9, 1971.

77. Mark Evanier, "POV," *Comics Buyers' Guide* #1379 (April 21, 2000).

78. Barks wrote two more stories featuring the ducks: "Horsing around with History" was published in *Uncle Scrooge Adventures* #33 (ser. 2) (Prescott, Ariz.: Gladstone, 1995). Barks wrote the script with art by William Van Horn. "Somewhere in Nowhere" was based on a story idea by Barks, with the script completed by John Lustig and art by Pat Block. It was a Donald Duck story featuring Scrooge and was published in *Tesori* #3 (2000) in Italy.

79. Barks, interview by Ault, June 3, 1999.

80. *The Duck Man: An Interview with Carl Barks* [videotape] (1996).

81. P. Maroveli, E. Paolini, and G. Saccumano, *Introduzione a Paperio: Fenomenologia Sociale nei Fumeti di Carl Barks* (Florence, Italy: Sansoni, 1974), 211, quoted in Donald Ault, "Visual Synchronicities in Carl Barks' Comics," *Comic Art* 4 (Fall 2003): 50.

A CARL BARKS FILMOGRAPHY

1. Notes for *Carl Barks Library*, 1987.

INDEX